RUNNING
YOUR
BEST

RON DAWS

RUNNING YOUR BEST

THE COMMITTED RUNNER'S GUIDE TO TRAINING AND RACING

Illustrated by the author

THE STEPHEN GREENE PRESS
Lexington, Massachusetts

Copyright © Ron Daws, 1985

First published in 1985 by The Stephen Greene Press, Inc.
Published simultaneously in Canada by Penguin Books Canada,
Limited
Distributed by Viking Penguin Inc., 40 West 23rd Street, New
York, New York 10010

LIBRARY OF CONGRESS CATALOGING IN PUBLICATION DATA
Daws, Ron.
Running your best.
Includes index.
1. Running—Training.   I. Title.
GV1061.5.D38   1985   796.4'26   85-7614
ISBN 0-8289-0559-2

Printed in the United States of America by
Fairfield Graphics, Fairfield, Pennsylvania
Set in Caledonia
Designed by Mary A. Wirth

To the memory of Sherman Anderson
for helping shape my values
and steering me in the right direction.

ACKNOWLEDGMENTS

During the preparation of the manuscript several people were kind enough to read portions of it and made valuable suggestions and comments: Bruce Brothers, David Cassell, Phil Jeni; Kathy Shulga and Tom Begner for their editorial assistance; and Mary Hanson, to whom I am especially indebted for her tough criticism and patience.

"It is not the critic who counts; not the man who points out how the strong man stumbles, or where the doer of deeds could have done them better. The credit belongs to the man who is actually in the arena, whose face is marred by dust and sweat and blood; who strives valiantly; who errs, and comes short again and again, because there is no effort without error and shortcoming; but who does actually strive to do the deeds, who knows the great enthusiasms, the great devotions; who spends himself in a worthy cause; who at the best knows in the end the triumph of high achievement, and who at the worst, if he fails at least fails while daring greatly, so that his place shall never be with those cold and timid souls who know neither victory nor defeat."

—THEODORE ROOSEVELT,
European and African Address

CONTENTS

INTRODUCTION

*T*his book is about reaching for the stars. You say you don't have the Olympics in mind as a goal? Neither did I, once. I never broke 2:20 in the marathon, nor 4:25 for the mile. My coach at the University of Minnesota even booted me onto the outside of the track when the "good runners" showed up to train. Nevertheless, I made the 1968 U.S. Olympic Team.

This book is not my story, however. Instead, it explains from the vantage point of the "average" athlete how I made the most of my abilities and how *you* can do the same. Not only can most runners dramatically lower their race times, they can actually advance to levels of excellence. You may never come close to a world record, but you can get the best out of yourself.

It is surprising how runners underestimate their capabilities. They look at current performances and fail to realize that their limits could be far beyond anything they've envisioned. They never venture forth; they never strive for that which could be theirs. Others believe in themselves but are confused by an avalanche of conflicting information.

This book contains no complex physiology or esoteric theories. It is a practical guide. It will explain training: how to do it, when to run what, and why. Not the workouts world-class athletes do, but what *you* should do given your set of circumstances. Runners are generally aware of the different kinds of training methods, but don't understand how to apply them. They confuse their reasons for running a particular workout, often choosing it because a friend is running it or they heard that someone famous does it.

In spite of a constant avalanche of running ideas from all directions, most runners do not know how to translate those ideas into day-to-day training. This book will try to resolve that. However, it is not possible to offer mass-produced training schedules that can be used successfully unless you re-tailor them to your personal needs. The schedules in this book demonstrate the principles behind the training. Once you understand the principles, it shouldn't be difficult to structure workouts around them.

More than just help you put together the best training, this book suggests what to do when things go wrong. No strategy can anticipate everything. We get injured or sick, our resolve temporarily wavers, or things just don't progress the way we think they should. Occasionally, workouts and/or races seem to fall apart for no reason. When running temporarily nosedives, you have to ferret out the causes and decide what to do before things get worse. Should you ease back, work harder, work differently, race less, eat differently, sprint more? This book provides the insights you will need to face those questions.

There is nothing easy about running your best. There are no gimmicks or short cuts. But hard work is not the lone solution. Success is not guaranteed by thrashing yourself harder than others in training. Undirected grueling workouts more often bring frustration than anything else. Successful conditioning means knowing precisely when to work hard, when to rest, and how to match various kinds of training to your specific needs.

There are also the matters of motivation, persistence, improving, learning from mistakes, defying the odds and the whole subject of mental preparation. Some of these issues are the deciding factors in getting you to accept the challenge in the first place, and the rest will steer you free of trouble when things could go wrong.

This book is for serious male and female distance runners of all ages and their coaches. It is for the talented and those who did not pick their ancestors carefully. The common denominator is that you want to be the best you reasonably can and are willing to work for it. This book is not so much for runners who just want to keep basically fit (although there is nothing wrong with that). I am concerned with running excellence at your particular level.

I didn't want this to become another training puzzle with many of the pieces missing; therefore, I've included many "extras" that you will need to run your best. The additional time spent getting it right is better than charging out half-informed, misinterpreting what's to be done, getting injured, or at best, not getting as much for your effort as you should.

Although the chapters are in a first-things-first sequence, this is also a resource book.

Relative beginners may, at first, perceive this book as being "high powered." But, as you improve, you will need increasingly specific and advanced information. Rather than have you outgrow the material after a few races, training programs are provided for the relative beginner to the elite runner. Hopefully, if you are a relative beginner now, you will advance.

One thing no guide can do is eliminate thinking on the part of the reader. Nor can it instill in you the basic urge to try. You must set your own goals. You must be responsible for your own future. This book provides the tools you need to excel, and I hope it will inspire you to shoot for the stars. Even if you only get to the moon, you will venture into worlds never dreamed of.

PART I
GETTING THE MOST OUT OF TRAINING

1.

GETTING SERIOUS

*M*ost runners are capable of far better performances than they suspect. While you may think you have no realistic chance of improving dramatically, the annals of sport are laden with those who succeeded even though on paper they had no chance. The genes you inherited may determine your ultimate limits, but how you apply yourself determines how close you get to those limits. When Arthur Lydiard told his runners, "It's not the best athlete who wins, but the best prepared," he understood that the most superb physical specimens can still be beaten. That's what is so fair and inspiring about running. Even though you might have inherited average physical equipment, if you persevere, you will win over the talented who aren't as tenacious.

Whether you ever win a race is not important. What matters is striving for your best at your level. The marvelous revelation you can then experience is that almost without exception your capabilities are far greater than you ever suspected. As David Moorcroft, world-record holder for 5000 meters in 13:00:42, says,

"There's not a lot you can do about your natural ability, but there's a hell of a lot you can do about the way you apply it. . . . At the ripe old age of 29, I've finally produced the performance level of which I was capable . . . so I can retire happy. For I've always thought that the most important thing is to fulfill your potential. . . ."

THE AVERAGE RUNNER'S POTENTIAL

How well could a man or woman with average athletic endowment run during his or her peak years? Although it's difficult to define average talent, a male with no physical problems is capable of a 2:30 marathon and a 32:00 10km, and comparable times for a woman are 2:45 and 35:25. I know that sounds fast, and you would have to be determined and train smart, but it wouldn't require becoming a running zombie.

For women, distance running is still relatively wide open, but the gap is closing rapidly. Only in recent years have women seriously begun to contest the longer distances. One has only to glance at the record book to see this. Women were not even officially permitted to race a marathon before 1972. In 1969 when Derek Clayton ran 2:08:36, the fastest recorded time for a woman was Anni Pede Erdkamp's 3:07:26, set in 1967. During the eight years between April 30, 1977, and April 21, 1985, the woman's world marathon record was broken nine times, resulting in a reduction in time totalling 14 minutes, 10 seconds (2:35:16 to 2:22:42). The men's record dropped by only 1:25 during the 16 years between 1969 and 1985.

Similar improvements have also occured in women's shorter distances. When Tatyana Kasankina set the 1500-meter record of 3:52:45 in 1980, faster than the great Paavo Nurmi's world record, it was equivalent to a marathoner running 2:23. When women catch up with Carlos Lopes' 2:07:11, their record will be 2:18. And that implies times like 3:46 for the 1500, 8:09 for the 3000, 14:08 for the 5000 and 29:36 for the 10,000. As it is now, women are about 30 seconds per mile slower than comparable men from the mile to the marathon. But that gap will close to about 25 seconds. Now that the women's 3000 meters, 10,000 meters, and marathon have been added to the Olympics, and the 5000 and 10,000 meters to several world championships, we will see fantastic improvement in all distance events from women in countries where there is not yet much emphasis.

I believe that the following times are realistic, but tough goals for serious runners of normal physical ability at their peak years. (It is not implied that one could run these times over the entire range of distances).

						DISTANCE				
	Mile	3km	2-M	5km	10km	15km	20km	25km	30km	Marathon
Men	4:27	8:52	9:34	15:20	32:05	49:30	1:07:20	1:25:30	1:44:00	2:30:00
Women	4:59	9:52	10:38	17:00	35:25	54:30	1:14:00	1:33:45	1:54:00	2:44:00

Exploring your potential doesn't mean dropping everything to become a full-time athlete, but taking it seriously enough (although not without humor) to carefully look into how you are applying your time and effort. George Sheehan, one of the most important philosophers of the sport says, "And out on the roads, and whenever you play, there is fitness and self-discovery and the persons we are destined to be. There is the theater where we can write and act out our dreams. . . . Running reminds me that at any age, man is still the marvel of creation. . . ."

After I graduated from college I had to decide how seriously I wanted to run. For eight years of high school and college I had been a mid-pack runner at best. I had shown some talent in cross-country, but otherwise my performances suffered because I didn't understand training. Most aggravatingly, I would run reasonably at the beginning of the season and then my races would begin to disintegrate. The slower I became, the harder I trained, and the harder I trained, the slower I became.

At the University of Minnesota I improved meagerly: a 4:30 mile, a 9:43 two-mile, and three miles in 15:22, but felt that I could do a lot better. So after college I decided to give it my all because there was nothing to learn from half a commitment. I had no illusions about world records or the Olympics, but rather, I wanted to see how far I could go given the talent I had.

That meant that if 80 miles a week would put me close to the leaders, I might as well go for 120 a week and try to win. Otherwise, I would always know that whatever I did accomplish, I could have done better. It didn't matter that my 120 miles would only put me on par with the talented who ran 80, and that the talented who ran 120 would beat me. You work with what you are given and who you are.

That proved to be one of the most rewarding decisions of my life. By eventually coming to understand training and expanding my concept of how much work I could handle, I was treated to a great learning and growing experience. I never set a world record, but I did win and place several times in the Nationals, set two American track records, placed in the top 10 four times in the Boston Marathon and made the Pan-American and Olympic Games team. That I was not a contender for an Olympic medal never mattered. Any 4:30 college miler can tell you that the Olympic *experience* would be the medal.

FIGHTING THE ODDS

Looking back, it's frightening how close I came to not trying for the Olympics. The odds against succeeding were staggering. The year before at the Pan-American Games I had injured my sciatic nerve and was told I would never run again. I did run, but won only one local race that Olympic year. I placed fourth in a regional marathon trial that was used to select 20 runners for altitude training in Colorado, where Olympic selection would take place. I ended up 19th on that list.

Yet if trying for the Games seemed hopeless, the remaining choice was terrifying. What if the third-place qualifier ran a time I thought I could better? I would have to live with the knowledge that I had let a chance to run in the Olympics die because I had not dared to accept the challenge. Better to try, fail, and know I had given my best.

"The fear of not succeeding," according to the Swiss psycologist, Paul Tournier, "is, for many people, the biggest obstacle in their way. It holds them back from trying anything at all. And for lack of trying the never give themselves a chance of succeeding—the very thing that would cure them of their doubts. It is not, after all, such a terrible thing not to succeed straight away in some new undertaking. What is serious is to give up, to become stuck in a life that just gets emptier."

Dr. David Viscott takes this theme a bit further in his book, *How to Make Winning Your Life Style*, pointing out that many

"Winning" occurs not only at the front of the race, but any-time a runner does that which he or she sets out to do.

people are afraid to win. Losers, he says, have a tendency to asso-ciate with other losers. They flock together, point fingers at win-ners and waste their time finding fault with them.

"There is such a thing as luck," admits Dr. Viscott, "but luck works only for those people who have worked to receive it. Op-portunity knocks all the time. It's just that some people don't hear it because they haven't prepared themselves to take advantage of it when it does come knocking."

YOU MUST REALLY WANT IT

You cannot fake commitment. If the urge to run doesn't gush up from within you, it's hopeless to pretend it's there. The researcher Turk says, "How you think is how you perform." The validity of that statement seems to be mirrored in former mile world-record holder Herb Elliott's statement when it was implied that when he retired at age 22, the world had not seen his best.

"You did see the best of me." Elliott countered. "This is where people make the mistake, and why I continually re-emphasize that training should focus on the mental rather than the physical side. Mentally you saw the best of me and therefore totally you saw the best of me."

Elliott went on to describe a couple of times he started to train properly again after retiring. The object was to go against Peter Snell at either the 1962 Commonwealth Games or the 1964 Tokyo Olympics. Elliott says, "After a few weeks I realized it just wasn't there. . . . There was just no excitement, no tenacity and no enthusiasm. It was an absolute drag. I just couldn't see myself going through all the build-up that would have been necessary to run against Peter Snell and beat him. I just wasn't interested enough."

What drives some of us to run 80 to 140 miles a week while others won't walk up a few flights of stairs? In my case, it was probably overcompensation for earlier athletic frustrations. Perhaps there were a few personal quirks there too—why else would one choose to hammer out 30-milers on Sunday mornings when a myriad of other less excruciating pleasures await one's choosing?

Running is made in our minds. We runners know we must run. This is understood. No other reasons are needed, nor when others ask, "Why?" are we ever able to answer directly or satisfactorily. When you are full of running it is a craving, and the feeling can put you in pursuit of the most improbable of quests. It is that exquisite feeling that no matter what, nothing can stop you. It is born out of purpose and grows into dedication. Neither I nor anyone else can instill desire if your own spirit doesn't move you. Only after the desire is there will other motivational tactics and encouragement work. This is what Elliott spoke of and what we all know. When the thought of running your best ignites that drive in you, there's practically nothing you cannot do. If it isn't there, or

Running knows few boundaries; the masters and the blind can also excel.

temporarily abandons you, the probability of an Olympic medal couldn't entice you to run five miles at any speed.

Making a commitment to run comes down to how badly you want to explore your limits. It means honestly confronting your excuses. It means making time to train. Unless you go all out for something, you may conclude your life without actually having lived it. It doesn't have to be running, but it should be a quest for excellence, and it need be for only that period of your life that it takes to fully explore it. That's how you find out what you are made of. That's how you find out who you are. To live your life your way, to reach for the goals you have set for yourself, to be the you that you want to be, that is success.

SETTING GOALS

In many of life's pursuits we fall short of our potential because we don't define our ambitions. Often runners just want to "get in shape and see what happens." It's a step in the right direction, but not very inspiring. Half-committed expectations provoke only half-committed training. Bob Timmons, who began working with 15-year-old Jim Ryun in 1962, understood this when he saw Ryun jump from a 5:38 mile to 4:26.4 in six months. Timmons had what some thought was the unmitigated audacity to tell Ryun he was capable of cracking four minutes before graduating from high school. "It's my feeling that as track coaches, many of us have a great many negative thoughts about achievement," Timmons said several years later. "We still have a tendency to talk about things that can't be done instead of things that can be done, are being done, will be done. Very few noteworthy achievements come about by happenstance. They're accomplishments of thorough planning, determined sacrifice, genuine effort, and continuing hard work, all of which give direction and purpose."

My own competitive goals are not as intense now as they were during the late 1960s and early 1970s, when I was searching for my best, but when I learned I would be facing Ron Hill in my age group during the 1982 Maratona Atalantica Boavista in Rio de Janeiro, I wanted to challenge him even though he had outrun me by 15 minutes in the London Marathon three months earlier. It was an absurd mission, perhaps, but it drove me to train better than I had in years. "Get as fit as you can," I told myself, "and should Hill show up unprepared for heat or run a misjudged race, you might nail him at the end." At any rate, I knew I would run better. Caught up in the challenge, I developed a marvelous sense of purpose. I never resisted beginning a tough session; difficult workouts seemed easier; and I was excited by the imagined presence of Hill shadowing me during the training.

The matchup never materialized. Hill got stranded in France

due to a mixup with the airlines, and I competed without him. Still, it was my best race all year, in fact in several years, as I placed 29th out of 5500 runners in unusually muggy conditions. Whether I could have threatened Hill seems academic now because I am reminded of something I had temporarily forgotten: the power that is released when you commit to a tough goal.

You won't run your best unless you set goals, because without a specific challenge that you've written down and can see yourself accomplishing, there's no real reason to do the work. For goal-setting to work, your targets must be specific and have an outside chance of believability. With impossible goals, you know you are just fooling yourself. Wishful thinking never accomplished anything. But neither have expectations so low they reach no further than your immediate grasp. As Robert Browning so eloquently said, "A man's reach should exceed his grasp, or what's a heaven for."

Billy Mills' reach certainly exceeded his grasp when 20 months before the 1964 Olympics he wrote his goal for the 10,000 meters in his training log: 28:25. Just before Mills wrote that, in 1962, he had left Kansas University with a modest 4:11 mile and a 9:03 two-mile. With those credentials, even making the Olympic team seemed presumptuous.

The rest is now legend: before the Games Mills had never broken 14 minutes for 5000 meters; in two of his five 10,000 meter races he did not break 30 minutes; none of the six experts in *Track & Field News'* pre-Olympic issue had predicted Mills even finishing as high as sixth; Adidas denied him complimentary shoes on the grounds they were giving them only to possible medal winners. In the Olympic 10,000 the indefatigable Mills clung to Mohamed Gammoudi and Ron Clarke for 24 laps, Clarke knocking Mills into the third lane with 350 yards to go, and then on the last curve Gammoudi bursting between Clarke and Mills, nearly knocking Mills down. Mills recovered and shattered Clarke and Gammoudi with a devastating sprint to take the lead in the last 50 yards to win in 28:24.4, his best by nearly 50 seconds and an Olympic record.

Mills, part Indian, grew up among alcoholism and despair at the Pine Ridge, South Dakota, Oglala Sioux reservation. "No one I knew had goals, a reason for living," he said later. "There was nothing to commit to ... the hardest thing I had to do when I began training to be a distance runner was to say no to my friends, my peer group, when 'socializing' meant going out and drinking."

In his book *Psycho-Cybernetics*, Maxwell Maltz advances what Mills sensed all along: when the mind sets a tough goal, the body works to fulfill it. But if you set low goals, the body will accept and fulfill those, too. Runners often go to a race, see who is at the starting line, then figure where they will place. If someone has beaten them, they figure they will be beaten again. They literally think themselves into a place in the pack.

INTERMEDIATE GOALS

Goals are of two kinds: short-range and long-range. Your long-range goal may be ultimately to run a 2:40 marathon or to chop 30 seconds off your 10km best by season's end. Your short-range goals would be the training targets—so much mileage and certain training times along the way—as well as target times for preliminary races.

I recall laying out five months' training leading up to the Boston Marathon, but was nearly paralyzed when I realized I was in for 2200 miles of running. So I looked at the first week. It entailed 40 easy miles and I said, "Well, you can do *that*, can't you?" And I went out each night and ran about five miles. Then I said, "That wasn't so bad, so you can make those few additional miles this week." And then I did that.

Although the program in its entirety was overwhelming, when I broke it into smaller segments, concentrating on one run at a time, it was possible. As I became successful in meeting short-range goals, I gained confidence and momentum, developed a new self-image, and grew confident I'd eventually achieve my long-range goal.

SET YOUR OWN GOALS

When you set goals, evaluate your motivations and don't judge yourself by society's standards or the expectations of others. Your goals should be true to your own aspirations and limits. You don't have to prove anything to anyone but yourself. It is you who will be doing the work and making the sacrifices, so you don't need to dance to anyone else's tune. Get used to the fact that there are those who would love to see you fail so they can say, "I told you so." Success, quite appropriately, has been defined as, "The one unpardonable sin against one's fellows." Brendan Foster, British

1976 Olympian, said, "It's wrong to think that every race has only one winner. Running is about improving yourself, and if you ran faster or finished higher than last time, then you're a winner no matter how many others finished in front of you." Frank Shorter says, "I don't consider coming in second (or whatever) losing. It's just not winning."

Setting goals means taking risks. If you dare to take risks, that in itself is a success. Eventually, if you take enough risks you will get results, and, if nothing else, you'll get the maximum out of yourself. Most goals should be short-term and fairly attainable because you will need successes along the way. But in some corner of your head store away a few "wild-ass dreams"—just on the fringe of lunacy—that might be possible. The great thing about tough goals is even if you don't quite reach them, you still go further than you would have had you no goals at all.

PERSISTENCY AND CONSISTENCY

In Bud Greenspan's television series *The Olympiad*, he featured a select and exemplary few athletes he called "The Persistent Ones"—those whose motto seemed to be, "If at first you don't succeed, try, try again." One of those dauntless souls was France's Alain Mimoun, whose career in running was nearly stopped before it began. He was wounded in the left leg while fighting with the free French in the battle of Monte Cassino in Italy during World War II. Mimoun was destined to run, however, and fought his way to international standing soon after the war.

In the 1948 Olympics he placed second in the 10,000 meters to Emil Zátopek and was nearly lapped. So he trained for four years to race Zátopek, whom he idolized, in the 1952 Olympics. Mimoun chased Zátopek again in the 10,000, and this time got within 16 seconds of him at the finish. In the 5000 meters, Mimoun was again second to Zátopek, but by less than a second. So Mimoun trained hard for four more years. In the 1956 Olympics, Mimoun, now 35 years old, finally won the marathon, defeating Zátopek, who was sixth. At the finish Mimoun waited for Zátopek. Mimoun jubilantly slapped Zátopek on the back and announced that he (Mimoun) had just become a father, the news of which was kept from him until the race's conclusion.

Everyone wants instant success, but sometimes profound persistence is required to achieve one's best. Even a runner of Rob de

Castella's stature spent many years working his way out of the pack. "When I first started running I was fairly average," he says. "There were many others who had a lot more ability than me. However, Pat's [Clohessy] guidance and careful development with my consistent approach have perfectly complemented each other. I think training every day is so important, and I really make an effort to do a session every day of the week, every week of the year."

It *is* possible to shift the odds in your favor, but it requires tending to details and doing things most runners don't bother with. This will look like you outsmarted the others, but it's just a matter of *attitude*.

My approach was to untangle what I was doing wrong in training, innovate to get the workouts I needed, invent motivational tricks to keep me going, and treat mistakes as learning opportunities.

When, after eight years, my best mile was 4:30 and my 3-mile was 15:22, I knew I wasn't blessed with physical talent. But my high-school track coach had provided a clue to another kind of talent after I pestered him every afternoon for a pass to get out of my study period to run. Finally, annoyed with my hounding him, and yet pleased by my determination, he snorted, "Geeze, you're a persistent son-of-a-bitch!"

Most of the difficulty in making yourself train consistently is that terrible dialogue runners have with themselves when deciding whether they have to do a particular run. No wonder they say that turning the doorknob is the hardest part of the workout. But there are all sorts of mental tricks you can use to keep yourself going.

When you resist starting a workout, tell yourself, "Just go out for 15 minutes, and if you don't feel good, come back" (knowing full well that once you get going you'll keep going). While it's tough to envision running for say, 1½ hours, it's easy to say yes to 15 minutes. If that fails, say, "Okay don't run, but (your main rival) is out there getting one in on you. And when the race comes you'll kick yourself for letting this one go."

Consistency is the glue that holds your workouts together. When the physical work becomes regular and balanced, and when you commit to a realistic but tough schedule and then make yourself do it, there's an awesome feeling of inner purpose and confidence. You may be balancing on that thin edge between your limits and exhaustion, but after you accept and handle the workload, the excitement of discovering you can do what you set out to pushes back the limits to being the best you possibly can be. Emil Zátopek has said, "If I miss one day I can tell I'm several seconds slower." Liquori says, "The first day you miss training, you begin a backward slide." Obviously, if exhaustion is about to set in, a rest is needed, but that's not what Zátopek and Liquori are getting at. While no one actually loses conditioning in one day, if you lose too many sessions, you not only develop a sloppy attitude, conditioning does not progress on schedule. Pianist Arthur Rubinstein made the point in admitting, "When I take a day off, I notice it. When I miss two days, the audience notices it."

When you come to the starting line knowing you have done everything possible, you can live with the outcome because there was nothing you could have done to prepare better. That is a terrific incentive to run a smart, competitive race. Win or lose, you can accept the result.

INNOVATING

The great Zátopek possessed no innate physical advantages over his adversaries. It was his unbelievable will power and unparalled desire to win. Zátopek experimented with all types of training. He would gallop through the forest knee-deep in snow, wearing army boots. He would run or walk the telephone poles on his way to work holding his breath until he became so mentally tough he would pass out. He ran with his wife, Dana, on his shoulders (until it resulted in a hernia). He never let himself get bored—or miss a workout. When one night he was faced with the prospect of missing training because family responsibilities prevented his leaving the house, the indomitable Zátopek simply turned up the radio, filled the tub with water and dirty laundry, and ran in place on it for two hours.

Inspired by Zátopek's resourcefulness, I ran my morning work-outs at work up and down a nine-floor spiral fire escape staircase when I couldn't afford the time to dress and run outdoors one winter. That spring I won the Nationals and made the Pan-American Games team. By the following winter I had constructed a treadmill in my basement from junk parts. It not only enabled me to get in runs after I got kicked off the fire escape, it rescued one of my key indoor workouts when I couldn't get on the track. In exchange for 10 × 1-mile at 5:00, I ran 10 hard five-minute repetitions on the treadmill. To keep from going bonkers during the two-hour workout, I pumped just about all the music I owned through my stereo earphones.

I also tinkered with my racing shoes. Early on I built my own from scratch. Later, when commercial racing flats became better, I carved those down until I knew they were lighter and more responsive than anyone else's. In the moment of truth during a race, when I would desperately search for any signal or reason why I should be able to fight off or pass another runner, I would say to myself, "We may be equal, but my shoes are faster and I'm going to nail him." A suffering body will grasp at any logic. The result was that I made the decision to have a go, and making that decision justified the shoe chopping. In some corner of my brain I probably knew that an ounce or two didn't make that much difference, but in a race I would buy it every time.

As I later discovered, Ron Hill thought along these same lines. In fact, Hill was (and still is) a man obsessed with detail. One of the sport's foremost innovators, he popularized carbohydrate loading, light shoes and fishnet singlets. He has recorded and pondered every footstep he has taken. Even so, when Hill lined up as the favorite to win the 1972 Olympic marathon, Frank Shorter did a double take. Decked out in seemingly metallic shorts, singlet, and shoes of his own design (to reflect heat), Hill looked like the Tin Woodsman about to set off for Oz in aluminum underwear. Moreover, Hill had ripped the tongues out of his shoes (to save weight), shaved his legs (to slip through the wind), and trimmed his hair to the "exact millimeter." Taking this all in with some incredulity, Shorter thought to himself, "Now there is a man who's precise!"

Hill also has not missed a day of training since December 20, 1964. As of mid-1985 (when this was written), that's double workouts every day except Sunday for over 7500 consecutive days. It is not surprising, therefore, that Hill says, "I just don't believe anyone who says they've got no time to train. I've found time. . . . even in airports. . . . You have to say, 'This is what I've got to do, so how am I going to do it, and when am I going to do it?' " Hill was able to fit his training into his life before the elite of the sport were subsidized by shoe companies and prize-money races. It proves that a runner who works a 40-hour week, like most of us, can do it.

By running four to six miles of the way to work and various

routes back in the evening, you may have to leave only 20 to 30 minutes earlier in the morning than when you drive all the way. For years I wasted time driving and then running when both could be easily combined.

LEARNING FROM MISTAKES

Mistakes cannot be avoided, and often, repeated mistakes are a necessary detour on the road to success. Success requires taking risks, and risking invites failure. But to risk is to grow, even when things backfire. A mistake that teaches a lesson sends a better-equipped runner back into the game. We often learn more from failure than success. Mistakes and failures are worthless if you just accept them and deny the lessons they teach.

The mistakes I made in dealing with the sciatica I encountered before the Pan-Am Games in 1967 taught me how to overcome the same affliction when it returned ten days before the 1968 Olympic Marathon trial. Before the Pan-Am Games I mistakenly persisted with a 20-mile run that left me injured and unable to run in the Games. It was the worst defeat I had suffered, and I couldn't imagine any good in not being able to compete with the only national team I'd probably make. But without my experiences with sciatica on the Pan-Am Games team, I wouldn't have made the Olympic team. And I'd gladly trade the Pan-Ams for the Olympics.

For every defeat, there is a victory waiting to be released if you are willing to dissect what went wrong. Too often we make the same mistakes—as though it was beyond our capacity to change things. Some runners habitually charge out too fast in races and crawl in without getting the message. They commit tactical errors in races and would just as soon forget about them afterward. They repeat the same training mistakes and never ask themselves what went wrong. Mark Twain knew that even a cat that sits on a hot stove will never do it again.

Perhaps it is the nature of the beast. Many times after repeating a mistake I've told myself, "You should know better by now." We are less apt to heed advice when things seem to be going right, even though we may be on a collision course with disaster. But after we get into trouble we are ready to listen. When my high school and college track performances disintegrated as the racing season progressed, I began to research various training methods until I discovered the Lydiard approach. But even after I studied everything he wrote, I had to learn a lot on my own—often by trial and error.

There were other lessons. Seventeen days before the '68 Olympic Marathon trial at 7640 feet I ran a 15.6-mile time-trial. For the first 10.4 miles I was faster than I had time-trialed 10.4 miles the week before. I anticipated an excellent final time, but the pace was too fast, and before I could finish, I got sick in a service-station men's room. I couldn't run the next day, but it gave me time to think. Instead of being upset, I realized that a valuable lesson had been revealed: In the trial I *had* to run even speed. That led me to devise a special workout which drilled in a sense of the pace. Thus, what could have been a disappointing time-trial, instead was a key factor in putting me in the Olympics.

So, I had learned training and even-paced running. But there would be other lessons—heat training, tactics, surviving slumps, overcoming defeat—and even today, new ones continue to emerge. That is life and racing: mistakes . . . learning . . . triumph . . . different mistakes. . . .

2.
THE
ABCs OF
TRAINING

BELIEVE IN YOUR PROGRAM

A poor program, if you totally believe in it, is far better than a good program run with doubt. Runners often don't understand how to approach workouts. Not because of a paucity of information on what to do, but because everyone in the game and all the running literature keep giving conflicting advice. As more information is dispensed, runners become more bewildered. Everyone from physiologists and world-record holders to runners at your elbow have a theory about training. Many of their concepts are diametrically opposed: Train on grass; train on roads. Interval work is good; it's bad. You have to work hard and hurt in training; you should never go all out in workouts. A hundred miles a week is minimum for top performances; quality is more important than quantity.

When Percy Cerutty trained Australian mile and 1500-meter record holder Herb Elliott he was able to mold Elliott into one of the fiercest competitors of all time. But Cerutty's training of Elliott was not scientific. It was based almost purely on emotion and his ability to convince Elliott that if he trained like an animal, fearing nothing and energetically tackling anything, he would be unbeatable. Elliott was never beaten in the 1500 or the mile (unless you want to count a loss to 17-year-old Ray Walters when Elliott was 14). Elliott, recently reflecting on meeting Cerutty in 1955, says, "Percy excited me as a person. I found him believable, which a lot of people, particularly on first meeting him, didn't find so. . . . I could feel Cerutty stir emotions in me that must have been already there somewhere. Percy had the ability to fan them up from a dormant spark into something a lot stronger."

Because Elliott never doubted that his preparation was better than anyone else's, the idea that anyone could beat him was totally unacceptable. Also, because Elliott believed without reservation in what Cerutty preached, he was able to perform and survive the rigorous training that Cerutty prescribed.

Doubt is the killer of enthusiasm. The most perfect program is useless if the runner doesn't believe in it. Who can make himself do a difficult or unappealing workout if he doesn't believe it will help? There can be no sacrifice without reason. The runs become dull and uninspired, and eventually the energy to do them dissipates. John Sinclair, one of America's best road racers, cautions runners that "Once you've chosen your plan, you'd better believe in it. Once you lose confidence in it, you're finished."

After I got into heavy-duty training I believed that 100 miles per week was the minimum with which I could reach my potential. If the week's mileage was recorded using two digits, I felt I was backsliding. I argued with a friend about the actual difference between logging 99 or 100 miles, especially after telling him I would often squeeze in a mile or whatever to reach the magic figure. He said there was no difference between running 100 miles and 99. And for me to insist that there was, was only playing a mind game.

It did matter immensely whether I clocked 100 or 99. For one thing, if I could settle for a mile less one week, I could part with two the next. If I didn't hold the limit somewhere, I felt the whole program would come apart. To me, three-digit weekly mileage was magical. And it *was* because I believed it. If I hadn't believed it, then there would have been little, if any, significant difference between 99 and 100.

COACHING

I spent my first 11 years using hit-or-miss training until I discovered what Arthur Lydiard had to say in his book *Run to the Top* (London: Herbert Jenkis, Ltd., and New Zealand: A. H. & A. W. Reed, 1962). Later I wrote Lydiard for help, but it never came about. Undoubtedly, had I a good coach I would have reached my peak much earlier—say in my mid-20s rather than my early 30s, and I would have run faster. Conversely, by prodding, experimenting, and searching on my own, I learned a lot of lessons I probably wouldn't have if all my ideas had been spoon-fed to me.

The problem was that I couldn't locate anyone whose advice I trusted more than my own. That may sound pompous, but, like believing in yourself, you must believe in your coach. Rob de Castella says of his coach, Pat Clohessy, "It's so important to have someone in whom you can have complete confidence."

Even once having been a great runner does not mean that the spark can be transferred to others. Czechoslovakia's Emil Zátopek learned this after setting 18 world records and retiring in 1957 to become a national coach. The ever-candid Zátopek admits, "I was not good at coaching . . . when one of my boys was beaten, I went to congratulate the winner and oooh, my boy says, 'My coach goes and congratulates my adversary because he has beaten me.' The really good coaches are frantic for their boys and arrange everything—I cannot be fanatical. Nurmi was never anxious to be a coach . . . Arthur Lydiard was no record holder but was a very modern, nice man. There are many wonderful coaches who were never world-record holders. And many world-record holders and Olympic champions who were never good coaches."

Zátopek is right. Often the best athletes make the worst coaches. Part of the reason is that they have little firsthand insight into the average runner. World-class runners are physiological freaks. If their abnormalities were visible like, say, "the man with the alligator skin," they could draw top wages in any carnival freak show. They are wired like practically no one else, and can survive training that would wreck the rest of us.

Many athletes do not see the value of a coach, fearing that it would stifle their creative energies, or else they aren't quite sure a good coach could make a difference. Others simply think they know it all or can't accept the idea that they might need outside help. They say they are working about as hard as they can anyway. Peter Coe, Seb Coe's father and coach, says, "What goes on between your ears is as important as what goes into your legs and lungs in training terms."

A good coach understands this as well as how to motivate the athlete to set tough goals. Sometimes the coach or mentor does no more than provide that extra confidence the athlete needs in a critical moment. In 1954, on his journey to Oxford to attempt the first four-minute mile, Roger Bannister ran into Franz Stampfl, the Austrian coach. Bannister had briefly met Stampfl earlier, and until then no coach had impressed him much. Now Bannister saw Stampfl as someone he "badly needed at that moment."

"I would have liked his advice and help at this moment," Bannister wrote later, "but could not bring myself to ask him. It was as if now, at the end of my running career, I was forced to admit that coaches were necessary after all."

Stampfl's presence at that moment proved critical. Bannister wanted to postpone the attempt because of the wind, but Stampfl convinced him he was capable of 3 minutes 56 or 57 seconds and therefore should maintain his resolve. It was, said Bannister, "that bit of nudge" he needed to get on with the attempt.

One of the best illustrations of an athlete floundering for years and then dramatically reaching world-class status in one year after being coached is New Zealand's Allison Roe. She developed from an inconsistent club runner one year to winner of the Boston Marathon. Six months later she held the women's world marathon record. But it wasn't until someone else got her to believe in herself that she could do it. Until Roe came under the influence of Garry Elliott, a local club runner in Auckland, she was known in New Zealand as a spotty trainer and competitor.

Elliott knew he was dealing with a great natural talent, but also someone who was inconsistent and who tended to become bored by intensive training. Elliott says, "Getting Allison ready for New York [the marathon where she ran a world-record 2:25:29] involved preparing her mind to handle the pace, and preparing her emotionally to handle that situation." He went on to set up a "stepping stone" approach, to prepare her emotionally by having her succeed at progressively more difficult training and time-trials.

One thing he did to ensure her success was to lay out a downhill, wind-aided road course where she was able to run world-class times in training. Roe, who avoided the track, apparently believed that these times were legitimate. When I asked Elliott about the validity of Roe's times, he replied, "It's reasonably accurate. Whether or not it's one or two seconds out doesn't matter . . . she believes she's doing it." Right up until the New York Marathon Elliott kept working on Roe's head. The final mental boost was listing "all the positive things we'd done in her preparation." It contained all her fastest workouts, best race times, and her training mileage over the last six months, which was a personal record. Elliott finally told her that 2:28 would win, and that since she was obviously capable of that, she should just go out and enjoy the race for the first 17 miles and then put pressure on Grete Waitz, who they reckoned would be her main competition. And that's pretty much the way it happened except that Waitz was forced out at 13 miles by shin splints. After that, Roe took off to run the second half faster.

So in Roe's example we see a runner of great natural talent, but who was not consistent or confident in her training or racing, come under the tutelage of someone who could dispel her fears. After Elliott thoroughly convinced her that she was unbeatable, for most of 1981, she was. It demonstrates that once she visualized herself as a winner, she became a winner. But the kind of training they did, with no real build-up, was conducive to injuries, which began to pull Roe down. She trained sporadically and lost her confidence and drive. After her fantastic 1981 season, Roe has never performed at that level since.

Steve Cram, British 3:49.95 miler at age 21, and gold medalist in the 1983 World Track Championship 1500 meters, says he needs "somebody to talk to when things are good and when they are bad. You need someone to praise you or to tell you what you did wrong. Even if you don't agree with them you still need someone to put out other views. . . . Some people say, 'Oh, I just train myself,' and I think you can get away with that, but it's the other aspects—the motivation side—that are possibly the most important."

Arthur Lydiard says, "I've never yet seen a great athlete at the Olympics who didn't have a coach. I've seen great athletes who've failed because they never had a coach—I think Ron Clarke is a typical example. He should've won Olympic medals, and he didn't [Lydiard means a gold medal; Clarke won a bronze in the 10,000 meters in 1964]. So all these people who are aspiring to be great, they need guidance. Otherwise they're going to make costly

Coach Pat Clohessy (left) and Rob de Castella discuss the upcoming training and racing.

mistakes. But I think that once an athlete gets a fair basic knowledge, he doesn't need so much a coach as a mentor—someone he can sit down with and talk things over, and make the decisions to eliminate mistakes."

Lydiard hit the nail on the head. In the case of world-class athletes, the coach may not necessarily know that much more about running, but is a source of inspiration, and by arranging the training, takes a lot of pressure off the athlete. Moreover, as Lydiard found, "Simple psychology is a big thing. Those boys [Snell and Halberg] had faith in me. If there were any little doubts in their minds, the fact that I could tell them to do something about them seemed to allay their fears." The athlete in the thick of training often cannot see things objectively. Emotion overrides cool assessment. Even when the athlete is capable of deciding what to do, it's a mental boost to get confirmation and a good send-off from someone whose judgment can be trusted. Rob de Castella says that Clohessy doesn't dictate or take charge. "Rather," de Castella says, "he consults, he discusses, and persuades." World-class runners don't have coaches because they don't know what to run, they have them because two heads are better than one.

Many times the coach is outright responsible for getting an athlete to believe enough in him or herself to make the decision to tackle seemingly insurmountable odds. Such is the case in the career of Steve Scott, who, when he left high school, didn't even want to run bad enough to go to a college an hour away from home. But when he met Len Miller, coach at U.C. Irvine, Miller not only got Scott to come to Irvine, he began to tell everyone that Scott would be the "next great American miler." That strategy—of prodding Scott—boosted the athlete's confidence. And as Scott took the bait and got better, Miller would dangle increasingly higher goals in front of him. Finally, Scott clocked 3:31.96 for the 1500 meters and a 3:47.69 mile to break Jim Ryun's American record. Says Scott of his coach, "He is undoubtedly responsible for any success I have had. I probably wouldn't even be running now if it weren't for him."

COACHING YOURSELF

It is often difficult or impractical to find a good coach, especially one who can be with you or train alongside you. The solution is to coach yourself, but objectively, almost to the point that you assume two identities: the runner, and the coach who monitors the runner in his or her best interests, but without the emotionalism of the runner. This simply means that when you play the role of the coach, you must consider the runner side of you as another person, *objectively* deciding the best course of action. After the "coach" has decided what's best, you, the runner, have to decide how many of these decisions are acceptable.

This perhaps sounds a little crazy, but it works. When I used to seriously race the Boston Marathon, for example, I carefully evaluated how fast I was running at the beginning to make certain I was on correct pace. The first 10 miles of Boston are downhill, easy to over-run. Then you die somewhere after halfway. So, at the gun, I would move out lively enough to clear the melee of frenetic arms and legs and then at about one mile I'd pretend I was an impartial observer watching myself run by. I'd say, "Can that guy keep that up for another 25 miles?" Judgment would not be based on my time at one mile, but rather my effort. If I couldn't see myself running at that pace all the way, I'd slow to what I thought I could handle. Others would scoot by, but around halfway I'd begin to reel them in. Looking back, I never once wished I had not followed my initial assessment. I've finished fourth, fifth, ninth, and tenth at Boston and each time it was because the "coach" told me to cool it initially, then apply the pressure. In the heat of competition the runner side of me wanted to go with the pack, but had I, I would have died like all those I hauled down at the end.

The coach side of you must decide what is best for you, the athlete. He or she weighs what is understood about how various kinds of training affect the runner, isolates past problems and their causes, and tries to work past them. It requires understanding your strengths and weaknesses and customizing the training and race strategies accordingly.

One of the purposes of this book is to acquaint you with the thought processes that are involved in coaching, whether you are advising yourself or others. The problem with written schedules, especially when presented in a book, is that there are many ways to interpret and apply them.

If you coach yourself, understand each workout's purpose so you can interpret how to run it. When the objective is to take a rest, go easy no matter how many old ladies on crutches pass you. Impress them the next day when it's your turn to get moving. Use your head when deciding how much is enough. If you are trying for 15 × 400 and you begin struggling and losing form, or your calves are knotting up, stop. Cut the workout. This is different than copping out. It is recognizing the difference between a commitment to finish a difficult session, and foolishly persisting when your body and common sense are telling you that by continuing you will do more harm than good. When Salazar finds he can't handle a workout, he says he'll "just stop. I now realize that there's just no use digging my grave any deeper than it already is." A good coach would stop you or Salazar at this point, and I'm hoping that in lieu of a good coach, this book will show you how and when to make these decisions yourself.

INDIVIDUALIZED TRAINING

At each stage of your development there is one best way to train. While the basics of physiology are the same for all (and therefore the basics of conditioning will be the same), the differences in what each runner actually does—and there are many—are in the application of the basics. Runners differ widely in experience, talent, speed, endurance, durability, likes, and dislikes, to name a few of the obvious. Therefore, although two athletes might use the same general approach, one might run 100 miles a week and another 60; one might work hard one day followed by two easy days, while another alternates hard and easy days. One might use the track, another runs intervals elsewhere. There are many ways to interpret and apply any schedule.

"Different runners must have different programs, even if the principle is the same," says Rolf Haikkola, who coached Lasse Viren. Bill Bowerman agrees: "Types of application differ," he says, "but principles don't." That the program must be tailored to the needs of the athlete is neatly revealed in a conversation between Frank Shorter and Garry Bjorklund. Between the 1976 Olympic trials and the Games, Garry studied and adapted the training of Shorter, who ultimately emerged the victor when the two raced. Finally, perplexed that he did not derive the same benefit from the training as did Shorter, Bjorklund asked him, "Frank, why do you always beat me?"

"Because," Shorter answered, "I train Frank Shorter to run Frank Shorter's race, and you train Garry Bjorklund to run Frank Shorter's race."

There is no shortage of programs and schedules for runners to follow. Like the endless procession of new, miracle weight-loss diets, scarcely a month passes without running literature offering another scheme for cracking the three-hour marathon, the 40-minute 10km, or taking on Mary Decker and winning. Some of the schedules are basically sound; others are not. Many are misleading or just sheer nonsense. Most promise the greatest results for the least involvement. Everyone, it seems, wants a gimmick. Everyone wants to go to heaven, but no one wants to die.

If your program is based on sound psychological and physiological principles, the differences between what a world-class runner does and what you do should reflect only your individual differences.

It's tempting to copy what the world-class do, especially with the market saturated with "how they train" literature. This is where many runners go wrong. What we all tend to forget is that the elite did not train that way while they were coming up. People forget that Salazar, de Castella, Rodgers, Waitz, and Decker did not begin by running 120 miles a week or 15 × 400s in 60 seconds. Dick Beardsley, who ran the 1982 Boston Marathon in 2:08:53, was a 4:35 miler in high school. Before that marathon he ran 7 × 4:34 with 2½-minute rests.

After Frank Shorter won the marathon at the 1972 Munich Olympics, many aspiring runners began to copy what Shorter reportedly ran before the Games. They forgot that Shorter got his start racing the track distances and cross-country in high school and at Yale University. Later he moved up to and became world-class at 10,000 meters. By the time he tackled road running and the marathon, he was out of school and had a well-rounded background of distance training, racing, speed work, and solid mileage. Only then did he run the marathon, and when he did, he excelled straightaway. Even runners with just as much experience as Shorter probably wouldn't train the way he did. You have to consider the total organism. We all are so complex and individual that considerable program personalizing is necessary. This doesn't mean you can't learn from Shorter, but that you should extract that which suits *you*.

When I first began to help runners with their training, I soon realized the one athletic talent I had: I could string relatively tough workouts together for days and even weeks without getting permanently run-down or injured. I'd get tired, certainly, but not exhausted, and by merely cutting back for a day or so I'd be ready to hammer again. I later found that most others could not do this. I could, for example, run 30 miles on Sunday and seven sets of 10 × 100 fast striding on Monday, but I would never ask anyone else to try that.

Although I rarely got injured, others who tried to duplicate my patterns would have. It soon became obvious that in working out a program for other runners, I could not just give them what I did, perhaps watered down by 10 to 30 percent. Whole patterns had to be re-assembled. In the case of Lorraine Moller, I found that while I could use fartlek to my advantage, she was too competitive when we ran it together and tended to race, either pushing too hard when leading or getting discouraged if she fell behind while following. I had to substitute a similar kind of workout with more structure, like intervals, so she knew what was coming and how much pressure to apply.

TRAINING SCHEDULES

Training according to a schedule that has been carefully constructed in advance is the surest way to balance your training. This entails blocking out what you want to do, and then revising and fine-tuning it to smooth out the kinks so it progresses logically. A realistic schedule reflects the basic concepts of sound physiology and is mentally stimulating. It ensures that you make the best use of your time and efforts between the start of training and the races you are shooting for.

I often spend a week or two fine-tuning my schedules after the initial draft. I do this by calibrating them against what I've done in the past and what I've learned since then. I go over my training logs searching for mistakes, isolating combinations of workouts that seem to work, and progressing the workload so that the demands are realistic.

It's difficult to describe exactly how this is done. It requires that you or the coach become something of a detective, searching out clues from the past to apply to the future. You must weigh what you understand about how various kinds of training affect you. You must not violate the basics of physiology. You must use your intuitive powers in deciding how much is enough but not too much. In short, it means thinking and evaluating in realistic terms. It is one thing to write fierce workouts on paper and quite another to do them.

Antero Raevuori, in describing the approach Lasse Viren and his coach took toward Viren's program wrote, "It is not enough to write numbers on a sheet of paper: 'Today, 35 kilometers. Tomorrow, 20. The day after tomorrow, 50.' Every single moment, Rolf Haikkola must know the limits of Lasse Viren's body and the state of his mind, his very emotions."

Haikkola explains how he used to plan Viren's training around the races they anticipated: "The racing schedule will be the backbone of Lasse's training program. It is much easier to draw plans around the exact dates of races. Unless I know the number of competitions, I can't make up a schedule. And the number is not enough; I must know the distances. Every now and then the organizers have not provided a race according to Lasse's training needs. We have to look for another race. If the right distances are not set up, the whole system becomes absurd."

What Haikkola is saying, and what I've always thought, is that you can't develop an effective training schedule unless you know what you are working toward. A schedule is a blueprint for constructing something. If you were drawing up plans for a building, you would have to know what kind of structure it will be and the number of floors. In running you must know when the important races occur and what the distances are. Then you plan your training around them. This doesn't mean you have to know the exact dates and distances of all the races, just the big one(s). It's enough to know that there will be other "tune-up races" during your sharpening. If there are no developmental races scheduled when you need them, you will have to write time-trials or other special workouts into your program.

When you make up your training as you go, perhaps waiting to see how you feel before you train each day, it's much like looking at individual pieces of a jigsaw puzzle and trying to imagine the picture. Each day's training, like the puzzle pieces, must be arranged in the proper sequence. Workouts interlock in precise ways. Some runners and coaches can balance programs intuitively. But for that to work, the one calling the shots must have considerable experience and a sound, intuitive idea of how the workouts are progressing. Although the program isn't written, the rationale is there. Otherwise training is hit or miss, inefficient, and likely to underwrite all sorts of mischief.

Writing out your workouts, or types of workouts, makes it easier to spot training mistakes. It increases the odds that you get the optimum amount of each kind of training within the time available. Without a schedule it's easy to panic, take shortcuts, and jump into workouts you are not ready for or do not yet need.

This is especially tempting when your competition has jumped ahead into track-type work, and you are still supposed to be putting in the miles. When you assign a particular kind of training to each of the weeks between the beginning of a season and the major races, it's easier to balance your work.

Smooth transitions between different kinds of training minimize your chances of injury, because sudden jumps into unfamiliar territory are eliminated. In making it up as you go, you might, for example, get the urge to test your speed without sufficient background and wind up injured. You should also make sure that stress days are balanced against recovery days, so that each week unravels as a finely orchestrated event. That way you don't erroneously work the same muscle systems two days in a row. You won't, in a fit of unguarded zeal, string tough workouts together until exhaustion or injury sets in. You get variation; you get enough rest because you worked it out that when your head was screwed on right. Without rests you get weaker instead of stronger.

Successful use of schedules requires, however, that they be flexible enough for you to respond to unforseen developments or planning errors. Things go wrong to upset schedules—illness, injury, or temporary loss of drive. These are the times that plans need to be revised. Sometimes you will need more rest than scheduled after a hard workout or race. It's important that you intercede at this point and rearrange your runs. Otherwise, impaired performance or injuries await you down the line. Having a schedule to adhere to when the going gets tough is like having someone give you a push to get you going. But it's equally important to recognize the need to cut back if you start getting in over your head.

When Arthur Lydiard published schedules in *Run to the Top* in 1962, they were the best I had seen, and I couldn't wait to try them. He had cautioned that they were just examples of the principles governing conditioning and should not be strictly adhered to. It was the principles that counted, he said, and so long as one balanced and ordered the workouts, any number of variations, all of which would produce the same results, could be developed.

This last point was lost in many runners. They overlooked the reasoning behind the work and slaved to the schedules. It ruined many in the United States because in New Zealand the road, track, and cross-country seasons are in a different sequence than here. Moreover, at that time, most of the U.S. runners competed for high schools and colleges which required coping with intense, short competitive indoor and outdoor seasons for which there was relatively little time for preparation. In New Zealand, everyone ran for a club rather than a school, so there was time for the long build-ups that Lydiard demanded. Coaches and runners in the northern hemisphere began to say that Lydiard's methods were suited only to "down under." Fortunately, I had re-read the text until I thought I understood what he was driving at, ran to his schedules until I gauged my reactions to them, and then rewrote them to fit my own individual needs.

When I understood what each workout was supposed to accomplish, it enabled me to eliminate a lot of the guesswork and indecision from my training. I developed new faith in my ability to work hard, and set goals previously unimaginable.

But it had been difficult to interpret what Lydiard was getting at. For example, Monday's workout might be to "run one mile at three-quarters effort." No mention of warming up, or how much, if any, supplementary running should round out that workout. When the workout was 20 interval 440s or 20 interval 220s, his tables of effort would have me running faster during the 440s than on the 220s for the same level of difficulty. No mention was made of what kinds of recoveries to take between the fast sections. That may not seem important until you realize that 20 × 440 at 70 seconds with a 100-yard quick jog recovery is worlds apart from 20 × 440 at 70 seconds with a 440 walk between them.

Which means that when you study the schedules in Chapter 13, look at them in their entirety—in terms of various blocks of training and weekly patterns. Don't just say to yourself, "Well, the schedule says to run hard anaerobic repeats with short rests today." Ask yourself (if I haven't adequately explained), "What's the purpose of that kind of workout; how does it relate to what I'm trying to do at this point in my training, and how does it balance out the other workouts?" When you have the answer, you know how to set up several different workouts, any of which would accomplish the same thing. At that point you can begin to tailor the schedules to your own particular needs and circumstances, which is better then running something just because a piece of paper tells you to.

Some runners don't want to take the structured approach because they fear it will take the spontaneity out of training. It doesn't. It takes most of the worry and mistakes out. There is a greater sense of well-being and enthusiasm when you know where you are going. When you are working on one thing, such as basic conditioning, you don't wonder whether there will be time for everything else. You have provided for all that. It also forces you to look at the program as a whole, rather than just a series of separate workouts, stretching your knowledge, intuition, and imagination to their fullest in deliberately working to serve up the best batch of training you can, so you run what you *need*, not what you *want*. You don't get that by making it up as you go.

TRAINING LOGS

It is difficult to make connections between the proposed future and the fading past if you don't keep records. Our memories often betray us. How we think we trained before a good race or injury is often not the way it went. The only way to be sure of knowing what you did is to record it.

When I began running seriously, training logs were not popular. Running itself was not popular. I recorded my workouts in a diary, one or two days' worth on a page. Several drawbacks emerged, however, when I tried to evaluate what I had done. It was the separate pieces of the puzzle syndrome all over again. So I got a small sketch book, roughly 10 inches by 12 inches, and ruled off a calander of rectangles on each page to show a whole month's work at a glance.

Record in your log what you will need to reference. The essentials usually include distances, times, efforts, and how the work was performed, such as intervals, steady pace, fartlek, hills, and so on. It's also valuable to keep a record of your morning pulse, working pulse (to be discussed) and your weight. You will want to remember how you felt. Were you energetic, or were you tired? Note when you stretch, weight-train, or do other supplementary work. Beyond that you might note unusual conditions such as heat, cold, poor footing, or wind. I like to keep a cumulative daily mileage total as the week progresses.

Training logs, besides being fun to read years later, are valuable in timing your peak condition. If, for example, you had hit your peak too soon last season, or conversely, hadn't allowed enough time to complete your sharpening, this time around you can make the necessary adjustments.

A schedule and log in no way ensure that if you plan your workouts and then analyze them, you will execute perfect training. But it is an approach, and by pondering the logic of what you are doing, you can't help but gain insight. This will speed up learning, and that gives you special adaptive advantages. Ultimately it makes training and racing more fun.

TWICE-A-DAY WORKOUTS

Double workouts are nothing new. England's Alfred Shrubb, who set every amateur world record between six miles and the one-hour run during one race in 1904 ran them. But except for the exceptionally dedicated, few runners in the first half of the twentieth century trained twice a day, and they were mostly ultra-distance runners. Until the 1950s, few serious runners averaged one workout a day. Roger Bannister usually trained on his lunch hour five days a week. A medical student at Oxford, he felt he could afford no more time than that. Nevertheless, he was first to break the four-minute mile.

Most serious runners run twice daily because they believe it helps in competition. While many athletes swear by double workouts and rise at ghastly morning hours to do them, there is little, if any, conclusive research demonstrating that they are beneficial. Some studies even suggest that they might make you slower.

What is the rationale behind double workouts? Lydiard considers any running you do of benefit. If the main workout is supplemented with another relatively slower run, you run more miles per week, thought to be a determinant of success. Moreover, Lydiard says the second workout "assists in the recovery from low blood pH that may have developed from anaerobic training." In other words, if you've had a hard track workout, a light run the next morning loosens you and flushes away some of the legs' residual waste products before the main run that evening.

If you want to go in circles checking something out, review the research on double workouts. While most runners and coaches intuitively recognize that *if applied correctly*, twice-a-day runs can improve you, the scientific world hasn't been able to prove it, mainly because it's difficult to control other variables affecting performance. That's why training remains basically an art rather than a science.

A friend of mine from New Zealand, Roy Stevenson, recently wrote his Ph.D. thesis on twice-a-day workouts, and his experiences illustrate the experimental problems typically encountered with studies of this sort. He formed two groups from 26 males and females (ending with 18) who were already running 30–40 miles per week and could run 10km in 33 to 43 minutes. He had both groups run five days a week, but one ran four miles in the morning and evening, the other eight miles once a day. After six weeks, various physical and performance changes were measured. The result most significant to me was that pre- and post-study times for runs over 440 yards, one mile, and the maximum distance covered during 12 and 30 minutes, revealed no statistically significant differences between the two groups.

Stevenson was hampered by the reluctance of elite runners to volunteer for any study which would compromise their own training. Moreover, the subjects who dropped out of the study probably were not randomly distributed, and even if they were, fewer numbers lowered the statistical significance of the results. He concluded that, "The results confirmed the null hypothesis that there would be no significant changes between groups . . . this means in effect, that splitting one's set daily running mileage into two sessions does not incur any special benefit over completing the miles run in one single workout. . . ."

Does this mean that twice-a-day workouts don't help? Although science doesn't seem to think so, let's see what common sense and experience tell us.

If I coached runners who ran 40 miles a week as did those in Stevenson's study, they would not run twice daily. Considering that roughly the first mile and a half of any run is basically warming up, and that most physiologists agree that the training effect kicks in only after about 20 minutes, two four-mile runs would not appear to be as effective as one eight-mile run. Hal Higdon advises, and I agree, that unless one is already running for about an hour in the main workout, there is no point in adding a second workout or splitting less than 60 minutes' work. My gut feeling was that of Stevenson's two groups, those who ran eight miles once a day would, if anything, benefit most.

The answer to the twice-a-day workout question is "yes" under some circumstances, and "no" under others. If you are a beginner or running less than 50 to 60 miles per week, double workouts probably are of no benefit, and perhaps a drawback. Double workouts mean more time spent changing clothes and cleaning up. Ask yourself if that time could be better spent extending one good workout.

Double runs probably are most valuable during your build-up when mileage and aerobic training are important. Most runners can tolerate more miles by running twice a day. Personally, I find it easier to run five miles in the morning and 12 in the evening than one 17. When I feel that a continuous 17 is more beneficial than five plus 12, I will either run 17 plus another easy run, or skip the second run.

A rule of thumb for adding a second run to schedules designed for one run a day is to subtract *half* of the second workout's mileage from the main run. For example, if the schedule calls for a 10-mile run and you ran four miles in the morning, run eight in the evening. When half of the second run's mileage is subtracted from the main workout, the total stress is about the same, provided the supplementary run is relatively easy. Ron Clarke said that when running twice a day, one workout should be relatively easy. I agree. Two tough runs a day will usually begin to tell on any runner.

One benefit of double workouts is they teach you to recover quicker. Much of the training has to do with rate of recovery. Running twice a day requires that you recover between runs on an average of every 12 hours rather than 24. When beginning morning workouts after you are used to just one in the evening, it's grating to crawl out of bed and hit the roads. But after a week or two you get used to it. Lydiard claims that slow morning runs provide a "message." Higdon feels that double workouts not only increase the mileage during the build-up by splitting the miles into two shorter runs, they enable you to run faster.

Len Miller, Steve Scott's coach at Arizona State University, recommends, however, that no runner do double workouts year round. High school runners, he advises, should stop double workouts at least a month before their main competiton. Grete Waitz, an extremely experienced athlete, also eases up on double workouts before competition. But because her competitive season is not as compressed as a high-school athlete's, she trains hard between races. Still, she says, "To run a good race you mustn't feel tired. To east down, I train just once a day for five days before the race."

Now that we have all these ideas, I'll suggest a practical approach to double workouts: Until you've been running two or more years, don't bother with them. Don't do them at the beginning of a new season when there's enough stress in running once a day. Do them after you can handle at least 50–60 miles per week, and then start with two or three double workouts a week until you can tolerate or want to do more. Don't break your longest run of the week. Keep that one intact, for reasons I'll get to later. It's generally not economical. to run much less than four miles or 30 minutes at a time, unless you are just loosening up or recovering from an injury. Drop double workouts at least four to five days before serious competition. If you are losing sleep to run in the mornings, either go to bed earlier or forget them. If you have morning races, morning workouts teach you to function then. Bill Dellinger, for one, puts his runners through hard intervals every Thursday morning because he believes they prepare his team for the stress of morning cross-country races.

Keep the supplementary run easy and shorter than your main run. Harry Graves, track coach at Penn State says, "Only experienced, developed athletes should do morning runs, and those runs should be easy. A 30-minute run at the seven-minute pace is adequate for most runners." If you are scheduled for 12 miles, and want to split it into two workouts, you would probably be better off with four and eight rather than six and six, although there are many exceptions depending upon the type of workout. While two recovery six-mile runs would be okay, an easy four and a hard eight would be better than two hard sixes. When quality becomes more important than mileage, cut back on the morning runs except to loosen up after a hard track or road sessions.

WINTER TRAINING

On December 19, 1983, Michael Krantz, a 23-year-old geology major at Carleton College, Minnesota, stepped out of his apartment at 7:34 A.M. for a 35-minute run at 8- to 9-minute-mile pace. He wore a T-shirt, briefs, long-sleeved polypropylene jacket, cap, gloves, and running shorts.

"It didn't feel especially cold to me," he said later, "and I don't recall feeling the wind, so the wind may have been at my back." During the run Krantz said he experienced no discomfort on his bare legs, but "at one point . . . noticed that part of one ear was frostbitten." It was back at the apartment that he got a real shock. His thighs were swollen, the skin unshapely, hard, and literally frozen white. This is not surprising, considering that the temperature was 35 degrees below zero and the windchill was in excess of −60 degrees.

Krantz began to go into shock and sought help at another apartment. He was rushed to the hospital and immersed in warm water and taken by ambulance to a Minneapolis hospital burn unit where it was feared he might lose part or all of his legs.

"I suppose some people would think this was stupid," Krantz said a week later when he took his first steps, "but it just didn't seem any colder than usual when I started out."

It's guys like Krantz who give winter running a bad rap. They forsake common sense, naively venture half-naked into one of the Midwest's worst winter storms of this century, and then leave us with horror stories about the perils of winter running. No wonder so many runners ditch their running gear and worship their fireplaces when the first snowflakes fall. If they run at all, it's at the YMCAs, health clubs, shopping center malls, and in Minneapolis, the repetitious hallways of the Metrodome sports center. Just the thought of scurrying from the house to the car in January produces shivers that rumble from the tips of their parkas to the very depths of their insulated overshoes.

Most of these runners have either never ventured out in the winter to run, or else embarked without the correct clothing and mental approach. I've run through 25 Minnesota winters and reckon I've experienced everything Mom Nature offers below the Arctic Circle, and I still say give me any January rather than a hot July. If that sounds like the rationale of a frozen brain, let me explain.

Straightaway, understand that you can't freeze your lungs. In the time it takes −40 degree air to get from the mouth to the bronchial tubes, which connect the throat to the lungs, it will be warmed by more than 100 degrees, easily adequate to protect the lungs.

Air sucked through the mouth is warmed by blood under the surface lining of your bronchial tubes. A running body also has a lot of *heat to get rid of* and much of it escapes through the body's large and efficient radiator—the lungs. Even at the slowest running speeds of 11-to-12-minute miles, the body's metabolic rate is five to 10 times that at rest. And given the body's exceptional ability to conserve heat by constricting surface blood vessels, and that when dressed properly you exist in a portable semitropical microclimate, keeping warm while running isn't difficult.

HOW TO DRESS

If you can remember two words, light layers, you should have little trouble with any temperature this side of the Arctic Circle. (Footing is another and more difficult matter, which I shall get to later.) Most beginners dress too *heavily* for the conditions. They pile on thick sweats, bulky underwear, and down jackets. Down jackets are particularly inappropriate because when they absorb sweat, they lose loft (the dead air spaces) and their insulating properties, and in time begin to reek.

Don't pile on cumbersome, heavy clothing. Use various layers of light clothing according to the conditions. Three considerations govern keeping warm at any given temperature: insulation provided by dead air space between layers of clothing, keeping the wind out, and the amount of heat generated. Although there is a marvelous array of materials available for winter clothing, such as Gore-Tex and polypropylene, you can keep quite warm with judicious use of "ordinary" clothing.

What you protect most depends on where you lose heat fastest. Because of the prodigious blood flow to the head, in extreme cold, 40 to 50 percent of the body's heat loss can occur right out the top. If you keep your head and neck warm, you've solved half the problem. Considerable heat is lost through the hands and wrists, and while the connective tissues in the knees and Achilles tendons don't radiate heat, they can be a source of injury if not kept warm. The legs and feet can probably withstand the cold most, especially the feet because you constantly stomp them.

HEAD

The key here is a sort of "dickey" that covers the neck and lower face. You can buy them or make an excellent one by opening the top of a *wool* stocking cap so you can pull your head through it. Synthetics are useless because they lose their shape and insulating properties when wet. Depending upon the conditions, cover your neck, chin, mouth, and nose, breathing through the wool at the beginning to warm the incoming air before you begin to generate heat. One-piece masks aren't as versatile and too hot for all but the worst conditions. Some runners wear hooded sweatshirts, but they scoop up air like a windsock, and when you turn your head to watch for traffic, you find yourself staring into a cave. The best cap is a wool stocking cap or two. Some runners apply petroleum jelly to their face, which undoubtedly helps them to keep warm, but I've never had to resort to this somewhat slimy device.

UPPER BODY

A light polypropylene shirt next to the skin "wicks" the sweat to the outer layers, thus nearly eliminating that wet, clammy feeling. A cotton fishnet shirt works pretty well, too. Over that wear one or two long-sleeve, turtleneck T-shirts or a regular T-shirt. Over that, a nylon or Gore-Tex windbreaker. It's essential to protect your neck and shoulders, otherwise you involuntarily hunch your shoulders and run stiffly.

HANDS

Mittens are warmer than gloves. Some runners use wool-lined leather choppers, and some invest in Gore-Tex mittens. I've had good luck with rubberized cotton work mitts, one inside the other at extreme temperatures. Mitts should extend up your wrists unless you want misery on frigid, windy outings. During mild winter days, a wool sock on each hand makes a good mitt.

HIPS AND LEGS

Down to about freezing, briefs, running shorts, and nylon windpants are enough. When it gets colder, add lightweight flannel pajama bottoms (ones that fit tight at the ankles) under nylon pants. Pajama bottoms are virtually weightless and warm because your legs don't sweat much. Several companies make flannel-like lined pants with a wind-resistant outer that both breathes and keeps out the cold.

Men should always wear briefs and running shorts *inside* their pants. I could name several local runners who without realizing it during the run, froze their, well, . . . ah, "naughty-bits" as the Monty Python cast would say. People snicker, but if you are the one involved, besides experiencing severe pain during the thaw-out, you could wind up the tallest soprano in the Vienna Boys Choir.

FEET

No problem here. You can use the same shoes and socks you wear in the summer except that wool and wool-blend socks are better than cotton because they retain warmth better, especially when

wet. *Never* wear nylon next to your foot. It's been known to freeze
to the skin.

Keeping warm in the worst winter conditions is not difficult,
but if you act totally incompetent like bare-legged Krantz at −35
degrees, you risk severe freezing or worse. The first time I ran at
−28 degrees I couldn't complete the run because I overheated in
my extra sweatshirt. You generate so much heat, you should feel
the cold the first few minutes of the run. If possible, run into the
wind on the way out. If you start *with* the wind and sweat heavily,
when you return into a 20- to 40-degree colder windchill, you
could become a human icicle.

You can enjoy and greatly benefit from outdoor winter running if you convince yourself you can do it. It seems impossible
that you could go out in a few T-shirts, cap, mittens, a light nylon
suit and keep warm, especially after freezing in heavier normal
dress. Yet it's a whole new ballgame once you get moving. The
toughest part is not the cold but the footing. Ice is the worst.
There are no shoes that provide traction on ice, especially on
downhills. A light dusting of snow on iced sidewalks and streets
camouflages and lubricates already challenging footing. Ice is
worst when rain freezes or snow melts and refreezes in the evening. But, like the Eskimos who develop a sixth sense about tun-
dra, one soon learns to sense and negotiate icy patches. You fall
occasionally, but usually only your ego gets hurt. Besides, it isn't
icy often.

Snow is fun. My most enchanting runs have been during light
snowfalls. It's soft, crunchy, and at night, a jeweled wonderland
where I can leave footprints behind. Hard-packed snow is an excellent cushioned surface, much nicer than hard sidewalks and
roads. Salted snow, known as greasy skid stuff, on the other hand,
transforms streets into skating rinks and can make any run frustrating.

When traction is bad, don't try to run hard, no matter what
the schedule says. When your feet give way under you, the action
on your Achilles tendon resembles snapping a wet towel. When
the roads are salted, run the sidewalks, shoveled or not. Galloping
through uncleared walks is frustrating initially because you reckon
people should shovel, but actually it is valuable resistance training. The effect is compounded up hills. Now, rather than swear

under my breath at homeowners who don't shovel, I accept these stretches as a beneficial, challenging exercise which toughen me. Snowbanks at the corners, often three to four feet high, effectively render any run a steeple-chase. Leaping up and over these obstacles is wonderful strength training.

You've probably realized already that in the winter, course times don't mean much. On some nights 7- to 8-minute miling would be tough for the world-class. Years ago I found timing the same routes I used in summer discouraging, so instead I go by effort on slow footing. This is not to say one cannot run quality stuff in the winter. Normally conditions are quite good, and some of the hardest workouts I've run have been winter hill workouts, 30-milers and fast repeats on a cleared stretch. Long runs in the winter are easier than in summer because dehydration is rarely a factor.

Cold and snowy winters are best for base training. Until recently there was no outdoor winter racing in the Northland, which was good because it provided a natural break from competition. Even if one raced indoors in January and February, there was no temptation to do anything other than train in November, December, and early January. This was perfect for recharging the mental batteries and building a mileage base.

Likewise, the indoor season was ideal for developing speed and experience at the shorter track distances, because until March there were no road races. During January, February, and part of March one can really get fit combining two days a week of track work with outdoor running. After a few days outdoors you look forward to stripping down indoors. After a hard indoor workout, the roads look good again. When road racing begins, you possess both speed and endurance.

TIPS ON WINTER RUNNING

1. Try to avoid open areas on windy days. (Always check the conditions.)
2. When the weather is especially bad, consider running loops near home rather than getting into trouble near the turn-around of an out-and-back route. Tell someone where you will be running and when you should return.
3. Carry money in case of an emergency.

4. Run on paths or sidewalks if possible. On roads, run against traffic, close to the curb. Be prepared to "bail out" if cars are sliding. Run defensively at all times.
5. Wear reflective clothing. Windshields are often frosted up, so don't depend on motorists to see you.
6. Once you start a winter run, you are pretty much committed to keep running. If you have to walk, you will soon become chilled. When planning winter routes, anticipate how you would get back if you got too tired to run, injured, etc.
7. As soon as you finish a winter run, get out of your wet clothing, shower, and dress. After a run your resistance is at its lowest, an ideal time to become chilled and sick.
8. If you have to race in cold rain or sleet, sandwich a dry-cleaning bag (with head and arm holes) between a long-sleeved shirt and a singlet. It will absolutely stop all wind. However, it doesn't breathe and is clammy. If it gets too awful you can rip it off.

3.

SUPPLEMENTARY TRAINING

I believe that good running requires more than running. But what else is needed varies from runner to runner. Individual strengths and weaknesses play a huge role in the decision, as do the distances over which you compete. Any exercise can help or hurt, depending upon how it is performed. You can get hurt or stronger lifting, bounding, or stretching. But you can also get injured running too many miles or sprinting.

This chapter cannot be an exhaustive examination of all the ways you can supplement your running. I do not have enough pages; you do not have time for more than the essentials. But you should be familiar with four broad areas of activity: 1) stretching, 2) strength training, 3) resiliency exercises, and 4) running alternatives.

STRETCHING

The top runners who stretch are too numerous to list. The stretching and gymnasium programs of track athletes such as Seb Coe are already legendary. A chiropractor showed Rod Dixon how inflexible he was and how running itself was making him tighter and slowing him down. Frank Shorter says, "I've made it a point to become as flexible as I can," and Bill Rodgers says, "Flexibility exercises are an important part of monitoring a runner's program."

Running tightens muscles and that restricts their range of movement. To get greater acceleration, "You must become more mobile," says George Gandy, Coe's trainer. "To me that means a long-term investment in stretching ... I encourage runners to stretch all the time. . . . At every opportunity, stretch, stretch, stretch."

There are two approaches to stretching: *ballistic*, which you probably learned in school, and is characterized by bouncing movements. The problem with ballistic stretching is that bouncing often causes over-stretching, which triggers the stretch reflex—a contraction of the muscle to protect it from extending too far. This, ironically, tightens and shortens the very muscle you are trying to relax.

The correct stretch is *static*. After getting into a good stretch position, relax and *hold it* for about 30 seconds. If you overstretch, you will feel pain, your muscle will quiver or you will not hold the position. Never force yourself beyond what is reasonably comfortable. It's not a contest; don't be influenced by others. Some of the most unlikely looking specimens can fold themselves like pretzels, but the only way you may be able to touch your toes is by assuming a fetal position.

Runner's stretches loosen the back, hamstrings, quads, butt, groin, Achilles tendon, ankles, and feet. The stretching sequence doesn't matter much, and often two areas can be worked simultaneously to save time. If you can stretch only once a day, do it after a distance workout, and before fast interval work. If you can, also stretch a little after a fast workout to reduce stiffness and speed recovery. When stretching alone, I like to listen to music or practice the visualization exercises described in Chapter 7.

BACK AND HAMSTRINGS _____

The most relaxing stretch to begin with is the plough, which begins as position 1,* relaxes into 2, and progresses either into 3 or 4. This stretch loosens your back, neck, and hamstrings. Bend back as far as you comfortably can to get a good stretch, but if you can't keep your legs straight or reach the floor with your toes, don't force it.

* Drawings (except 4 and 8) excerpted from *Stretching*, © 1980 by Bob and Jean Anderson. Shelter Publications. Distributed in bookstores by Random House. Reprinted by permission. For a free catalog of Stretching Inc. publications, write to: P.O. Box 767, Palmer Lake, CO 80133.

GROIN

Position 5 helps prevent groin injuries. Sit and put the soles of your feet together, pull them comfortably in toward the crotch with your hands across the tops of your feet. Now gently pull your upper body forward from the hips (don't roll your head and shoulders over) and hold for 30 seconds.

GROIN AND HAMSTRINGS

Lie on your back as in 6, bring the knee of one leg forward and clasp it just below the knee and hold. Switch legs and repeat.

Position 7 also stretches the groin and hamstring. By rotating your ankle clock- and counterclockwise, you can also stretch out tight ankle ligaments. Keep the extended leg straight with the toes up.

HAMSTRING AND QUADS

The single most valuable stretch may be the hurdler's stretch (8 and 9). By leaning back the quad is stretched; when forward, the opposite hamstring. An alternate hamstring position is 10, which also stretches the groin. Reverse the position. Note that the toe of the outstretched foot points up.

BACK AND HAMSTRINGS

Position 11, with your feet pointing forward and your knees unlocked, stretches the back and hamstrings. It is similar to the plough in a standing position. If you can't comfortably touch the floor with your fingers, don't force it. Don't bounce up and down. Hold the position for 30 seconds.

When using position 12, don't raise your leg so high you can't keep it straight. The leg should be slightly bent at the knee with your toe pointing forward. This is a convenient stretch just before a workout or race.

ACHILLES TENDON AND HAMSTRING _____

Position 13 is known to almost every runner. It is a convenient stretch to use before a run. By keeping the rear leg straight, you stretch the calf and Achilles tendon. If you bend at the knee, you stretch the tendon only. The heel of the rear leg remains on the ground. You can stretch both Achilles tendons together by keeping both legs back, but make sure that the stretch is equally distributed.

QUAD AND GROIN _____

Position 14, resembling an elongated sprint start, stretches the quads and groin area. Reverse the legs to complete it.

ANKLE AND QUAD _____

Position 15 is another convenient stretch before a run. Simply grasp the foot in the opposing hand, pull it up to your butt and hold it. By standing a few feet from a support and bending from the hip (keeping the support leg straight), you can stretch the hamstring of the other leg as well.

The stretches described certainly do not exhaust the list, or may not include your favorites. But they will loosen essentially all the muscles runners use, and because most stretch a combination of muscles, you can get the full treatment in 20 to 30 minutes. Never use any stretch that pulls on an injury or sore tendon. Don't do any stretch that hurts. It's best to go through a set of stretches twice, the first time to get into position and relax, and the second time through you will be much looser.

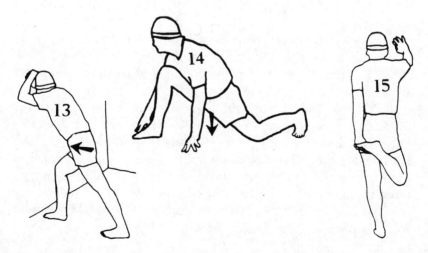

STRENGTH TRAINING

Running normally does not build a great deal of upper-body strength and endurance. Distance running, in fact, does not particularly strengthen the legs. You need to move them fast against resistance in order to strengthen them. Leg strength is essential for developing speed. While pushing weights around is one way to develop strength, the most efficient way is with hill bounding, springing, and resiliency drills.

When we were kids we climbed, wrestled, threw things, and did a lot of upper-body activities. Then we became "runners," ignored everything above the waist, and let our upper bodies atrophy and weaken. This indicates that as we get older, strength training becomes more valuable.

Weight training increases muscle flexibility if the muscles are worked through their full range of motion. Running does not do that. A strong, flexible muscle is less susceptible to injury, especially when there is a near balance between antagonistic (opposing) pairs of muscles.

Runners who do strength training today comprise a virtual track who's who: Steve Scott, Alberto Salazar, Joan Benoit, Seb Coe, Steve Ovett, Eamonn Coghlan, Craig Virgin, and Rod Dixon. Herb Elliott observes that "Many distance runners have . . . a bony-looking chest, with absolutely no muscle, which sits on a fine pair . . . of legs. For that person, weight training is essential. They need to build good pectoral and arm strength. In addition, they need good [abdominal] muscle and back strength. . . ."

Often, however, runners don't seriously try other modes of training until serious injury lays them up. Such was the case with Joan Benoit, who after having both Achilles tendons surgically repaired in 1981, began riding a stationary bicycle and using Nautilus machines. When she resumed running in 1982, she was faster than ever.

Professor Jonda, a neurologist from Czechoslovakia, thinks distance runners lose their explosive power because of imbalances between the strong fast muscles such as the calf, hamstring, some back and quad muscles (phasic muscles), and endurance muscles used to maintain upright posture. Distance runs shorten phasic muscles until they are unable to contract strongly. That is why many runners could benefit from an all-around weight program for the upper body, and hill work for the legs.

Building strength can be approached in two ways, 1) working against the resistance of free weights such as dumbbells and barbells, and machines such as the Nautilus or home gyms and 2) calisthenics that use the body's weight as a resistance. Each has its advantages and disadvantages. The best activities for non-full-time runners are those which offer the most benefit for the least money and time. No point in buying an expensive gizmo or driving to the Nautilus center and shelling out big bucks if you can accomplish nearly the same effect in a fraction of the time with calisthenics and your $29.95 vinyl-covered concrete weights.

NAUTILUS MACHINES _____

Nautilus enthusiasts claim their equipment overloads the muscle better than free weights in far less time. Nautilus machines do not require much technique. The runner (or your instructor) selects about a dozen machines, each of which applies a constant stress to a specific muscle or muscle group that you as a runner use. Eight to 12 repetitions on any machine should exhaust the muscle it works. The Nautilus people say you should work out two to three times a week, allowing at least 48 hours between sessions. Nautilus machines *can* improve running, but unless you are a full-time runner with considerable spare time and dollars, this method does not provide the best bang for the buck. Moreover, the workouts were originally designed for power sports—football, basketball, and such. Runners don't seem to need that kind of strength. Many runners think there's something unnatural about working so hard the muscle will be driven to failure after 8 to 12 repetitions. The total work is not great, and too slow to improve muscle speed (although it does improve strength).

Kirk Pfeffer, for one, believes that runners need endurance-strength, and doesn't do 8 to 12 repetitions with the heaviest weights. He does up to 100 repetitions using the lightest (probably over the strong protest of his Nautilus instructor). Additionally, some machines like the adductor-abductor, which works the inside and outside of the leg, may be dangerous for runners, who unlike soccer and football players, do not need lateral agility.

Along the same line, but a leap down in price from the Nautilus, are various compact home gyms. By changing the machine's configuration, you can work various muscles. Some designs use weights, other use gigantic rubber bands for resistance. The advantage of a home gym is its convenience. No membership fees, driving, or wait. If this interests you, research the equipment carefully to ensure that you get the most for your money.

FREE WEIGHTS

These are of two basic types—barbells and hand weights. Technique is important in using free weights, but their advantage is that you're exercising not only the primary muscles involved in making the lift, but many peripheral muscles as well. Machines don't provide much of that. Barbells often require a spotter—someone who will hand you and take away heavy weights. Dumbbells, which are held in one hand, won't "trap" you underneath them.

Lifting won't add much muscle bulk unless you want it to. Strength is developed using three sets of 5 to 8 repetitions or one set of 8 to 12 repetitions to a point of total fatigue. More repetitions during that session (even after a rest) won't provide additional strength. Muscular endurance is gained by doing more repetitions with lighter weights. Classic theory specifies that lifts be done slowly, with each repetition lasting about six seconds— two seconds lifting and four lowering. That way momentum cannot help out. By eliminating explosive jerking, you reduce the risk of injury.

Slow lifting has its disadvantages, however. The Russian researchers Werschosanski and Semjovov believe that the ability to produce power as fast as possible is far more important than maximum strength with no time limit, because when running there is not sufficient time to develop maximum strength. This means, they advise, exercising with 40 to 50 percent of the weight you could maximally handle, using fast initial movements to develop explosive strength. This seems to make sense, although I'd strongly advise that you work into this gradually, keeping the stress moderate at first.

As with Nautilus exercises, all lifts should involve full-range movements with sessions never occurring on consecutive days or more than three times a week. Most runners prefer lifting after running, when they're warmed up. Add weights only when what you are using becomes too easy. It doesn't matter whether you inhale or exhale during a lift, but never hold your breath.

A convenient weight workout directly related to running is carrying a one-half to a one-pound weight glove or Heavyhands during a run. I've used steel bars weighing three pounds apiece and agree with Craig Virgin, who found that "a pound in each hand was enough." Even that's too much for Frank Shorter, who says, "They throw your center of gravity off." The two three-pound weights I've carried certainly affected my form while I carried them, but I doubt that one pound in each hand every other day on morning runs or warmups and cooldowns could permanently throw you off. The value of hand weights is that they strengthen your arms so you can use them better when you are tired at the end of a race. That should improve your kick.

CALISTHENICS

The good news is that they don't require much, if any, equipment. They can be performed by anyone at any level of fitness most anywhere at any time. And they produce results. As in weight training, the larger muscles should be worked first because the smaller muscles are often needed to assist in large-muscle exercises.

I believe that the most important calisthenic is the sit-up (also called curl-up and sit-back). Most back problems are a result of strong back muscles and weak abdominal muscles. Strong abdominals improve upper-body carriage. They help prevent a runner's torso from flexing back and forth like a fishing pole. Your trunk should remain stable while running. Strong abdominals also enable you to get your knees up during fast running and help you maintain form when tired.

The key to good sit-ups is bent legs, a flat (not arched), "rolling" up and down one vertebra at a time, and not rising more than 30 degrees (so as not to activate the primary hip flexors and put strain on the back). Physiologist Laurence Moorehouse says the lowering phase is most important and should be done slowly.

Leroy Perry, unofficial chiropractor to the 1976 Olympic Team, further recommends that you keep your heels together, toes flared out, pubic bone rotated up, hands crossed on chest, chin to chest and curl up only until the shoulder blades are slightly off the floor.

There are other variations: sit-ups performed on inclined boards and benches that increase the difficulty, abdominal flexes done while hanging upside down, and raising your legs off the floor so than your stress position resembles a "V." Because sit-ups are a strength exercise, do enough repetitions to really feel it, perhaps two or three such sets, and never on consecutive days. If you do no other lifts or calisthenics, do sit-ups.

I do not favor leg calisthenics, especially squats. You can strengthen your legs more effectively with uphill running and springing drills. Chin-ups and pull-ups strengthen the upper back, biceps, pectorials, shoulders, and triceps. By lying face-down, hands clasped behind the head, and rising the head and chest off the floor and holding, you strengthen your back. There are other calisthenics, designed for special muscles, but the above list should suffice for most runners.

RESILIENCY EXERCISES

American distance runners have only recently discovered what sprinters and Europeans have practiced for years—jumping and sprinting drills. Lydiard has espoused hill springing for at least a quarter of a century, but I discovered that even few New Zealanders do them. On several occasions I have shown them exercises that originated in their own country.

Although most runners know that Seb Coe has used "circuit training" (a combination of weight training, gymnastics, jumping and springing drills), few know what he actually does or that many of these exercises could help them. Coe uses depth jumping— jumps from vaulting boxes to the ground and immediately up again to increase muscle resiliency and develop what Gandy describes as "his [Coe's] feather-light contact with the track." Coe also practices sprint drills and uphill running to develop strength and flexibility. "What we're doing," Gandy says, "is developing . . . muscle groups [that] receive and can tolerate larger forces on landing, while responding with bigger forces than they would in normal running . . . we're trying to encourage energy exchange systems with the body."

Uphill springing and bounding, as per Lydiard, are described in Chapters 5 and 10. This section is confined to the drills I feel benefit middle-distance and distance runners most. Resiliency exercises put the snap into your legs that distance running removes. With better drive-off you travel a little further through the air between strides. An extra inch per stride adds up in a race. Begin resiliency exercises before or at the onset of regular training so that you are used to them when you start hill and faster training. Not only will you progress quicker, there will be less risk of injury. Since beginning them, I've experienced none of the usual stiffness associated with the transition into speed work.

Skipping and bounding drills, unlike calisthenics and weight training, are fun (but weird-looking to the public). When you do the drills described below, get on a smooth surface, preferably a 100-yard straight stretch of grass or dirt. I cannot overemphasize beginning cautiously and easily, doing only about half of what you think you should do the first several sessions. At first, just aim for the general movements over no more than 30 yards at a time. When you can make the basic movements, work on getting good lift and power while remaining symmetrical and smooth. Have someone check that you execute the same moves from both legs. No matter how good you become at these drills, never go until you lose spring and form. When fatigue sets in, *walk* until recovered, then do a different drill until fatigued again, walk, and so on.

SKIPPING

If you've never skipped, think of it as a series of hops, alternating legs. The key to skipping is taking off and landing on the *same* foot. While one leg hops, the other knee is up. The better the skip, the longer you remain in the air. While airborne there is a pause, a moment when the body, arms, and legs hold the position before you land. Most probably, you will be aware of your arms holding their position at the extremes of their swing. It sounds complicated, but it's easy if you begin with modest alternating hops.

As you get used to skipping, try to spring to greater heights, bringing one knee high while pushing down hard with the take-off foot. Try to keep your trunk rigid rather than flexing forward and back. Work your arms vigorously forward and back with your elbows at a 45-degree angle. If you throw your arms around you won't develop good technique. Getting your knees high requires strong abdominal muscles.

Another variation of skipping emphasizes distance rather than height. Concentrate on an elongated horizontal stride rather than springing upward. Make sure you travel a straight line.

Skipping. Starting out, most runners cannot get their knees as high as these runners. Begin with what is comfortable and gradually try to get greater height.

PRANCING

This is similar to running in place, and advancing about one foot per stride, bringing the knees high, getting up on the toes, pumping your arms and moving your legs fast. You may notice a feeling of leaning backward, which is necessary to counterbalance the knee life. Try to stay "tall" with your head up and toes aimed straight ahead. Imagine you are tiptoeing across hot coals. As you gain finesse, you will be able to move your legs fast.

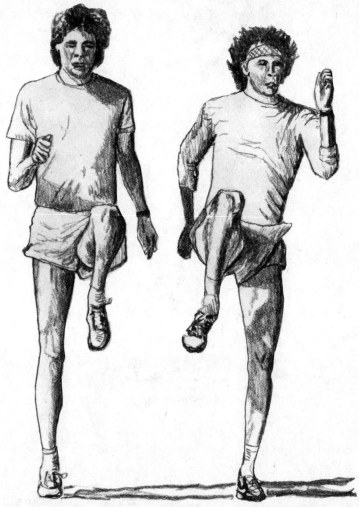

Prancing. The object is to get your knees up, arms pumping symmetrically, and a fast cadence that moves you forward only about one or two feet per stride.

JUMPING

With your feet together and arms bent at a 45-degree angle, jump straight up while snapping the elbows back, bringing the knees up and touching the heels to the butt before landing. During the descent your arms swing forward. The idea is to make several jumps

Jumping. A rapid series of energetic jumps is the most tiring of the drills. Do them in sets of 10 or so with full recovery between them.

in rapid succession, getting your knees and heels high. It's like exaggerated rope jumping without the rope. Do them in sets of as many jumps as you can manage at one time. Notice how the abdominals come into play in getting your knees up. This is the most exhausting of the three drills.

Because resiliency drills are anaerobic, do them on your hard workout days before cooling down, not on recovery or consecutive days, or more than three times a week. Unlike calisthenics and weight training, these drills are fun, but may prove to be a curiosity to the public. One evening as I skipped vigorously past a guy with a cigarette dangling from his lip, he smirked and called out, "Don't you feel silly doing that?"

"I can imagine that this appears odd to you," I replied, "but think how silly you look to me sticking leaves in your mouth and setting fire to them."

MASSAGE

"A good massage is the best thing a runner can do for himself," says Rod Dixon. "It stimulates blood flow and gets that tired feeling out of the muscles." Massage is reputed to have saved Mary Decker from at least one date with the surgeon. Alberto Salazar travels with a private masseur; Mat Centrowitz used deep massage as *the* treatment for torn hamstring fibers after trying many other approaches.

Massage may seem to be a luxury, but there's no denying it soothes body and mind, speeds healing, and makes you feel great. Massage works, apparently, by increasing circulation and flushing waste products from the muscles. With deep massage, fingertip pressure (one masseur I know of in New Zealand uses a stick) is used to spread muscle fibers and break up scar tissue, elongate the tissues, and relieve spasms. It works wonders if you can stand the pain.

The Europeans rely heavily on massage. In the 1950s Russia's 1956 Olympic five- and ten-kilometer gold medalist, Vladimir Kuts, claimed he never could have recovered from hard workouts without a massage. But these runners didn't and don't foot the bill, which can run to $35 an hour. Even if you cannot afford regular massages, it's not difficult for runners to learn the basic techniques and trade off massages among themselves. It's also not difficult to massage your own legs. Your technique may not be perfect, but almost any massage is better than none.

RUNNING ALTERNATIVES

There are numerous activities and sports that either aid running or substitute for it if you get injured. Grete Waitz trained on a stationary bicycle for three weeks after a stress fracture before winning the 1982 New York Marathon. "I didn't like it," she admits. "I did it just because it was good for me. . . ." Alex Ratelle is a notorious stationary biker who got his start after an Achilles tendon tear took him off the roads. New Zealand's Jack Foster got his athletic start bicycling competitively. He reserved Fridays for riding rather than running. And I've already cited Benoit's successes after riding the stationary bike.

Shorter, Benoit, and Liquori are among those who simulate interval training on the bike. By monitoring their pulses, they can compare their work rates to running. Stationary biking becomes increasingly important as one gets older and your legs can no longer take the pounding of running. Even Shorter now admits to this.

Running or bounding up stairs in stadiums, hotels, and so on are excellent substitutes for hill running and running itself when injury prevents running. If you cannot run back down, find a place where you can use the elevator. I'd love to try training up a down escalator, either to see how long I could remain aboard, or to do intervals by running to the top, drifting down, and so on.

Most runners in northern climates already know that cross-country skiing is an excellent running supplement or replacement that provides a terrific cardiovascular and strength workout for the entire body without any pounding. Swimming, similarly, works the upper body, and running in waist-deep water provides gentle but taxing resistance work for your legs.

SUMMARY

I rate stretching and sit-ups as indispensable for any serious runner. Those racing 15km and less will especially benefit from the

Stair running and bounding is an excellent substitute for (or supplement to) hill running and springing. Don't just run up, but rather "spring" with a lot of drive from the ankles.

zip that skipping and prancing return to the legs, as well as the resistance to injury from fast training and better drive-off. Resiliency exercises also prepare you for a smooth transition into the hill training described in Chapter 9. Those exercises and hill training are the best weight training for the legs. Unless you have a lot of time, restrict any other weight training to your upper body.

The value of stair running and hard stationary bike intervals (with toe clips) are much underrated by most runners. Many successful runners use the bike for their second workout of the day. Several use it in place of running when injured and have raced better afterward. Cross-country skiing is an excellent all-around conditioner, as evidenced by the high VO_2 max's (higher than runners') of the top competitors. In the winter, there is no reason why a serious ski session, which works the arms, back, and abdominals without pounding the legs, couldn't replace some runs.

Weight-training, and stationary biking, although beneficial, are boring to many. You can make these activities more palatable by working out to music, reminding yourself that you will race better, and sticking to it for a month, or until you see results.

4.
RUNNING TECHNIQUE

*A*lmost any running book contains photographs and drawings showing what you should look like while running. Instructional film loops scrutinize the world-class in action. In the laboratory, physiologists and biomechanical researchers probe the way we move, isolating and measuring such things as foot impact, symmetery of arm and leg movement, and efficiency.

What are they looking for? What are they trying to show? It's mainly that how we move has something to do with how fast and how far we move. There seems to be general agreement on that. There is far less agreement on what constitutes correct style.

Emil Zátopek, who clawed and thrashed his way to four Olympic gold medals and 18 world records, once told a television interviewer, "Track and field is not ice-skating. It is not necessary to smile and make a wonderful impression on the judges." Zátopek was not so concerned about how he looked on his way to the finish line as he was about getting there first. Yet, had Zátopek's shoulders and arms not rotated to and fro like a washing machine agitator, would he have run faster? And if so, by how much?

Ken Doherty, writing for his *Track and Field Omnibook*, gets to the core of the question and presents it effortlessly and succinctly: "Running technique is primarily an individual matter. It began when the athlete was two or so years of age, and over the course of a dozen or a score of years it had become so natural—or at least so fairly established—as not to be changed without disturbing a [runner's] inner as well as outer balance and relaxation. A second rule of thumb when it comes to running technique is to leave it alone. The technique of some . . . can and should be improved so long as we remember that improvement is related to a [runner's] competitive performance—not whether . . . technique is aesthetically pleasing. Do what comes naturally, as long as 'naturally' is mechanically sound. If it isn't, do what is mechanically sound until it becomes natural."

One difficulty with that logic, however, is determining what is mechanically sound. Even among the world's best, there are as many styles as runners. Bill Rodgers is aware that when he runs, he swings his right arm a lot. Yet when he was studied by Dr. Peter Cavanagh and his crew at the biomechanics lab at Penn State, they were unable to determine what caused it, "but they said I shouldn't try to change it." Rodgers said. "It was obviously something I did to counter some imbalance. They couldn't pick out exactly what it was."

When I was in high school I already "flapped" my left arm the way I still do. The coach would pull me aside, grasp my elbows from behind, and swing my arms neatly forward and back to demonstrate where they should go. I could reenact these movements while I concentrated on them, but as soon as my thoughts wandered, my arm resumed its original path. Now I don't worry about it. I realize that my arm counterbalances some idosyncratic movement in the opposite leg.

That we don't run the same with both legs is obvious from the way our shoes wear differently. In many people you can spot it by just watching them run. Arms, having less mass than legs, exaggerate their movements when balancing out the legs. Forcing my arms to swing aesthetically merely masks the cause and is, I believe, detrimental. If Rodgers or I want our arms to swing "properly," we will first have to isolate and change whatever is causing the asymmetry.

There are two aspects of style which ought to concern us. One is corrective, for example, replacing wasteful movements with those that move us furthest with the least effort. The other involves perfecting what we are already doing more or less correctly. The distinction isn't perfect, since movements that are basically correct but not refined could be termed wasteful. The distinguishing differences is that in the first instance something needs to be corrected before the preferred movements can occur.

Beginning runners are seldom efficient. Most, however, do not need to correct anything as much as perfect what they are already doing. Beginners overstride, and in general exaggerate their movements. It's natural. We develop by replacing gross motor movements with fine-tuned motor movements. For example, in playing the guitar, chord changes that at first require frantic groping up and down the fret board soon give way to dextrous, efficient movements.

Elite runners move this way. When I watched Carlos Lopes win the 1984 Olympic marathon on television, where it is difficult to gauge speed because the telephoto cameras foreshorten distances, I thought how easy, if not leisurely, Lopes looked. Yet, these were five-minute miles. That was his trick—to run fast and make it look easy.

Pat Clohessy (who worked with Billy Mills before his Tokyo win before advising de Castella) feels that relaxation is *the most* important principle in training and running technique. "I believe it is essential to success, and especially sustained achievement over several years," he says. "While tension and pressure limit one athlete's fulfillment, relaxation can transform another into a superior athlete. Physical relaxation is very important and takes the form of adequate sleep, recovery runs, and relaxation in training rather than being overcompetitive."

BASIC MECHANICS OF RUNNING

Running, as Brooks Johnson, the sprint coach, reminds us, "is a series of falls and recoveries." You place the body in jeopardy by leaning forward over the center of gravity and move the arms and legs in order to keep it from falling over. Arms are a source of speed and power; the faster the arms go, the faster the legs go. Arms also absorb much of the rotation that is created when we run. Elbows poke out slightly rather than oscillate neatly forward and back to counterbalance the feet, which are pulled under us to land in front of each other under the center of gravity.

The flawless marathon running form of Carlos Lopes. His whole attitude exudes relaxation; the symmetrical arm action, his gaze on the road ahead, his untensed shoulders and foot plant.

As they approach the finish, the lead runner's arms have "come up" as he feels the strain. Usually, this restricts movement and wastes energy.

Dr. Peter Cavanagh said that if the least economical runner he studied could make the correct changes in style, he could cut 20 minutes off his marathon time. Cavanagh found on almost 30-percent variation in efficiency among recreational runners, which means that a mechanically inefficient runner who clocks a 3:05 marathon actually did the work necessary to run 2:45.

Many runners also waste energy using a stride which is actually a succession of stop-and-go steps rather than continuous forward motion. Because they bounce, they come *down* rather than *forward* when landing. This acts as a brake, momentarily slowing them before they accelerate into the next stride. Efficient runners also have spring and bounce in their stride—even more than inefficient runners—but they use it to propel themselves *forward* rather than upward. One stride flows into the next.

"A great deal of energy can be wasted if you move up and down excessively while running." says George Gandy. "When you watch Seb run at speed, you can see he is driving off much closer to horizontal than the majority of comparable athletes. . . . In Seb this ability is associated with range of motion, and specifically with good hip extension. He consequently runs very low to the ground, so he's getting a long drive from behind. Look at most of the world's top athletes; nearly all have a fairly long 'dig' from behind. This is . . . good leg extension, which is a matter of range of motion."

It is also using the resiliency in the legs to recover much of the energy that is lost in cushioning one's stride. If you make wasteful vertical motions between strides, you "settle in" as you land, and lose much of the forward momentum for the next stride. It's as efficient as bouncing a marshmallow on a waterbed. Too bad we can't run like the red kangaroo. It uses less oxygen at fast speeds because at fast speeds it can use the resiliency in its legs during bounding that is lost at slow speeds.

In humans, as the foot strikes the ground, the knees and feet flex to cushion the impact. Energy is stored in the flex for when the leg straightens and the foot drives off. This is free energy recovery. Computer studies show that energy stored in the elastic tissues during the downward part of the stride allows them to be released like a spring to aid muscular contraction for the next stride. The leg muscles contract before the foots hits the ground to absorb and store energy for driving the runner forward. Elastic energy may produce 50 percent of the total energy to do work. Effective use of this elasticity requires some speed. If you move too slowly, you waste energy trying to contain elastic energy. "The elite athlete is more efficient than the average runner," the research concludes, "because he stores more elastic energy. This can be likened to the difference in the energy required to bounce a properly inflated basketball [elite runner] to that required to bounce an underinflated basketball." To recover this energy, many runners, such as Coe, perform various bounding exercises, both up and down boxes, and by running with exaggerated springing up hills and on the flat. This is the idea behind Lydiard's hill springing workouts. It's a subject further discussed in Chapters 4 and 9.

Flexing the knees and ankles is not the only way road shock is absorbed. Shoe manufactures claim that thick soles do it, but Brooks Johnson claims that "the best way to absorb the shock is through proper running technique." Perhaps this explains why elite runners are able to race in light flats, and tail-enders stick to their heavier training shoes.

Besides the trauma to the muscles and joints caused by road shock, there is another—pseudoanemia. It may be a false anemia, but the result to much the same. The most common reason for pseudoanemia is that runners have about an extra quart of blood, but not quite as many red cells. Another reason is that repeated pounding on the feet during long runs can burst red blood cells and decrease the oxygen-carrying capacity of the blood, especially in vegetarians and women. Cushioned training shoes, running on grass, and good technique help greatly to prevent it. Pseudoanemia may be one reason it takes so long for some to recover after a marathon, especially those who are not able to maintain form in the final miles and stomp in.

Evidence that it is the physical pounding and not the exertion that traumatizes the legs was reported by Dr. Robert Hikida and a team of scientists who used an electron microscope to examine leg muscle fibers from marathoners and top cyclists after racing. Biopsies from the marathoners showed signs of muscle death and inflammation within the muscle. Many of the substances normally confined to the inside of the muscle cells were found outside in the fluids that bathe the cells. Even red and white blood cells were found outside the blood vessels, and red blood cells inside the muscle fibers. There were also small tears in muscle fibers and membranes. None of this was observed in top cyclists.

Jack Foster seems to know this instinctively. When we went to run the sheep paddocks near his home in Rotorura, he stuck to the grass, jumping every concrete driveway until we got to the fields. Although he avoided hard surfaces in training, he had no trouble with the roads during a race.

That fast long runs on hard surfaces can traumatize the legs shouldn't surprise anyone who has raced a marathon (especially a hilly one) and discovered that the only way to get down stairs afterward was to descend them backward. The muscles are damaged and must be given time to heal. Easy jogging, or better, cycling, helps speed healing because increased blood flows brings nutrients and carries away impurities. Too much running, however, only beats up already injured legs.

Getting down the stairs after a tough, hilly marathon.

UPHILL TECHNIQUE _____

Running up hills is especially difficult. But you may be making it harder than necessary. Minor idiosyncrasies in style that are inconsequential on the flat eat up energy on the hills. Fortunately, uphill running technique is fairly simple. Above all, uphill running must be fluid, because while propelling yourself forward, you must hoist yourself higher. When leaving the flat to begin a hill, technique changes. Lower your center of gravity rather than "run tall" as when clipping along on the flat. Crouch slightly, with your rear tucked in, shoulders forward, head down, arms low and stride short. Imagine yourself six inches shorter than you are.

Running uphill requires a slight forward crouch, lower arm action, and a short economical stride. On uneven grassy hills it is more difficult to maintain an even rhythm.

Overstriding and bouncing waste energy. Instead, "flip" yourself forward from the ankle and drive with your foot by pushing from your toes at the end of each stride. The ability to get drive out of your ankles and feet is acquired by doing the bounding and springing exercises discussed in Chapter 9. Don't bound, of course, in a race, but use the drive and power these exercises develop. Land on the balls of your feet so that the Achilles tendon works like a big rubber band stretching as your heel drops and snapping back for acceleration. If you land heel first, you'll lose much of this recoil.

In a way it is possible to fall uphill if you keep *just forward* of your center of gravity. It's much the same as cross-country skiers learning to get their weight over their leading foot. Beginning skiers usually alternate sliding their skis forward with their weight positioned in between. Were they to lift the trailing ski they would fall backward. The concept is the same for uphill running. But don't bend forward at the waist as in skiing; bring the whole body's center of gravity forward into each succeeding stride. You won't actually fall because the trailing leg comes forward, plants, and sets you up to fall into the next stride. John Lodwick, who has run the Boston Marathon in 2:10:54, says that the mental trick he uses on the uphills is to look at the pavement directly in front of his feet rather than the hill in its entirety. I do that, too, and the amazing thing is that when you look down you lose reference to what is level and sometimes forget you're running uphill. It sounds complicated on paper, but if you develop a short, quick stride, stay low with your weight forward, get "flip" out of your feet and ankles, pump your arms down as you drive off, and experiment a little, you'll discover a style that works for you.

A good way to perfect your technique is to tuck in five yards behind someone on a hill during training, and see which style enables you to gain on him with no extra effort. Remember what you did when this happens so you can practice it.

DOWNHILL TECHNIQUE _____

Fast uphill running is damn hard work. Fast downhill, for many, is terrifying. Coach Bill Squires, who worked with Bill Rodgers, Salazar, and Beardsley over Boston's infamous grades says, "Running uphill is a science, but running downhill is an art. To run well downhill demands almost no strength at all, but two other things ... an excellent sense of balance and sheer courage. In other words, to run well downhill means to have total confidence in yourself."

Two things make downhill running frightening. One is the fear of taking the brakes off and letting go; the other is the slamming that occurs when you do. All the effort expended in getting to the top is theoretically recouped on the descent, but herein lies a problem. Whereas a cyclist can freewheel down without moving a muscle, a runner cannot. Gravity might be doing most of the work, but you must move your legs fast or fall. The impact gives your legs—especially the quads—a hell of a bashing. Runners fear falling, so they keep the brakes on. And that is where the work comes in. That's why you can't come close to gaining back the energy you used on the way up. It's rather like our cyclist pedaling down with the brakes on.

Exercise physiologists Jack Daniels and John Hayes, experimenting with the oxygen demands of uphill and downhill running, discovered that "The up versus downhill experiments revealed that it costs roughly 12 percent more energy to run up a one-degree grade than it does to run on the level. But running down the same grade is only seven percent easier than running on the flat." Moreover, when Tom Clark at the Nike Performance Laboratory studied 10 well-trained runners at various grades from six percent uphill to 10 percent downhill at 7:00 pace, he found that at the steepest uphill grade, the shock was only 85 percent of that experienced on the level. The steepest downhill resulted in 40 percent more leg shock.

David Costill describes what happens to the legs during descents in language gruesome enough to make you want to walk: "In downhill running," he says, "the tension developed in the leg muscles to resist gravity is enormous. The muscles are attempting to shorten, but are literally pulled apart. Consequently, the connective tissue in the muscle membranes are physically torn apart . . ."

Before you get queasy thinking about all those muscles you've pulled apart, read on, because Costill offers hope: "There's no evidence that the damage is permanent," he adds. "It also seems that the more you perform this type of exercise, the less soreness and muscle trauma you experience. Though we have no explanation for adaption, it may simply be that you are able to coordinate the muscle tensions and the muscle fibers to the sudden shock of the eccentric contraction."

Which means that the keys to running down hills economically and fast without injury are relaxation and practice. The way to begin is to get on a soft surface—grass or dirt—that is free of holes and lumps so you can relax without fear of turning an ankle. Then practice free-wheeling, progressively taking off the brakes. Remind yourself that even were you to fall on grass (which you won't), you won't get hurt. At first it may seem that you can't get the hang of it, and then perhaps after several days or weeks, all of a sudden you will be flying down practically effortlessly. Bill Dellinger tells his runners, "You must learn to run downhill and then progress to a point where it feels comfortable to run fast downhill."

Realize also that if you go *easily* at the beginning (the first week) and then faster each succeeding week, your legs will adjust by developing "shock absorbers" to minimize the risk of injuries when you really let go. The normal tendency when running downhill, as Dellinger reminds us, is to break with the heels, holding the arms high while leaning backward. You can save your quads by landing instead on the ball of the foot. This is especially important during a long race such as the Boston Marathon, where if your quads have had it by 21 miles, you can't take advantage of the remaining long stretches of downhill, and will have to tiptoe down. The same applies to the first time you try to jog after the race. You'll have to get up on your toes to protect your quads.

Downhill speed is controlled by forward lean. Think of your body as a lever. When you want to go faster, push the lever forward (and your center of gravity). When you want to go slow, ease back on the lever. Inexperienced hill runners run with the lever way back, digging in with their heels, causing more trauma to the legs than if they were able to just let go. Some say the body should be perpendicular to the ground, but even on a reasonable slope I doubt that is possible. Besides, you can't see yourself from the side, so how would you know what angle you are making?

The arms are used mainly for balance. Don't pump them; keep them low and in counter-rhythm with the legs. On uneven trails your arms will be all over, perhaps shooting out to the side, lifting and dropping like flaps on an airplane to maintain balance. When you no longer fear these free-wheeled descents, your movements will become natural, and the sensation—as I like to imagine it—an effortless hang-gliding descent.

RUNNING FAST

Two aspects of running fast that continue to astonish me are: 1) how poor at it most distance runners let themselves become, and 2) how quickly one's speed can be improved. Many runners train at 7:00 per mile and slower and then seem surprised that a 37-minute 10km (approximately 6:00 miling) felt like sprinting. Running fast is not all cardiovascular. Much is mechanical, knowing how to relax and remain smooth at a fast pace.

Each winter I am amazed by how fast my speed returns when I begin indoor track workouts. The most dramatic example occurred years ago when I began running indoors twice a week after logging 1000 miles outdoors. I had excellent endurance, but could barely run 75–76-second 440s during the first workouts. I doubt I could have raced a 5:00 mile. During the first two or three track sessions I felt clumsy and couldn't get going. I wanted to run faster but couldn't remember what to move in order to do it. Over several weeks the *effort* originally required for 75-second 440s soon produced 73s, then 70s, and finally mid-upper 60s. After 13 track sessions in six weeks I ran 14:00 for three miles.

Part of this improvement was adjusting to anaerobic metabolism, but there's more to it than that. What happens when you begin to pick up the pace is you relearn the movements necessary for faster speeds, get more drive from your feet, use better arm movement, relax the antagonistic muscles (those opposite the ones doing the work) and lengthen out. Instead of fighting yourself while applying the pressure, more effort goes into moving forward.

Films of top distance runners such Clayton, Rodgers, and Salazar show that at no time, even during sprinting, do they fully extend their drive-off leg. Sprinters, on the other hand, get greater drive from the explosive extension of the knee and ankle at the moment of toe-off, and stay in the air longer between strides. Distance runners, therefore, can't cover the same distance per stride as sprinters, even when running flat out.

At the paces run in a distance race, a distance runner is more efficient than a sprinter running at the same speed. Distance runners use their arms less and get less vertical height between strides. However, when distance runners sprint, they bounce more and are *less* efficient than sprinters. Although distance runners can never become sprinters, they can learn to run fast with greater

Even milers must run like sprinters at the end of the race. These world-class runners are able to retain their form even though powering into the finish.

efficiency. It's a matter of developing and practicing neuromotor patterns in training that become automatic during a race.

Many runners mistakenly see themselves as being "naturally slow," and incapable of getting much faster no matter what they do. If they try some stride-outs, or time-trial a lap or two on the track, they'll tell you, "I tried it and just couldn't get going."

Imagery plays a big part in developing speed. When starting faster work, try to "see" yourself sprinting slowly rather than just running your road speeds faster. There is a big difference. At aerobic speeds it's economical to shuffle, but when you stride out, that doesn't work as well. Anyone who has done speed work with Lydiard knows he insists that you "run tall." Bill Bowerman, who trained several world-class dash men at Oregon, long ago came to the same conclusion and says, "A forward lean might be useful to someone trying to bash down a wall with his head. But in running,

*The impeccable striding technique of England's Seb Coe, 1980
and 1984 Olympic 1500-meter champion.*

it merely gives the leg muscles a lot of unnecessary work." He contends that one's posture should be so erect you could drop a plumb-line from the ear and it would fall "straight down through the line of the shoulders, the line of the hip and then to the ground." The way to accomplish this, he says, is to pull the shoulders back and buttocks in. "While sprinting, keep your arms low and pump them hard and rapidly."

Bud Winter, former sprint coach at San Jose State who trained John Carlos, Tommie Smith, and Lee Evans, agrees that "sprinters have to run tall. To do this, they must push the chest out, pull the caboose in and run high on their toes. The position is similar to that of a soldier standing at attention." The hands should be cupped and relaxed. "Now bring the arms to almost 90 degrees, palms upward a bit to keep the elbows close to the sides. Force is applied in bringing the arms forward—like punching." Studies show that the arms move fastest in their forward drive. As the arms drive forward, the opposite leg drives back, helping propel the runner forward.

That advice seems to make sense out of an encounter I had with Gordon Pirie in New Zealand a few years ago. I was running repeat 800s on the track. Pirie was there with one of his athletes and waved me aside as I approached the next 800. With all the directness and lack of tact that is the Pirie trademark, he called out to me, "You'd run better if you sawed your bloody arms off!" I felt insulted, but interested, so I heard him out.

"I'll show you something," he continued. "Make your hands into fists."

I made fists.

Then he held his palms out at chest level and said, "Now swing your arms back and forth and punch my hands."

I punched.

"Harder and faster."

I did a reasonable imitation of an emaciated Muhammad Ali working over someone's midsection.

"That's the way your arms should go," he said, satisfied. "Now run another 800."

As you go faster, your heels come up higher behind. The trailing leg folds at the knee to swing up toward the buttocks to shorten the pendulum which allows you to bring the leg through faster. That's why sprinters and middle-distance runners have high heel kick, pull through, and get good knee lift. Sprint technique

Toward the end of a race when extreme fatigue sets in and the legs lose their power, the tendency among many runners is to exaggerate arm action. In a sense, they revert to "running with their arms."

works the calves because as you get higher on your toes, it puts more tension on the Achilles tendons. In fact, until recently it was thought that the calves drove the body forward. But high-speed photography has revealed that the calf muscles are not significant in forward propulsion of the body. A complete absence of these muscles does not prevent forward motion. The calf muscle actually acts as a brake, and it is the airborne leg that pulls the body forward. The Achilles tendon and calf stabilize the ankle so that a runner does not fall forward before he or she gets the other foot planted. One of the reasons your calves get sore when you sprint is that the force exerted on them is roughly three to eight times the body weight.

POINTS TO REMEMBER ABOUT STYLE _____

Style is an individual matter. Although it doesn't matter what you look like as long as you get from point A to point B the quickest, there are basic tenets of form that everyone should consider:

1. Never run so fast or so hard you are out of control or strain. If you don't feel smooth and relaxed at fast speeds, back off.
2. Don't tilt your head back, especially when kicking at the end of a hard run or race. It means you are tying up, and it interferes with relaxation and speed. Your gaze should fall 10 to 30 yards in front of you.
3. Don't stick your rear out in back. Keep it under you. Runners who "lean into it" most often make this mistake.
4. Don't rotate the palms of your hands down and let them flap at the wrist. Even some classy runners make this mistake. Flapping dissipates whatever drive you could have derived from your arms. Keep your thumbs on top of a cupped, relaxed fist. Rotating your palms down pushes your elbows out.
5. Efficient arm carriage is low. Lydiard says the thumb should skim the waist band of your shorts. Many beginners, especially women, hold their arms high and pump up and down near their chests. Your arms should form a flexible 90-degree angle at the elbow. But some world-class runners like de Castella carry theirs lower, and others like Salazar carry theirs higher. In each case the governing factor is comfort and nonrestrictive movement.
6. Don't swing your arms across the center line of your chest.
7. An asymmetrical gait may be due to a short leg or other physical irregularity such as a muscle imbalance. Can

your shoe be shimmed up, or are there any other corrective measures you can take?

8. If you carry tension in your shoulders and/or jaw (shoulders come up or you grit your teeth) remind yourself or
have a partner remind you to drop your shoulders, or
jaw.

9. Usually, your most economical stride length will be close
to what comes naturally. But not always. Bouncing is
usually associated with overstriding. At the end of a race
many runners "lope" (revert to a long inefficient stride)
at the expense of tempo (a short fast economical stride).

Don't allow your hands to cross the body's center line.

5.

STAYING OUT OF TROUBLE

EVALUATING WORKOUTS

Among the stories in the folklore of science is that of the biologist and the flea.

This particular researcher is studying the behavior of a large and unusually cooperative flea. By virtue of years of practice and self-denial, he has trained the flea to jump over a matchbox on command whenever he yells the word "jump." Being a true scientist, he wonders what it is that gives the flea the ability to respond in this way, and decides it must be the first of its three pairs of legs. To test his theory, he tears off the front legs and again gives the command to jump. The flea jumps. Revising his hypothesis, he then tears off the two middle legs. He yells "jump," and the flea once more successfully clears the matchbox. Finally in a fervor of experimental zeal, he pulls off the last pair of legs, and once more issues the command. This time the flea remains immobile. So the researcher draws the inevitable conclusion that pulling off the flea's hind legs has made it deaf.

This fable reminds me of a dilemma all runners experience: drawing correct conclusions from what we believe we have observed. Runners think that if they are running faster in training they are making progress. While this may be true, the ultimate objective in training is to *race* faster. No one receives medals for workouts. Hard training at the wrong time, while looking impressive, can wear you down before a race. Some training prepares you to train faster rather than race effectively.

Lydiard observed this years ago when the cliché workout of milers was fast interval 440s on the track. They ran 440s two or three times a week for weeks, systematically chopping the times down. Many, he noticed, failed to race well. "What they've done," Lydiard shrewdly deduced, "is train themselves to excel at fast repeat quarters, not race a fast mile."

If you don't understand what various workouts are supposed to accomplish, you'll waste time with the wrong training. For example, a local runner made the rounds of the "experts" to ask what improves speed most: hills, intervals, or sprinting. Most picked sprinting, but the question must be considered in a broader sense: If you've just come off of base work, hills lay the foundation for speed work. Later, intervals take you a notch further. Finally, with that background, sprinting itself develops speed. But if you go directly into sprint work without the background, it could contribute to your demise. Additionally, sheer speed doesn't necessarily produce the fastest finishes, something Peter Snell proved in the early 1960s when he raced George Kerr over 800 meters. Kerr had better speed than Snell. Were the two to race over 100 or 200 meters ten times, Kerr would have beaten Snell every time. Yet, at the end of the 800, Snell always outkicked Kerr. The reason was that Snell did the stamina training necessary to enable him to attain his speed *when he was tired.* Kerr, on the other hand, was excessively interval and sprint trained and could not use his speed when the "bear" was on his back.

When Lasse Viren won both the 5000 and 10,000 meters at the Munich Olympics and won both again four years later at Montreal, a defense never before or again repeated, it dramatized just how well Viren and coach Haikkola understood how to evaulate workouts. Viren trained on the track only three times before the Munich Games, and very little before Montreal. Haikkola put Viren on the track only to gauge his condition. Using time-trials and carefully controlled interval workouts, Haikkola evaluated where Viren was in his conditioning, and what needed to be done. The rest of Viren's track-type work was done on trails, using fartlek, because they wanted to minimize the pressures that circling the track and taking times created. It was enough for Viren to work hard, running freely, and then periodically check to see that progress was on schedule.

Haikkola says that "Lasse's problems before the two Olympics were entirely different. Six weeks before Munich he ran 5000 in 13:19, so he was ready. But was he too early? We had a test run in Stockholm and he broke the world record for two miles with 8:14. He was ready. But still the newspapers said the peak won't last. So we employed three tests which put Lasse's mind to ease. Each time it was the same. He would run 200 meters 20 times (with 200-meter recovery-runs in 45 to 50 seconds), and we would time him and take his pulse right after each 200. In June, he averaged 30 seconds and 190 beats per minute. In July, before the two-mile record, he averaged 29.3 and 186. In August, before the Olympics, he did 27.2 and 172. So we had real proof that there was nothing to worry about.

"Before Montreal, we gave Lasse the same test. He averaged 28.2 and 182 beats per minute, not his best. His training had been interrupted by a month-long sinus infection that had to be drained six or seven times. So we did another test to discover what kind of work was needed. He did 5000 meters on grass by sprinting 50 meters and easing 50 meters, sprinting and easing, 50 sprints in all. He finished in a time of 13:32* (better than all but a handful of runners can do while running an even pace). But his pulse was only 186. In perfect condition he would go over 200 after such a sustained stress—ease exercise. It was obvious that he needed additional speed training, but there were only eight days left before the 10,000 meter heats . . . three days later he was quicker; you could see the difference in the action of his ankles. He was reaching his maximum sharpness."

This is a much different attitude than most runners and their coaches have toward training. It was not enough that Viren trained or time-trialed fast. Clues were sought to gauge where he

* Viren's log shows he ran 13:50 with a 184 pulse. This would seem more realistic. Running 13:32, even if the jog 50s were at 5:00 pace, the fast 50s would have to be 3:42.7 mile pace. With either time, it's an incredible workout and the point is made.

During the 1972 Olympic Games 10,000 meters, Lasse Viren (left) and Mohamed Gammoudi stumble and fall after 4000 meters. Gammoudi never got back into the race, but Viren, up and running within three seconds, overtook the pack and was on his way to his first Olympic victory and another world record.

was in his development and what needed to be done. Most runners before the Olympics would have been content with a world record for two miles or 20 × 200 in 27.2. Haikkola, however, viewed these performances in terms of the Olympics. Two miles in 8:14 and 20 × 200 in 27.2 were excellent, but did they mean Viren was sharpening too fast? Five thousand meters of alternate sprint-jog 50s in 13:32 (or 13:50) was fast, but when Viren's pulse didn't go high enough, clues were provided for the remaining training.

On the eve of both Olympics, Viren knew he was ready. During the 20 × 200 tests, "the idea was to keep the same rhythm," Haikkola explains, "but open up for the last 200. Lasse ran that last 200 in 25.8 seconds, yet his pulse was lower than it had been in June. He was in better shape: more speed, less fatigue."

Further insight into Viren's training monitoring were revealed after Atlanta's Peachtree Road Race when author David Martin questioned Viren about his ability to so precisely gauge his form before the Olympics. Viren explained that another method was to time-trial 800 or 3000 meters every other week, closely monitoring his pulse afterward. Viren actually had a nurse do this, taking his pulse 30 seconds before he began the trial, immediately following, and at regular intervals afterward to check his rate of recovery. He kept a record of the results, looking for a lower reading after each trial run *at a given speed* (not faster), and for a more rapid recovery during the next few minutes.

One function of workouts is that they are a feedback system. They tell you if you are improving or digging yourself into a hole, because it can happen that the faster you train the slower you race. Dellinger reflects this attitude in his coaching of Salazar when he said, "We don't go about our training to break records. Alberto trains to compete at the best of his ability. Salazar says, "The winner isn't the person who could have been the best, the winner is the person who *was* the best, and if someone doesn't train smart, that's his problem."

Being on schedule implies a logical rate of progression. This doesn't necessarily mean you improve by uniform increments, but you also don't just see how quickly you can get faster, because you might reach your peak too soon. If you level off way before your target race, and then get discouraged and enter a slump because your improvement has stopped, that early progress seems pretty useless.

Much as been made of the East Germans' reputed monitoring of their anaerobic workouts by analyzing the athletes' blood lactate levels. The athlete runs another hard workout only after the lactates drop to a certain level. But Costill claims that the East Germans aren't as scientific and advanced as everyone thinks. I do know, however, that the East Germans rely upon the concept of somatic intelligence, which means that *you* know your body better than anyone—doctors, orthopedic specialists, podiatrists, or physiologists.

While blood analysis is beyond most runner's means, a coach or experienced runner can weigh factors such as the speed and degree of difficulty at which the workout was run, and the physical and mental residue fatigue experienced the next day (or two). If you feel like skipping workouts, or your training times are slowing, this is a signal to let up. Many runners mistakenly try to train harder, especially a week or two before a championship, when they feel they have to make up for lost workouts.

In 1979 and again in 1983 the Athletics West Club conducted tests and surveys of their long-distance runners to find simple predictors of overtraining, injury or illness. The best were pulse rate, fluid intake, change in body fat (weight), and time to bed and hours slept. With respect to sleep, it didn't matter so much when the athlete went to bed as that bedtime didn't vary by more than 30 minutes, and that the quality of sleep was good. Insomnia is a definite indicator of overtraining.

In addition to using one's pulse, Mary Decker's coach, physiologist Dick Brown, says that when she becomes unusually thirsty, her morning weight is down, or her percent of body fat (measured by calipers) drops, this a tip-off that she may be overworking or getting dehydrated.

Pulse rate indicates how hard you are working, whether you are ready for another hard workout, and when you have had enough during a workout. Taken immediately after awakening each morning, it's a good gauge of whether you are ready for a hard workout. Dick Beardsley, for one, keeps a sign near his bed reminding him to "TAKE PULSE" upon awakening. If it is elevated 10 or more beats per minute, something may be amiss; an emotional problem, or residue fatigue from a hard session, or too many miles. In any case, he cuts back that day.

As Viren did, periodically use your pulse to tell how hard you are working. Stop momentarily to check at what percent of your maximum heart rate you are operating. This roughly gauges at what percent of your VO_2 max you are working. During interval training take your pulse immediately following fast sections and compare them to those taken during the same workout previously. The same times run with a lower pulse, or faster runs with the same pulse, signals improvement. If your pulse is higher, you are probably overworking. If, during interval training your pulse fails to return to 120–130 after 1½ to 2 minutes of recovery, you've probably had enough.

A good example of this occurred when Dick Quax, former 5000 meter world-record holder and Olympic silver medalist, was coaching at Athletics West and running one of the athletes over six medium-effort 800s. The runner completed the first two feeling tired, but on target pace, and felt he could complete the workout. However, after the second 800 and a recovery lap, his pulse was still fairly high, so Quax had him jog for an extra 30 seconds before the next 800. The third 800 was again on goal pace, but after a recovery lap his heart rate was still elevated. Quax said, "Do another recovery lap." Still the runner's heart rate was elevated, so Quax cancelled the rest of the workout over the athlete's protests.

As you become more fit, you recover quicker after a given workout. After Viren ran those 20 × 200s, his pulse was back down to 96 after two minutes. But getting an accurate reading is tricky because your heart begins to slow as soon as you stop to take your pulse. When I raced a marathon in 1973 wearing an EKG monitor, my pulse dropped from 180 to 150 within *five seconds* after finishing. Two minutes later it was under 100.

What most runners do is put their hand to their radial artery on the wrist, or carotid artery at the side of the neck under the jawbone and count the number of beats during 10 seconds. Multiply the beats in excess of 20 by six and add to 120. Don't press hard on the carotid artery, which serves the head, because it increases the blood pressure there. Sensors will detect this and tell the brain to vasodilate (open) the arteries and slow the heart to regulate (lower) their blood pressure. This would give a false reading.

Even though your pulse is changing while you take it, at least readings are comparable over time. There are devices on the market that monitor your pulse, but only a few, such as the Coach™ Aerobic Fitness Monitor, provide readings while running. Even at $200 (in 1984), it's temperamental. I expect that the price will drop and performance will improve as the technology improves.

If you went up to use your pulse as a gauge of how hard you are working, use the table on page 89.

HOW MANY MILES?

In the winter of 1971–72 Gerry Lindgren, former teenage phenomenon who ran two miles in 8:40 and 5000 meters in 13:44 in high school, embarked on a 50-mile-a-day training program. The goal was a gold medal at the Munich Olympics. "More than anything else," Lindgren said before starting, "it's going to help my self image. When I get on the track, I'll know I've done more than anyone else out there, and I'll know I'm stronger."

Lindgren never got past the trials. Bill Bowerman says that runners think the farther and faster they run in training, the better it's going to be for them. A runner can have just as much success by finding what his limit is in relation to his progress. It doesn't make any sense to think, "I'm going to win a gold medal because I have run farther than anyone else."

Rob de Castella says, "If you train 60 miles per week and run three hours [for the marathon], it's not true that if you run 120 miles per week you'll run 1½ hours. Find your optimum training level and stick to it."

RUNNING EFFORTS BASED ON PULSE RATE DURING
OR IMMEDIATELY AFTER A RUN

Percent of Max Pulse	PULSE RATE PER MINUTE (Your maximum pulse is roughly 220 Minus your age)								EFFORT
100%	165	170	175	180	185	190	195	200	Very Difficult
95	157	162	166	171	176	181	185	190	
90	149	153	158	162	167	171	176	180	
85	140	145	149	153	157	162	166	170	Difficult
80	132	136	140	144	148	152	156	160	
75	124	128	131	135	139	143	146	150	Moderate
70	116	119	123	126	130	133	137	140	
65	107	111	114	117	120	124	127	130	Recovery for Intervals*
60	99	102	105	108	111	114	117	120	
55	91	94	96	99	102	105	107	110	
50	83	85	88	90	93	95	98	100	Recovery for Repetitions*
37	61	63	65	67	68	70	72	74	Resting, General Population
30	50	51	53	54	56	57	59	60	Resting, Recreational Athlete**
25	41	43	44	45	46	48	49	50	Resting, Fit Athlete**

* Pulse rate at which you are recovered enough to begin the next repeat.

** Resting Pulse is your pulse while sitting relaxed.

To find that level you must heed the law of diminishing returns and recognize that at some point (that changes over your career), another mile will put you over the edge. But as the poet William Blake said, "You never know what is enough unless you know what is more than enough."

Lindgren and many others have discovered what is more than enough. Overtraining afflicts more aspiring runners than undertraining as evidenced by the many runners who go through their competitive seasons half exhausted or injured. Much of this is due to misinterpreting Lydiard and developing a complex if not logging at least 100 miles per week. Many have become so hung up

Mary Decker runs down Tatyana Kazankina to win the 1983 World Championship 3000 meters.

on mileage they cannot bear to cut back even when it would provide needed recovery.

A runner who has been *forced* to monitor her mileage is Mary Decker. Since her pre-teens, she has had enough overtraining injuries to fill a small medical textbook. When Dick Brown took over her coaching in 1981, the first thing he did was study her training logs. He discovered she habitually got injured when she ran more than 65 miles a week. So Brown made sure her mileage never topped 60 miles.

"My philosophy of coaching is, 'When in doubt, be conservative,' " Brown says. "I believe in what Bowerman said, 'Undertrain and the adrenaline will give you what you need on race day.' " It was difficult for Brown to get Decker to cut back. Her habit was to prove herself again and again in the workouts, but Brown knew that if she only tried this approach one season it would cure her forever. Mary gave her word to hold back and the immediate outcome was four indoor world records for which she received the 1982 Sullivan Award.

It was relatively easy for Brown to gauge Decker's optimal mileage, because even though theoretically she *might* benefit from 70 to 90 miles a week, the point is moot because the warranty on her moving parts always expired first. Her body simply cannot withstand more mileage at the intensity she trains.

Allison Roe, former marathon record holder, told me much the same thing in describing how she and Gary Elliott experimented with high mileage after she won the Boston Marathon in 1981. "I came back home, and we ran 85 to 90 miles a week for four weeks," she explained. "It totally exhausted me. Perhaps I was running too fast, but what's the point of running slower just to get the miles in? I was also starting to find all sorts of aches and pains, little starts of injuries. I didn't feel like running. I was fighting myself."

Roe cut back to about 70 miles per week, modest for a marathoner destined to become the world-record holder four and a half months later. But mileage is personal. High mileage bored her. When her concentration faltered, she would skip workouts. Elliott knew this, and because he was dealing with a mature runner with 10 years' background in track and cross-country, he was able to emphasize quality rather than quantity.

Most elite runners can tolerate higher mileage than this and improve. When I began running with Lorraine Moller in 1979, the farthest she had raced was 5000 meters. But during her university days in hilly Dunedin, New Zealand, she had trained 100 miles a week with the guys. Consequently, two months after trying a 10km road race in April, 1979—twice her previous competitive limit, she went to the Grandma's Marathon to just run 20 miles. She started slowly and felt so good at 20 miles she ran the last 10km in 36 minutes to finish in 2:37:35, then the sixth fastest time ever by a woman.

In coaching her for the 1980 Avon Women's Marathon Championship in London, I first had to determine how much work she could do without breaking down. I was flirting with Blake's prophesy than you don't know what's enough unless you know what is more than enough. By careful monitoring her reactions to the workload, she was able to keep from dipping into the "what is more than enough." It turned out to be around 128 miles a week. But to experiment with mileage, we temporarily sacrificed quality. However, because she had been a track and cross-country runner, even when not fully sharpened, she was still faster than her marathon rivals. Her road races in the 10 km range suffered somewhat, but I thought it would be worth it the next year when the plan was to trade mileage for quality.

For most runners it is difficult to determine optimum weekly mileage because the variables governing it are varied and constantly changing. Ten common factors affecting mileage are:

1. Previous running experience.
2. Mental tenacity.
3. Durability (resistance to injuries).
4. The event(s) for which you are training.
5. The speed at which you train.
6. Outside activities (40-hour week, desk job, manual laborer, "professional" runner with no other job, etc.).
7. Amount of sleep.
8. Emotional pressures.
9. Phase of training (goals in training).
10. One or two-a-day workouts.

One nice thing about high mileage is that once you have run it, even after getting out of shape, the body remembers how to do it. Lydiard mentions this in *Run to the Top*: "It is a big job building up to 20 miles the first time," he wrote, but in succeeding years, there will be no difficulty whatever in reaching the distance again, even with comparatively light training."

I cannot tell you how many miles you should run each week. You are going to have to answer that yourself. It will change as you get into shape, develop over your career, emphasize speed, and rest for races. But it may be beyond what you anticipated. I never dreamed I could run 100 and more miles a week until I read that Lydiard's runners, who he claimed were of average talent, did it. When you push back the mental limits, your body is free to let loose too. Go at it gradually, cutting back when about to overdo it.

It will be incredible—running and *improving* from mileage formerly thought beyond your ability. When you do overdo it, look back in your log and see at what point you got into trouble.

Ask yourself, "How did I feel after that workout?" If it was hard to get going for several days, or you were constantly stiff and aching, then you were probably training too hard and needed to cut back. On most workouts you should feel as though you could have gone a little further or faster. By trial and error you eventually will get good at predicting how much you can take *and still improve.*

After Dick Beardsley ran 2:08:53 at the Boston Marathon in 1982 he began to think he was indestructible and on a "big roll" going into his 1984 Olympic preparation. "I'd run a marathon on Sunday," he explained after the Games that he sat out injured, "and I'd be back training hard three days later. I'd run a hard race on Saturday and I'd go out and do a hard 20-miler the next day. . . . For a while my body held up to anything I did with it. But all it takes is one little miscalculation, just something here or there with your training."

Never make your target mileage a contest to see how much you can run. If you run so far you never run fast, you are doing it wrong. Grinding out miles neither fully develops stamina, nor prepares you for a smooth transition into interval work and racing. More and more miles will perhaps look impressive in your log and make you a good mileage runner, but nothing more.

New Zealander Jack Foster, who took up running in his mid-30s, set the world record for 20 miles when he was 38, and at age 41 was silver medalist in the Commonwealth Games with a 2:11:18 marathon, based his training on the Lydiard principle, but always kept the emphasis on quality rather than quantity. He says that more than 100 miles per week would never have produced anything to surpass what he did get out of his thin frame. "Besides," he says, "I didn't want to put all that much time into it. I had a family to spend time with." Furthermore, Foster doesn't believe that the high mileage his countrymen Terry Manners and Kevin Ryan ran was good for them. "I told Terry time and time again he ran better on 100 miles a week than 140 miles. He'd tell me, 'Done 140 this week,' and I'd say to myself, 'Great!' because I knew he was going to be easier to beat."

In summary, mileage is important, but it isn't everything. If enough is good, it doesn't follow that more is better. During your aerobic build-up it's much more important than while sharpening when speed becomes increasingly important. During your build-up ideally you should run the highest mileage you can without injury or exhaustion. Trial and error will locate this limit, but if you err too far, you may experience an annoying delay in training. Other than at the beginning of your season when mileage is the main goal, lots of slow miles will prove worthless when the races begin. Head the familiar adage of Lydiard and Bowerman, "Train, don't strain." Three simple words that imply that if the miles you run underwrite your best performances, they are training; if you end up on the sidelines exhausted or injured, they are straining.

LISTENING TO YOUR BODY

Your body speaks to you. It sends progress reports before you run, while you run, and after you run. It tells you when it feels good, when it doesn't, and when things are about to go wrong. Normally runners don't hear the body talking because it barely whispers.

The messages are transmitted in biofeedback, which is a closed-circuit return of biological and emotional information to your senses. Usually it is difficult to interpret. Ordinarily, you can't hear, see, taste, or even feel the activity of your muscle cells, metabolic processes, and the beginnings of injuries. Signals that you are overdoing it, or about to get injured, are often perceived as the fatigue and discomfort associated with physical activity. While running hard intervals your calves might get tight, but do you write it off as a normal consequence of running higher on your toes, or should you perceive it as a warning that you are about to pull a muscle? When stepped-up training makes you stiff, is that verification that you have subjected yourself to the stresses necessary to trigger the training effect, or is it an omen of impending problems?

If you learn to read various sensations in terms of possible outcomes and compare hypothetical consequences with past experience, predicting outcomes and verifying the results, you eventually learn how to answer questions like these. It's not a matter of intelligence, just being tuned in and knowing the language.

This is a vital advantage. If you consider that during a year's time roughly one-third of all runners experience an injury, then reading your body's signals will be of exceptional value. Even among elite runners, more performances are ruined by injury than by inadequate conditioning. In fact, the preponderance of injuries among runner allows one of New Zealand's top masters, John Robinson, to save face when meeting a runner whose name he's forgotten. When the other runner says, "Hi," John replies, "Hi, how's your injury?" Robinson says it works every time; he's never encountered a runner who either isn't injured or was recently, and is flattered that he remembered. England's Cliff Temple goes so far as to suggest that "there are only three normal states of health for a serious distance runner: injured, recovering from injury, or deciding which injury you'd like to have next." If you think that's tongue-in-cheek, when the next Olympics or World Games trials begin, note how many athletes are missing because of injury.

Everyone talks about listening to your body, but how do you do it? As mentioned above, when your calves get tight or you drag between workouts, do you carry on, ease back, or stop? Before we can address questions like that, it's necessary to state a premise from which I believe we operate. It is that nearly every injury we as runners get is due to having made a mistake. There may have been little discernible warning, and little chance of averting it, but nevertheless an error has been committed. If you accept that, it means that when we get injured, we are not innocent victims of forces we have no control over. But if we can't recognize that mischief is afoot, how do we sidestep it?

Although you can't eliminate mistakes and injuries, you can prevent most of them. When you consider that we often ignore *blatant* hints that things are going wrong, it's not surprising that we don't heed subtle warnings. Some runners almost ask for trouble. They let their shoes wear until they list to one side like the *Titanic* before her final plunge. Meanwhile, they complain that their feet, ankles, or knees hurt. They begin speed or hard downhill work without sufficient conditioning and wonder why everything hurts. They won't back off hard intervals between weekly races, but they'll wonder why they feel washed out. They'll run another hard workout before they've recovered from the last one.

It's easy to tune into errors like these, but to avert the subtle ones, you need to become a Sherlock Holmes. Once you begin thinking like a sleuth, many of the problems become, as Holmes might have said, "Elementary, my dear runner." The key to interpreting training feedback is not in the listing of symptoms and their probably meaning. It is a matter of *attitude*. It's being cautious, taking subtle symptoms seriously, and not letting pride sucker you into doing things that hindsight recognizes as foolish.

As an example, some years ago after a seemingly adequate build-up, I began track intervals. At first all went well, but, as the pace increased my hip began to act up. It wasn't persistent or even incapacitating, but intuition told me to get off the track before it became serious. Yet with races coming up, how could I do anaerobic work without running fast?

I considered substituting my hill workout, which involved hard up-and-down runs plus striding on the flat. But stride-outs and running downhill would stress my hip worse than the track. I compromised. Hard uphill runs wouldn't bother me, were anaerobic, and would build power. I could jog down. After two weeks of this, I was able to return to the track on schedule. Nothing brilliant about that, but it's typical of the way these things happen and the questions you need to ask. First it required taking the twinges in my hip seriously. Secondly, it meant drawing upon past experience to select a safe alternative. Third, it required mental flexibility. Sometimes our thinking becomes so rigid we forget we can (and often need to) change things. Actually, I almost overlooked hill running because the downhills meant pounding.

Here are five approaches to listening to your body:

1. *Distinguish between normal sensations and warnings.*
   This is tricky. Not every ache results in injury, nor does a bad day mean you are approaching a slump. Ask yourself what became of these symptoms in the past. It's trial and error. When training on the indoor track, I discovered I could overdo it with no symptoms until the next day. Therefore, I run indoor workouts with caution, beginning slowly, being careful with workouts that have bothered me in the past, and aborting any workout I think will be straining rather than training.

   Normally when your motivation temporarily wanders, train on, because when it returns, you will be upset over losing valuable work. However, during a hill workout one winter night, three miles from home and halfway up the first hill, I unexpectedly found myself just standing there. I hadn't made a conscious decision to stop. I just did. What are you doing! I thought.

   "I hate this," I replied out loud. "I don't want to be here." I knew from the intensity of my feelings that I should stop the workout. I would have stood there had I not frozen, and the jog home was so repulsive I didn't run the next night. It was well I didn't. I had been covering 90 to 120 miles a week for two months, and my body and mental batteries were demanding a break. I felt no guilt over dropping the two days because this time it was the right thing to do.

2. *Differentiate between a needed rest and malingering.* When you don't feel like running, ask yourself if you need rest, or whether you are subconsciously (or consciously) looking for an excuse to skip the workout. Is there a good movie around, a party, or does running just seem like too much trouble? Sometimes what you feel has little to do with physical fatigue, but is rather a conflict of interests. If there's any doubt, start the workout. If you don't snap out of it after warming up, cut back or stop.

3. *Struggling with one injury triggers another worse injury.* That's because you run cockeyed to favor the first one. Runners are such an irrepressible lot they will limp through a minor injury on one leg only to find that a few days later the knee or hip on the other side hurts worse. If others notice you limping, either back off or stop temporarily. While it's aggravating to lose workouts, it's better than prolonged injury. If you shouldn't run, admit it.

4. *Sometimes you won't recover from a hard workout as scheduled.* Occasionally your scheduled recovery is not enough, though you think it should be. If you aren't ready, no matter what the reason, either cut or reschedule. A good schedule includes a certain amount of duplication, so a few lost sessions shouldn't disrupt progress. Forcing yourself to adhere to your schedule when your body says rest is foolhardy. Steve Scott, for one, won't attempt hard workouts he's not ready for. "I don't do workouts that bum me out," he says. "They do more harm than good." Greg Meyer adds that "It's much better to bag a workout when you're sore and tired then to try and bull yourself through it. There's no use running a lousy workout."

5. *Admit that if you can have super days, you can expect incredibly bad ones.* It's frustrating but fair. No one knows why, but occasionally and for no apparent reason you won't be able to function at all. Even David Costill can't figure it out. "Tests show that every day it

takes a different amount of energy to run an eight-minute mile. I'm not sure why," he says.

When you should be able to perform, but can't, don't conclude that you condition has deteriorated. I once came to the track to run 3 X 880 in 2:09, and could barely run a 440 in 68. I thought I had fallen apart, but a few days later I ran those 880s. I didn't feel tired before the first attempt; it was just one of those inexplicable off-days. Occasionally you will have a string of off-days—perhaps for a whole week—for no obvious reasons. There's been no loss of sleep, no emotional stress, and the workouts haven't seemed excessive, at least on paper. If it isn't a signal that you are overworking, it will pass—perhaps when your body (or head) has had its breather.

Successive low-vitality days could also mean you are trying to train at a level over your head, regardless of what you think you should be able to do. Or you may be racing too often. Ask yourself if you are becoming bored with unimaginative workouts. Check your pulse, both resting and during standard workouts. If it's high, you may need to ease back on the workload, especially anaerobic work if you are doing any.

But realize that slumps of several days or a week are normal. Therefore, the greatest potential detriment is in believing you have suddenly fallen apart. Negative feelings have a way of feeding on themselves until fears become reality. Once you become convinced you can't run, depression, rather than any physically based problem, becomes the culprit.

Just as occasional off-days don't mean you've fallen apart, those days when you feel inexhaustible don't mean you are indestructible. The tendency with those super days is to get excited and run yourself over the edge. In 1968 one of those days coincided with a race in which I ran my best 3-mile by eight seconds. Two hours later, still energetic, I entered and nearly won the 2-mile, and then just for the hell of it jumped into the next 2-mile heat five minutes later. I was tireless that day, but useless the entire week. The next Saturday, trying to better my mile time, I ran 4:47—not even close to my 3-mile pace. So hold back when you feel super in a workout. There's no value in running over your head in one workout if it leaves you flat or injured.

TRANSITIONS

Some years ago in November, several women asked me to oversee their training for the upcoming road season beginning in March. Most of them were short on basic conditioning and speed, so I suggested they train for and race indoors during late winter before road racing. As a transition from road to track work. I scheduled three weeks of hill work, stressing that they must be basically fit before tackling hills, and even then with restraint. As a transition into the hill work, I suggested they run hilly routes during base training.

At first they kept in touch, but then I heard nothing. Several, I discovered, were injured from the hill workouts. Even before I checked their training logs, I had a pretty good idea what had gone wrong.

One of the basic tenets of training is that you make smooth transitions when increasing the workload or introducing new kinds of work. Don't run hard until you can run easily. Don't abruptly introduce hills, high mileage, speed or a new exercise. One kind of work melts into another. This is common sense, but one thing about common sense it that it is not very common.

These women got injured because: 1) not having established a good base, they weren't ready for hill training, 2) they hadn't been running hilly routes, and 3) they attacked the hills too hard too early. Which made a strengthening workout tear them apart. But that's the way training is. Done right it conditions, done incorrectly, it destroys.

Sometimes even a small slip in judgment can have catastrophic results. Recently a friend who is a 4:07 miler completed an excellent racing season, backed off, and then began rebuilding. But there happened to be a "Meet of Miles," so he jumped in one and clocked 4:19 which, he thought, was great considering he hadn't done any fast training. Nor had he recently done any of the skipping and "knees up" drills he used while warming up.

The next day it didn't seem as great. His Achilles tendon was throbbing, and after not being able to train for six months, he resorted to surgery.

To repeat, never abruptly introduce a new kind of work or try a race you are not prepared for. Increase mileage gradually; increase effort gradually. If you haven't been sprinting, and the others want to finish the workout with fast striding, tag along but just a bit faster than you've been doing, perhaps catching them during the recoveries. Put pride aside temporarily. Staying injury-free is worth it.

STAYING IN CONTROL

Actually, I've been talking about control all along. Staying in control simply means doing what you are supposed to be doing, and not allowing the runner next to you or your own pride sucker you into something there's no reason to do.

During a 10,000 meter heat at the Montreal Olympics, one of the Britons, Anthony Simmons, broke loose from the field and ran a spectacularly quick race, winning by over 10 seconds. As Simmons finished, he waved his arms in jubilation while the people in the grandstands gave him a roaring ovation. Some 60 yards behind Simmons, Lasse Viren approached the finish. He did not kick; he merely glanced around to make sure of his fourth-place position. To qualify for the final was enough. Many fans in the stands were disappointed that Viren had not made a race of it, and wondered if he was the same runner he had been in Munich.

Viren, on the other hand, couldn't understand why Simmons had wasted energy in a senseless sprint to the finish. "It is reasonable to insure a place in the final by kicking hard if chased by a cluster of men," Viren said afterward, "but I don't understand why *Simmons* kicked. He was followed by nobody. When one has to run flat out only two days later, it is completely maniacal to spend energy in the heats and unnecessarily tire the muscles. I shall never do that, for I haven't the slightest need to excel at the wrong moment."

Simmons entered the final as one of the favorites along with countryman Brendan Foster, Portugal's Carlos Lopes, and Viren. But, at the 5000 meter mark, reached in a sluggish 14:08, the pace quickened to a 13:31.4 last 5000, and Simmons could not respond. He finished fourth, out of the medals, 16 seconds behind Viren, the winner. There's no way to know how many seconds Simmons' grandstanding in his heat cost him. One thing is certain, however, it didn't help. If an Olympic favorite can lose sight of the goal during a lapse of sensibility, imagine how easy it is for the rest of us to be taken in.

Letting old ladies on crutches go past when you are already running as fast as you should be is exercising control. Entering a race as a time-trial and sticking to your predetermined effort when it's humiliating to let those you can beat go past, is control. Sticking to your pre-planned splits in a workout or race is exercising control.

When training with others faster than you, hang back and run what you set out to. Better to be seen bringing up the rear than to get in over your head and struggle through. It shows that you understand the concept of first things first, realizing you'll run faster later. You should know how long you can work at a particular effort. If you can't do it in a workout, there's even less chance during the heat of competition. When you can read the feedback your body gives you, you will enter most workouts and races with an excellent intuitive fix on what you can do at every stage along the way. If you can't, a speed that feels easy at the beginning becomes impossible later.

Decide beforehand how you are going to train, and then unless there's a reason to change, stick to it regardless of what the others do. Don't get fooled into doing something that is going to hurt you or contribute less than what you should be getting. Let the others go if they want to move on to fewer, faster miles in training before you have completed your build-up, lest you jump into something you're not ready for. The same applies to recovery days. When it *is* time to run hard, do it without feeling you are putting the screws to your partners. Beat them in races. That's what races are for. Many run fast workouts to impress themselves, teammates, or the coach without wondering how the effort relates to other workouts and races. They gloat over training times as though they were competition. If you always outrun your teammates in practice and lose to them in races, something is wrong.

This reminds me of a college runner I knew who had an insatiable appetite for leading workouts. He had run a 4:08 mile, so he was physically talented, but his teammates got fed up with his "I'm better than you" attitude. So they devised a secret game where during the repetition training each one would take a turn running hard enough to get in front of him while the others relaxed well behind. This guy always took the bait and raced them until he was exhausted. Although he was training faster than everyone else, his real races begin to disintegrate until he began dropping out, either by mentally giving up and just finishing, or eventually not even finishing. He was so competitively bankrupt from the training there was nothing left for the races.

Never train so hard you lose form and strain. This is so ingrained in the admonitions of coaching we are forced to accept that the problem is universal and far-reaching. "Train, don't strain," is Bill Bowerman's terse warning. Haikkola says, "It is most important to take training as training, not as competition." Bowerman advises that, "Even world-class runners . . . should stay within 90 percent effort. The all-out effort is saved for times when adrenaline is flowing, the band is playing, and the spectators are cheering, and the finishing line is in sight."

It is not necessary during training to run flat out to improve. New Zealand's Bill Baillie, in fact, told me that for years he had tried without success to beat teammate Murray Halberg, the Olympic 5000-meter gold medalist and former world-record holder for three miles. Baillie did, however, often duplicate Halberg's training times, but finally gave up and began to train at his own rate. Shortly thereafter, Baillie beat Halberg. Baillie swears that had he continued to struggle to match Halberg's training, he never would have beaten him.

You will improve with considerably less risk by running your track-type work at 4/5 to 7/8 effort rather than all out. When you need to know where you really are, occasionally runs a standard workout flat-out, like, but not necessarily the same as, Viren's 20 X 200, or time-trials, taking times and pulse. It's not necessary or even smart to time all your other interval workouts because the temptation is to race them rather than go for the greatest training effect. Check your pulse if you want to know how hard you are running.

As further proof that you don't have to kill yourself in training, after de Castella ran 2:08:18 to win the 1982 Fukuoka Marathon he said, "When I'm training, I go out and often do 10 miles in 60 minutes or something. I think, how the hell am I going to come out in a month or two and run through 10 miles in under 50 minutes and keep going for another 16 miles! If you stop and think about it when you're training, you can find it's too awesome."

Bill Squires, who coached Rodgers, Salazar, and Beardsley, remembers "crawling to the locker room and lying on the floor" after exhausting workouts in college. "What total nonsense," Squires says. "You have to leave something in 'em, or they burn themselves out." After Beardsley ran 2:08:53 at Boston, Squires told me he has no qualms about pulling a runner out of an interval workout when he feels that runner has had enough. "I can see by his shoulders." Squires said. "And I never get any lip. My athletes leave the track with something left. I want them to use that the second day, not burn it all off." Perhaps Lydiard captures the concept of control best when he said that "The essence of good training is when you're doing everything correctly, and at the right speed, the right time, and the right volume."

WARMING UP

In the old days, runners didn't warm up much, if at all. They went directly into fast workouts and races, then waited for that surge of power known as "the second wind" (when the aerobic metabolism kicked in to take over from the anaerobic system). When you begin any run, you produce all your energy anaerobically before the heart is able to pump enough oxygenated blood to the working muscles.

The efficacy of the warmup has been debated because there is no physiological proof that running around before a hard workout or competiton will enhance one's performance. Modern physiologists, even David Costill, writing as recently as 1979, reported that "while [the arguments for warming up] appear theoretically sound, very little research has been conducted that provide convincing evidence for benefits in distance running [presumably racing]." Costill concedes that because the Swedish physiologist Alstrand has reported a 5 percent increase in the VO_2* max following a warmup, a miler, or 2-miler, who relies heavily upon his ability to get oxygen, *might* benefit from a warmup.

My own experience tells me I cannot run smoothly and efficiently at any speed for at least several minutes after beginning, and often only after one or two miles. On some days, running is so difficult at first, I can hardly believe I'll ever get with it. Physiologists Jack Daniels and Robert Fitts recommend that every run

* For an explanation of VO_2 max, see pages 141 and 144.

begin with "five to seven minutes of easy running, a similar period of flexibility exercises, and then a few more minutes of easy running." Their research shows that after warming up the heart pumps faster and ejects more blood per beat to deliver more oxygenated blood to the muscles. It enables fat to be released from the blood and into the muscles, thus reducing the prospect of glycogen depletion. Warming up also raises your core temperature slightly, just enough for optimal metabolic performance.

Your warmup depends upon your workout or race and climatic conditions. Before a long steady run, the warmup is simply a slow first mile or so. After 10 or 15 minutes it probably would be beneficial to stop and stretch, but few runners do so because of the inconvenience.

What amazes me is how many good runners with back, sciatic, leg, or tendon trouble will start fast at the beginning of a run. Even if you don't suffer from one of these afflictions, this is a good way to attract one. Tendons and ligaments receive little or no blood supply, so it's risky to work them until they are warmed up. One way to warm up without doing any running is to ride a stationary bicycle. That way you are all ready to go as soon as you begin running.

When warming up before intervals, a time-trial, or race, there's more involved than just starting out easy. Another ingredient is required—anaerobic running. The warmup before an interval workout and a race should be identical. In fact, develop a standardized pre-race warmup by experimenting before your interval workouts. Once you find a suitable routine, time it so you know how long before your races to begin. If you begin and finish your warmup too soon, you have to keep moving or you will cool down. But if you warm up for too long, you risk fatigue. Inexperienced competitors often arrive at a race 60 to 90 minutes before the start, and then because they're nervous or else don't know what to do, they begin warming up. After they've finished, the race is still 30 to 60 minutes away.

After a warmup is begun, you are committed to keep moving. Jog until the last possible minute before a race. You can always slip into your appropriate starting position from the side. Unless it is hot and humid, keep your sweats on for as long as possible and then toss them to someone just before the gun. This is particularly important on cold days when you would cool down rapidly waiting for the start in shorts and singlet.

At road races make it a practice to find out whether the gun will go off on time in order to know when to start your warmup. When I ran track in college, I began my warmup during the low hurdles rather than follow the schedule. Invariably, they would be running late, but I knew the 2-mile started about 30 minutes after the hurdles.

Except for the marathon, try this warmup: One and a half miles of increasingly faster running, changing into your racing flats, stretching, four 80-meter stride-outs, a moderately hard 200, and about five minutes (or until lining up) of jogging which allows you to fully recover, but not cool down. The entire sequence takes about 30 minutes.

Norway's Grete Waitz takes a little longer. "I start jogging about 45 minutes before the start and continue for 15 to 20 minutes," she reports. "Then I do 10 minutes of faster strides and exercises, before putting on my racing shoes and doing a few more strides."

Seb Coe spends up to 50 minutes warming up before a cold winter race. He begins by "moving very easily, walking, bending, stretching, and then jogging," indoors if he can. Warming up outdoors in "the freezing cold is a matter of continually trying to keep warm, and the second you stop, you're often back to where you started," he adds.

The shorter the race or faster the workout, the more warmup you will need. Years ago I didn't include that 200 mentioned above in my warmup. However, during a workout of three hard interval 800s, I noticed that on the first one my arms would go numb at the end, and I'd cough during the recovery jog. But it didn't happen on the next two, which in fact, felt easier. It occurred to me that perhaps 4 × 80 meters was not enough anaerobic running, so I added that hard but not exhausting 200. It would seem tiring, but after five or so minutes of jogging, I would handle a fast anaerobic start better.

David Moorcroft alluded to this when he said, "During the warmup there's a certain amount of fatigue. At this point the work capacity is slightly decreased. But with a certain amount of rest there is increased work capacity [called 'super compensation']. The trick is to get the compensation side to coincide with the start of the race. If the warmup is long and fatiguing, recovery is slower. A long rest after the warmup is of no value."

Before a marathon, 5 to 15 minutes of easy running, a few

Seb Coe stretches his quads and shoulders before beginning a workout.

stride-outs and some stretching should suffice. If you keep your head after the gun, you should be running aerobically straight away. Don't include strengthening exercises during any race warmup. You'll see others doing push-ups, sit-ups, various leg-lifts, and so forth but smart runners don't because calisthenics do not impart flexibility or aid in warming up. These exercises involve fatiguing anaerobic bursts. If it is your day to do sit-ups, push-ups, and so on, do them after the race. Pre-race stretching is, of course, another matter. Stride-outs also improve flexibility as evidenced by the difference in how the first and last ones feel.

WARMING UP FOR HOT RACES

Most advice on warming up for hot weather races caution you to all but dispense with the warmup because it raises your core body temperature, a handicap, if not a health hazard, in the heat. Costill says, "It appears sensible for the runner to eliminate any warmup prior to a distance race in the heat where one of the major performance limitations is overheating."

This seems to make sense, yet my own experience tells me something else, something I first noticed when I won the National Marathon Championship in 96-degree heat. While most everyone else was hanging out in the shade before the race, I warmed up in the sun. This should have raised my core temperature, and no doubt did. I certainly felt uncomfortable.

At first. Then I made some sort of adjustment to the heat. Part of the adaptive mechanism the body goes through during heat training is to teach it to kick in its defenses at a lower core temperature than occurs in non heat-trained runners. After heat training, you sweat sooner, more profusely, but lose less salts and minerals. Dilute sweat means more evaporative cooling with less electrolyte loss. To compensate for a higher sweat rate you must, of course, drink more before and during the race.

I believe that warming up in hot weather triggers similar responses; after all, the purpose of any warmup is to prepare the body for what's coming up. So you feel hot at first, and then it doesn't seem as bad. You feel cooler and perform better unless the race is so long that dehydration sets in. The point is, I would not want to race before this coming-to-terms process, whatever it is, occurs. Use your head, however. If on a moderately warm day you warm up wearing a light sweatsuit or T-shirt, strip down long enough before the start to prevent being overheated when the gun goes off.

COOLING DOWN

Cooling down is treated by most runners as a bastard child after a workout or race. We all know or suspect we shouldn't just stop afterward, but when you can hardly stay on your feet, even running slow after you've caught your breath is unappealing and often inconvenient.

Once out of the finishing chute of a race, the tendency is to wander about either telling everyone how brilliantly you performed, or to establish excuses for why it wasn't your day. That's O.K., but socialize on an easy 2-mile cooldown jog. In 1981, Salazar, who tends first to his own needs, infuriated reporters by disappearing after winning the Falmouth 7.1-mile race. Eventually, he returned and explained his absence. Needing a cooldown before the press latched on to him, he continued for several miles.

He did it again in October in his first New York Marathon, won in 2:09:41. "Like after Falmouth," Salazar said, "I just kept jogging a couple of miles after the finish to warm down, and then I went to somebody's house to shower and change my clothes. I never got back to the press until two hours later and they were all freaked out and pissed off for me keeping them waiting. Looking back now, I'm glad I did that. The way I feel is, why should I be at their call the second I finish a hard race?"

After a race or series of hard intervals, the lactic acid in the muscles needs to be "buffered" by getting oxygen-rich blood flushed through them during an easy run. When you simply stop and your heart rate drops, the smaller feeder arteries, arterioles and capillaries, contract, shunting the flow of blood from the areas they serve. That makes it harder to get rid of the lactic acid, so you don't recover as fast.

Also, blood stays in the legs to compete with the needs of the heart and brain. The level of norepinephrine and endephrine, produced by the adrenal glands to raise blood pressure to exercise levels, raises sharply again during the first three minutes after stopping—even though your blood pressure is already up. It's a physiological mixup, according to Harvard scientists who discovered the phenomenon, and can be countered by jogging as soon as possible upon finishing.

After an exhausting marathon, running a cooldown is sometimes out of the question. But there are other ways to hasten recovery such as walking, a warm shower, and dancing.

Often after a marathon you are so sore, exhausted, or perhaps blistered, you can't even hobble anything resembling a cooldown. There are two other things you can do. One is to get into a warm shower or bath (but not after a hot race). After Sunday 30-milers I've barely been able to step over the side of the tub, but after a shower it's like new blood has been pumped in. In winter, hot water is best. In summer, cold water brings your core temperature down.

Dancing is another way to recover. It's somewhat embarrassing stiff-legging it out on the dance floor during those celebrations that invariably cap off marathons, but remind yourself that you don't have to impress anyone. Once on the dance floor it's amazing how fast sore legs loosen up. And you'll feel better the next day. Craig Virgin apparently came to the same conclusion after finishing second in the 1981 Boston Marathon. After the race, he tried to run a little, but could manage only two miles in 20 minutes. So later in the evening on a date "I went dancing," Virgin said. "It's great therapy; it helped. I couldn't run, but I sure could dance."

Finally, there's Jack Foster's horse method. Foster discovered that after a hard workout, race horse trainers hosed the horse's legs with cold water. "If it's good enough for horses," Foster reasoned, "it's good enough for me." Foster, who raced a 2:20 marathon at age 50, attributes his near injury-free career to training on hilly grass sheep paddocks near his home, and hosing his legs after interval workouts on warm days.

6.

MIND GAMES

THE THINGS WE TELL OURSELVES

Mental conditioning is a relatively uncharted side of athletics for most runners. Most don't have any idea what it is about or else think it sounds like a lot of hocus-pocus. This chapter includes proven, down-to-earth mental exercises that can dramatically improve your performance. You will learn to create images of the way you want to perform, how to program them into your subconscious mind and create reality from them. You will be alerted to negative statements you probably feed yourself (such as, "I tie-up in big races," or "I'll probably never get good at this, so why try?"), and will begin to replace them with positive statements. You will learn to deal with emotional stress, expand your limits, and improve your concentration. The cliché "It's all in your head," is probably far more true than you ever thought.

That we run means we first made a conscious decision to do so. The idea had to begin in your head before anything physical happened. Everything you do begins with your mind. The negative habits you develop as well as the positive. Self-images and expectations are primarily based on past experiences, learned information, what others have accomplished, and what others say we can do. Therefore, we often see ourselves in terms of our limitations rather than potential.

Ever notice that when an "impossible" barrier is broken, others follow relatively easily? After the Edmund Hillary expedition sucessfully scaled Mt. Everest, it opened the way for others. Five weeks after Roger Bannister cracked the long-awaited 4-minute mile, John Landy ran faster. Not long ago 2:40 was a barrier few women marathoners could break. Now it's commonplace among good women runners. No longer is even sub-2:30 awesome, and soon many women will be gathering momentum in the mid-2:20s to break into the teens.

When I was in college training 30 to 40 miles a week, my best mile and 2-mile were 4:30 and 9:43 respectively. I believed that was to near my limit until I read that Lydiard's athletes, who reportedly were ordinary guys like me, ran 100 miles a week and won Olympic gold medals. I began to see myself eventually running 100 miles a week and racing much faster, and when I believed it, it became reality. Afterward I realized that a new vision is required to push back the limits.

Many runners spend hours debating the latest shoe innovations and poring over information concerning every aspect of training, but forget that once they are properly shod and physically trained, what happens inside their heads controls how they use that knowledge and ability. If you are more concerned with color-coordinating your shorts and singlet before competition than your mental preparation, something is drastically out of proportion.

Runners usually approach races fit enough to run the times they want, only to wonder afterward why they didn't. Running is more than carefully orchestrated workouts and a physical challenge. You are, as has been said, the product of your thoughts. The messages you give yourself become the blueprint for performance. Without realizing it you may be underrating your abilities and feeding yourself negative messages. Contrast, for example, the statements of Nancy Conz and Patti Catalono before the 1984 Olympic marathon trial. Conz had run 2:33:23 and was ranked 15th. "I'm not in great shape," she reported three months before the trial, "and so many women who've come along are running so well. I kind of feel left out."

Patti Catalono held the American Record (2:27:51) in 1981, but floundered with injuries and other problems in 1982 and 1983 before qualifying for the trials with a 280-ranked 2:48:51. Yet Catalono insisted, "I really feel good. I'm renewed. It's like being born again. And I have all this energy stored up. I feel like I could move a mountain. . . . I think I have a good chance."

In the trial Catalono finished 16th in 2:37:13 and Conz became injured and didn't run. Before races have you said things like, "I'll die on the hills out there," "I'm nervous; I'm going to shoot for a slower time," or "Geeze, there's [your rival]. He's so confident; I bet he'll beat me"? Ever met a runner who *didn't* establish abilities before a hard workout or race? Before a hard indoor track workout I've complained (in jest, I thought) about the wind when I couldn't come up with anything else. Although I was joking, it revealed that I feared the workout and needed to shield my ego and confidence.

You may believe it's enough to think positively and develop a winning attitude only to discover that during competition's moment of truth, your positive spirit simply evaporates. Suddenly everyone else looks stronger, more confident and less tired than you. You think "Dammit, this is slow, but I can't get going!" As David Moorcroft observes, "You can kid yourself you're thinking positively, but really it's only what happens and what you feel in the race that matters."

Much of the rah-rah stuff runners try to swallow in the name of psyching up is counterproductive because it either has no substance or it triggers pressures that causes them to mentally and physically "choke." You may not need to try harder as much as learn to relax in order to get at the excellence within you. Let's examine the technique for gaining control over the way you see yourself.

VISUALIZATION

Nearly all top athletes use visualization in their preparations for competition. Before the 1979 AAU Championships, Steve Scott and his coach worked for two weeks on tactics to beat Don Paige, his main competitor in the 1500. Scott recalls: "I visualized where

I would be at every stage of the race. I saw myself racing completely relaxed, heard the splits I wanted to hear and pictured the exact point I would overtake Paige. The race came out exactly how I visualized it—right down to the splits."

Scott's advice to other aspiring milers is, "If you want to run a four-minute mile, you must see yourself as a four-minute miler and not as someone whose best time is 4:15. You have to actually see yourself running a four-minute mile in order to do it. You must train your body and mind to run fast if you want to run fast."

Research has shown that by picturing the successful completion of moves and actions you want to make, you can improve your performance. Bruce Jenner, the 1976 Olympic decathlon champion, kept a hurdle in his living room which he mentally "hurdled" during dinner. He understood that mental rehearsal would improve his actual hurdling. High jumpers prepare for each attempt for what often seems forever, concentrating on mental movies of the moves they want to make. If you observe closely (perhaps on TV), you can see their eyes dance about, their legs wiggle, and their arms practice liftoff as they "see" their approach.

If you think the whole idea of visualization is rather farfetched for a runner, you are in for a surprise, because we *all* use visualization to a degree, often without being aware of it or realizing how much difference it would make if done seriously. In 1979 I went to Harrisburg, Pennsylvania to speak at a pre-marathon clinic and use the race as a long training run. Part of the clinic featured a screening of Abebe Bikila's dramatic marathon victory at the 1964 Tokyo Olympics. If you've seen this footage, you may recall the sequence which zooms in on Bikila as he patiently "floats" away from Ron Clarke and the rest of the pack. His stride is impeccable, and his excellence so classic I gasped in awe as the image was imprinted in my mind.

When the gun released us the next morning, I had this uncanny feeling that *I* was Bikila. I ran easily, at what felt to be 7:00 miling. With the sun at our backs, I could see my shadow leading me. I imagined it belonged to Bikila and concentrated on it making it look smooth and easy. I was oblivious to the others (since I wasn't racing) and just let the shadow pull me along. What felt like seven-minute miles turned out to be nearly six-minute miles, and it became the easiest 2:39 marathon of my life.

USING VISUAL IMAGES _____

Before the 1956 Olympic 50km walk, New Zealand's Norman Read had a dream. "In my dream I saw myself take the lead at the 42-kilometer mark. And I dreamed I was on the victory dais getting a gold medal. When I *did* hit the front after 41 kilometers, I again began to dream that I could do it. It was a tantalizing thought."

Read won. This doesn't mean that if you dream of winning you will, but two prominent sports psychologists who interviewed numerous Olympic gold medalists discovered that there wasn't one who hadn't dreamed about winning before he or she actually did. Successful runners construct waking pictures that enhance performance. During the last half of the 1982 New York Marathon when Alberto Salazar got a stitch, and Rodolfo Gomez seized the opportunity to pass him, Salazar could have lost hope, panicked and allowed negative thoughts to overcome him. Instead, he thought, " 'All right, relax, hang back, don't press him, stay close but not too close and wait for the cramps to go away.' I kept thinking that over and over, relax, wait, and the cramps will go away. It was a long wait, a good eight or nine miles." By deliberately conjuring up images of running relaxed and outlasting the stitch, Salazar was able to recover and win.

You can also use visualization to keep workouts exciting, and prepare for racing. Bill Dellinger advises that "If you are by yourself, simulate race pace for 300 to 500 meters. Then imagine someone comes up on your shoulder. Pick up the pace and force yourself to run faster."

There were many workouts I ran on cold, lonely winter nights only because I visualized Abebe Bikila or my former teammate, Buddy Edelen, over in England starting their runs. Once, during a hard 3 × 880 track session, I lost my ability to hold the pace on the last one and fell 15 yards behind my teammate. It seemed impossible to catch up until I pretended I was running like I had a few nights before during some fast 110s. As soon as I pictured myself up on my toes, running tall, pumping my arms, I caught my partner so fast we nearly collided.

Don Kardong, who nearly got the bronze medal in the 1976 Olympic Marathon said, "In Montreal, I especially worked on seeing myself moving through the pack beginning at 10 miles." Kardong, who was back in the pack at mid-race, ran the second half faster to clock a lifetime best.

VISUALIZATION AND CONFIDENCE _____

"Running seems to go hand in hand with feeling good about one-self," observes psychologist Lynn McCutcheon, "mainly because it makes us feel better about our bodies." As self-confidence goes up, anxiety levels go down. David Costill believe that self-confidence may account for the biggest difference between physically talented runners. "The Derek Clayton of 1970 and the Alberto Salazar of today are gifted athletes," he says, "but others with similar laboratory scores do not necessarily achieve the same results. One thing observed in both runners, but which is not easily tested, was a high degree of self-confidence. Both men believed in their abilities to run fast and break records." Costill adds, "Self-confidence may be particularly important in the marathon where success depends to a large extent on the ability to concentrate."

VISUALIZATION AND CONCENTRATION _____

Joan Benoit attributes her success to "my mental concentration. My mental toughness. . . . Mental concentration is the biggest part of my running."

Concentration is being concerned with Now. It excludes everything extraneous. It's being "into it." You can't run relaxed, fast, and confidently while worrying about who is coming up on you or getting away. You *do* need to be aware of what the others are doing, your pace, and so on, because that is part of competition. But that concern must be translated into running better—and that's what visualization accomplishes—without the intrusion of unwanted pressures.

Years ago I learned that it is far easier to run difficult repetition workouts on winding, uneven, rolling trails than on the track. Trails keep your attention on the *now*—watching your footing so you don't trip, getting up this hill, keeping your balance on the downside, making the turns. When you are constantly focusing on the task at hand, it's difficult to think about how far you've got to go or how tired you'll be upon finishing. On the track, however, you're always aware of the laps and how tired you already are.

Recently, near the end of a race I was using for a workout, I caught a strong-looking runner whom I urged to get going. He took off, but as his concentration faltered he drifted back, whereupon I got him going once more. But at the finish we were together again. It struck me that if he could go whenever I focused his concentration, he could have kicked all the way.

You will do your best when totally absorbed in the task, not thinking about how good or bad you are doing. And when it's over it may not even have seemed like a big effort. Seb Coe, for example, reported that during his first 800-meter world record (1:42:33), "I had no particular sensation of speed, and I think I could have run faster. I wasn't exhausted at all at the end. It was strange—like being on auto pilot—I think I was mentally outside what my body was achieving and it was just beautiful."

NEGATIVE IMAGES

There is, in the language of *Star Wars*, also a "dark side of the force." Strong evidence shows that one's imagination is the most mighty of all human powers. Mighty enough to even wreak upon you real—*not imaginary*—clinically verifiable injuries.

I never believed that mental pressure could cause real injury until something unnerving happened in me. Ten days before I was to marathon in the 1967 Pan-Am Games, I developed the aforementioned severe case of sciatica. I dealt with it and considered myself cured until the next year, when precisely ten days before the Olympic marathon trial I developed sciatica again. A nasty coincidence, I thought, until 1970, when five days before the National Marathon Championship, my left quad became alarmingly stiff for no apparent reason.

This was more than coincidence, I decided. A pattern was evident: Under inescapable pressure from big races, I developed real physical injuries. My subconscious was saying, "I'm going to save you from this," while consciously I would be trying to do everything I could to remedy the affliction before race time. It illustrates that at times the one to be feared most before competition is yourself.

A more typical response is reported by Jim Lilliefors in *The Running Mind*. He mentions an elite runner who said, "Whereas in training I'd almost relished [pain], derive satisfaction from pushing to levels of pain, in races I'd worry abot it from the starting line, worry that it was going to happen too soon, and finally, in a somewhat hysterical reaction, would convince myself right out of running."

"Pressures build up," explained another runner who had retired briefly in mid-career, "and after a while, even going out the door isn't enjoyable. And when the physical act of putting one foot in front of the other isn't enjoyable anymore, you might as well hang it up."

PROGRAMMING YOUR SUBCONSCIOUS

Relaxation exercises are something I urge you to explore because they enable to gain considerable control over yourself and achieve goals you formerly considered out of reach. Relaxation is a kind of trance state, similar to that induced by hypnosis. You probably enter into and out of waking trances 200 or more times a day. You do it when you daydream. You do it when you automatically work your car's brakes, complete the correct turns, and find your way to where you are going without consciously thinking about it. I've done essentially the same thing while running familiar courses, especially alone at night in the winter. After I get going, I shift into automatic pilot, correctly making the turns while thinking about something else until suddenly I snap out of it and wonder where I am. I've had to look at street signs and landmarks to figure it out. I've even set off at hard effort, consciously forgotten what I was doing, and kept running hard.

Mental relaxation exercises work by first quieting the conscious mind. That gives you access to the subconscious, which, being very literal, doesn't differentiate between reality and fantasy. Your conscious mind is intellectual and rational; it makes decisions, analyzes and thinks. If you think you'd like to run a four-minute mile or a 2:30 marathon, your conscious mind decides if that matches your image of yourself as a runner. If it doesn't, the idea is rejected.

Hypnosis relies on relaxation, suggestion, and concentration to circumvent the screening process of the conscious mind. No one knows what hypnosis is, but almost anyone can learn to handle it. It has been called the most simple and practical proof of the existence of the subconscious. It is the suggestions you or the hypnotist plant that control physical and mental mechanisms normally not available to you. That may sound novel, but most of us know that hypnotized subjects can "see" normally forgotten past events in detail, or produce blisters when told the pencil they are holding is red hot. These examples are but a glimpse of the tremendous control the subconscious has over the body.

You will need to carefully control what you are asking yourself to do because the subconscious reacts the same to negative suggestions as to positive ones. Moreover, if the subconscious begins to react to an imagined situation in a way you don't like, it's difficult to stop the process by telling yourself it doesn't make sense. Let me offer an example: When I was a college track athlete, I also watched indoor track meets on TV. I could spectate until I'd hear the announcement that the next event would be the One-Mile Run. My heart would then begin to pound, and I'd tremble and tense. What's the matter with you, I'd think. You're not running. I'd tell myself to relax, but I couldn't.

Consciously I knew I wasn't going to race, but when my subconscious heard the call for The One-Mile, it couldn't distinguish between a race I was running and one I was watching. I was like the dog Pavlov fed to the accompaniment of a bell until the dog salivated merely at the sound of the bell, except rather than salivate, I readied my body for competition. You'll have a similar reaction visualizing a speech you are going to give, or an important race coming up. It's your subconscious treating fantasy as reality.

Emotional pressures cause real physical changes in the body long before the gun goes off. When just thinking about competition, the hypothalamus releases a hormone that tells the pituitary gland to release another hormone that stimulates the release of adrenaline, cortisone, epinephrine, norepinephrine, dopamine and other natural opiates into the bloodstream. Your muscles tense, your heart and respiration rates increase, and your digestive system shuts down, making you feel queasy. Blood gets diverted from organs and muscles not needed for "flight or fight." While this preparation is essential to raise you to competitive heights, it often creates other psychological and physical side-effects that, unless controlled, can ruin performances. A quick burst of energy from a squirt of adrenaline when you are trying to remain calm before competition merely revs up your motor while you sit there in neutral.

But this sort of thing can be put to practical use.

RELAXATION TECHNIQUE _____

Physical as well as mental relaxation is required, so find a quiet place where you will not be disturbed for 15 to 20 minutes (make sure the phone won't disturb you). Either sit in a comfortable chair or lie down (but don't become so comfortable you fall asleep). You can instruct yourself what to do, but in the beginning, I'd strongly suggest you review a few relaxation tapes and select one that suits you. One I like is by Dr. Arnold Lazarus of the Institute for Internal Living, 45 E. 56th St., New York, NY 10021. Not only is his technique good, he sounds like Rod Dixon. Or you could study the techniques described below and write and record a script which includes the instructions you will want to give yourself. The main concerns for runners are combating pre-race tensions that reduce you to a nervous wreck by race time; running confidently, fast, and relaxed during competition; and turning negative beliefs about yourself around so that once you decide what you'd like to do, you don't come up with a score of reasons why you couldn't.

A good way to relax (after you are comfortable) is to imagine yourself in your favorite, most carefree place (stretched out at the lake, a meadow, alongside a rippling stream, or whatever) and visualize *in detail* your surroundings. Feel the wind, hear the birds singing, or the water gurgling. Meanwhile, take several deep "belly" breaths, and as you exhale, imagine blowing out all cares and tensions. Tell yourself (or let the tape tell you) how heavy, relaxed, and good you are feeling. After you are relaxed, isolate and concentrate progressively on your feet, legs, back, arms, shoulders, neck, and finally parts of your face, telling yourself to let them relax even further. You don't have to do anything or force it—just let go and let it happen. When you get to your arms, for example, tell yourself they are becoming relaxed and too heavy to lift, and besides, it would be far too much trouble.

Next alternately tighten and tense the parts of your body, *experiencing how tension feels,* and then sighing, relaxing, and concentrating on how it feels to relax. This sequence might go something like this: Tense your left leg until you thoroughly feel the strain and fatigue. Concentrate on the feeling. Then say to yourself, "Relax," and let all the tension go from your leg, experiencing how it feels as it relaxes and how good it feels. Do the same with your right leg; make a tight fist and relax it; wrinkle and smoothe your forehead; clench and relax your jaw; tense and relax your shoulders. Do this in especially tense areas.

You not only want to differentiate between tension and relaxation, you want to practice how it feels to let go so that later, in stress situations, you will be able to let go and relax. This biofeedback teaches you to relax muscles you didn't know were tense and to gain control over the process. In competition, relaxation is not going limp, it's learning not to tense muscles that don't contribute to running.

ACCESS WORDS

If you start analyzing your form and thinking about how tough it's getting during competition, you can get so self-conscious that rather than running smoother and thinking positively, you tense. So the next step is to picture how you want to run, and associate an access word with the picture of yourself doing it. Through association you will be able to use that word in a race to automatically produce the same feeling and performance. Here's how it's done.

After you've induced a state of deep relaxation and practiced the tension-relaxation exercises, imagine a previous race or workout when you were running strongly, confidently and unusually well. Create a detailed mental picture. Notice how good you feel. The word I associate with this is "tempo," because I can chant it, stressing the syllables separately as each foot strikes. After you get into the rhythm, visualize yourself smoothing out and running faster. Concentrate on how smooth and relaxed you feel, how there are no other sensations or thoughts other than speed, relaxation, and exhilaration.

It may require several sessions, practiced for 15 minutes once or twice daily, to get good at it. It's easier to do these each day if you set aside the same time(s). At first you may think you can't be bothered, but remind yourself that it's only for 15 minutes, that you are going to feel good afterward, and that it will improve your running. Practice will ensure that during competition the responses you want will come automatically.

After you've practiced visualizing running well while chanting "tem-po," try the chant during the *final stages* of a workout or race when you begin to lose form and slow down. Your response should be to run with faster leg turnover and greater efficiency. If, however, thinking "tem-po, tem-po . . ." while running doesn't seem to work, stop chanting or you will form the wrong association. Instead, continue with the imaginary relaxation exercises until "tem-po" becomes strongly enough associated with how you want to move to trigger the effect while running. Don't give up if at first it's difficult to concentrate on "tem-po" and the images. When you begin thinking about how tired you are, or who's gaining on or getting away from you, refocus your concentration.

You can use the same technique to keep your composure before competition. Instead of associating "tem-po" with smooth running, program the words "let go" to trigger a calming effect. This is where the tension-relaxation exercises come in. During a relaxation session, try to relive as vividly as possible the worst case of pre-race jitters you ever had. Experience the nervousness, how your stomach churned, getting into the starting pack, waiting for the gun, the sickening feeling that "what if after the gun goes off I can't run?"

As you work yourself into an anxiety state, and I guarantee you will if you really get into it, concentrate on how awful you feel. Then think the words "let go" and clear the picture from your mind. Replace it with a situation where you were completely in control. Absolutely on top. Focus on how it feels to let the anxiety dissipate. Remind yourself that when you thought those words, the tension disappeared. Tell yourself that before a race or hard workout if you say "let go," you will relax as you just did. Repeat this exercise each day until you form a strong association between "let go" and calming down. Think about the worst that could happen if you ran lousy—that you wouldn't lose friends, your job, or self-respect. How you'd find another race and try again.

When giving yourself verbal suggestions, either with a tape you've recorded or your thoughts, there are certain rules and cautions you should observe. Your delivery should be slow and even—a soothing monotone. Introduce pauses when you will need time to visualize a scene or suggestion. Give yourself instructions in vividly detailed images so that your subconscious knows exactly what you are supposed to do. Don't do the "tem-po" or "let go" routines until you are 100 percent relaxed. Otherwise, when you tell yourself you are smooth, strong, confident, and so on, your conscious filtering system may inject the thought, Oh no, you're not. Also, when relaxed, you concentrate better.

Couch your statements in the present tense except when setting a targe date for a goal. Don't say, "I'll try to. . . ." Say, "I am . . ." as though it were already fact. The subconscious, being literal, works on messages as received. If they're vague, as in "I'm going to try to race hard on Saturday," you can't construct as vivid a picture of that as, "At the end of races I always maintain a rapid, efficient stride, my shoulders and jaw stay relaxed, and my finish looks and feels like those 400s I ran on Tuesday."

Avoid couching statements in the negative. Rather than tell-

ing yourself "I don't tie up," or "I don't choke before competition," say "I look forward to and enjoy competition," or "I remain
excited but relaxed before races." If you introduce thoughts of
tying up or choking, you will form images of tying up and choking
that will become part of your reality.

Emotion helps get things into your subconscious. You remember trivia and things you read that excite you and forget important
facts that bore you. Emotional reaction by the public to Frank
Shorter's 1972 Olympic marathon victory (especially *seeing*
Shorter's race on TV) helped launch the running boom in the
United States. Emotion sparks people's enthusiasm and keeps their
goals fresh. Emotion sets the stage for motivation. So when you are
visualizing goals or seeing yourself running, get excited about it.
Imagine how great you will feel when you reach your goal.

FINAL PREPARATIONS _____

It is one thing to practice relaxation and visualization during quiet
times when the pressure is off, but how do you cope just before
and during competition? Essentially the same, but you get your
exictement and emotion to work for you. The night before and the
morning of the race, use relaxation to calm yourself, and visualization to see the race. See yourself running the splits you want, remaining calm, relaxed and sticking with your race plan. Don't kid
yourself that near the end of the race you will automatically and
easily pass everyone. Acknowledge that it may require extreme
determination to keep the pressue on, but that you will remain relaxed and maintain "tem-po" into the finish. Regardless of where
you finish you can congratulate yourself afterward.

Rather than fear the race, plan to enjoy it. Remind yourself
that in most distance races, you don't experience unbearable fatigue during the first half, so all you need to attend to is getting a
good start, getting on pace, and relaxing. Know, however at what
point you are going to concentrate on your access words and imagery. Don't, for example, use "tem-po" for an entire race, just near
the end when it's difficult to maintain form and cadence.

On the starting line, take a few deep breaths and see yourself
blowing out tension. Inhale strength. Shake out and concentrate
on the gun and getting a clean start. Remain impassive and une-
motional as long as possible. Get emotional and determined later
when the going is not as easy.

If visualization doesn't seem to work for you, without realizing it, you may be negating your positive affirmations with counter statements you believe more strongly. Thus, although you do your relaxation and visualization exercises, the rest of the time you may be thinking and saying you gave up in Saturday's race, that you can't seem to do morning runs or stretch consistently, and that your goals are too difficult. Not being able to accept compliments, or always berating yourself for not having raced better, is a definite tip-off that you think you never live up to expectation. Don't become the one opponent you cannot beat.

Every time you catch yourself engaging in these kinds of thoughts, stop, because you will create reality from them (after all, they reinforce what you have unwittingly been feeding yourself for years) rather than the positive statements which are fighting for acceptance. Negative thoughts stifle enthusiasm, motivation, and encourage you to unjustly limit yourself. Tell your friends to alert you when you put yourself down, make alibis, see yourself in a negative light or doubt your abilities. This kind of feedback, either from yourself or others, is essential to breaking bad habits. Also, when others suggest that you are wasting time pursuing your goals, or that you won't succeed, dismiss them and substitute positive statements like, "My training is right on schedule; I'm getting faster every week."

You may believe that you are already positive and excited enough about running. And you may be. But use those emotions to balance out your physical training so that you don't run well only when you *happen* to be mentally right. Spend the 15 or so minutes a day programming your mind with positive images of the way you want to run, and I guarantee you will improve dramatically. You won't find all the solutions to running within your body. Look inside your head.

PART II
A BLUEPRINT FOR TRAINING

7.

MAJOR TRAINING METHODS

THE EVOLUTION OF TRAINING

The amazing thing about progress in sport, as Roger Bannister noted in the 1950s is that, "Training methods . . . being dependent upon more factors than it is possible at present to analyze, are likely to remain empirical." In other words, in Bannister's day they were largely guessing, and even today training is nowhere near a science, although there are many physiologists investigating every facet of it. Physiologists still do not make the innovative advancements in training methods; coaches and runners do. The physiologists nose around later, probing and measuring to find out why certain methods work. As Kenny Moore puts it, "Coaching knowledge developed through trial and error. The sport of track and field has been advanced by stubborn crackpots trying such deviant methods as flopping backwards over the high-jump bar or running 250 miles per week in training." The balance is slowly shifting toward the scientists, but the "stubborn crackpots" still lead the way.

Fifty to 100 years ago runners dabbled in training by today's standards. Britain's W. G. George, who in 1886 ran the mile in 4:12.75, trained twice daily beginning a month before a major race, but averaged only about 15 miles a week. His long workout was in the morning, perhaps a fast 1000 and 700 yards, and in the evening a fast 880 and 350. This was supplemented with brisk walks and his "100-up" exercise, a form of vigorous running in place.

Another British miler, Joe Binks, established the amateur mile world record in 1902 (4:16:8) training one evening a week, winter and summer. After a warmup consisting of a couple of short runs on the infield, he ran five or six 60 to 110 yard bursts and finished with a fast 220 or 600 yards. For the three-mile (which he ran in 14:10), he jogged two miles and capped it off with sprints.

By 1904 England's Alfred Shrubb was covering 30 to 40 miles a week in twice-a-day workouts. Among his many achievements was a 10-mile record that stood until Paavo Nurmi wrested it away 24 years later. Shrubb's training consisted mostly of continuous runs between two and eight miles. Three to four miles at "good pace" was common in the morning, and five to six at medium to slow pace in the evening, except when he ran a time-trial. (These were almost of race caliber and often consecutively as on the 24th, 25th, and 26th of October, 1904, when he clocked two miles in 9:17.8, 10 miles in 51:58, and two miles in 9:18.6). On November 5 he raced 11¾ miles in 60:32.2 coming past 10 miles in 50:46. Every clocking from six miles on bettered the world record.

Hannes Kolehmainen, first of the "Flying Finns," forerunner of Paavo Nurmi, founded the Finnish distance running tradition and laid the groundwork for modern distance training.

His season began with easy runs and walks to build general fitness. In preparation for races, he shortened the distance and intensified the pace, alternating easy and hard sections using the principles of modern fartlek and interval training. Although Kolehmainen's training was picked up and expanded on by Nurmi (under Kolehmainen's tutelage), it was overlooked by most of the remaining world. It would take 40 years for this concept to become popularized and used with devastating effect on competition and the record book. And, by then, some runners would be compressing a week of Kolehmainen's work into one day.

Paavo Nurmi's feats, which included 20 world records and 12 Olympic medals, are legendary. But as profound as his impact was upon the record book, he took great pains to reveal nothing of his training during his competitive years. On and off the track Nurmi was an enigma. He trained alone, avoided publicity and interviews, and when another runner was so tactless as to approach him during a workout, he coldly and promptly ran the intruder off his feet.

It would be difficult to summarize Nurmi's training because he modified it over a career that lasted 20 years. But it is enough to say that after he added winter training and speed work at the suggestion of Kolehmainen, Nurmi began to improve. Finally in 1924, he added 4 to 5 × 80-120 meter sprints and some 3-4 km hard runs with a fast last 400 meters.

THE SWEDES AND FARTLEK

Two important systems of training evolved after Nurmi retired that remained important components of today's conditioning programs. They are fartlek and interval training.

Fartlek is a Swedish word meaning, "play-of-speed" or "speed-play." It is a loosely structured form of interval training. Ideally it is performed away from the track over whatever challenges of hill, wooded path, sand dune, or snow are available. The idea is to alternate hard runs of 50 to 2000 meters with jog recoveries. The duration of the fast and easy sections are varied according to how one feels and terrain changes. The sense of exertion is lost in the fun of playing with these burst in the exhiliration of a natural setting.

Fartlek evolved. It was not invented by any one person or country. But it is heavily associated with Sweden, Gunder Hegg (world-record holder, 1500 to 5000 meters in the early 1940s) and Arne Andersson (former mile-record holder). Experts agree that Gosta Holmer, Swedish head Olympic coach in 1948, was the first to write about Fartlek. He said he decided to "create something new, something that suited our minds and the nature of our country. I rejected the American option that the runners should have fixed distances to run during their training schedule; I realized, of course the great importance of that, but I wanted to give the boys a feeling of self-creating, I wanted them to understand themselves, and then fix the training according to their individuality. Speed and endurance are the marks a runner should follow in his training. Following these lines I made up a system that I call *Fartlek* . . ."

A main principle of fartlek is its permissiveness, a refreshing change over the old system that embraced so many inhibitions. Slow running was supposed to sap your speed, hill climbing was supposed to stiffen your muscles and shorten your stride. Until fartlek, fast runs were measured and timed.

Fartlek recruits a wide range of muscle groups and ranges of movement. It also allows runner to judge their efforts according to how they feel rather than the dictates of the watch, both an advantage and disadvantage. Fartlek of the 1940s and 1950s included walking, although that has largely disappeared from today's interpretation.

Fartlek can be structured in many ways depending upon your needs. Early season fartlek should be aerobic, with no running faster than marathon race pace or 10km pace plus 30 seconds per mile. Gradually include faster anaerobic and leg-speed sections. To run nine miles of Fartlek, begin with 1 to 1½ miles of easy running, then add various fast sections of from 50 to 2000 meters (1¼ miles) with just enough jogging in between to recover before the next faster run. During these surges, work the uphills, downhills, or whatever you want. The last mile or so should be reserved for cooling down. If nine miles of fartlek takes about an hour, then warm up for the first 10 to 15 minutes, surge and recover for the next 40 to 45 minutes, and jog the last five minutes. One way to sharpen for races using fartlek while running with others of roughly the same ability is as follows: Split the time designated for surging among you. If there are three runners and 45 minutes of pickups, each runner would control a 15-minute segment. The leader picks it up and backs off as he or she chooses. The others must react and hold on. It teaches those in tow to respond to the kinds of unannounced tactics encountered during racing. It's important, however, that these sessions do not become competitive. This is a matter of attitude, not effort.

THE EUROPEANS AND INTERVAL TRAINING

Interval training means performing a series of relatively short, fast runs interspersed with enough jogging to provide a partial recovery. The runner becomes fit by running fast to develop speed, and with the recoveries, fast sections can be repeated many times to build stamina. The word "interval" actually refers to the rest periods, but most runners think of the fast sections when using the term.

Traditionally, intervals were done on the track over standard distances such as 200s, 300s, 400s, and so on. The fast sections are usually timed, the rests being timed and/or covering a fixed distance such as repeat 400s in 70 seconds with one-minute 200 jog recoveries between each. Nowadays many runners run intervals on roads, golf courses, trails, or whereever a fixed distance or variety of distances can be repeated with controlled rests.

Like fartlek, interval training evolved in several countries with many athletes and coaches contributing. Before World War I, Lauri Pihkala, an outstanding Finnish runner, ran with a "wave-like rhythm" in daily workouts. He said a middle-distance runner "profits more by dashing 130-200 meters four or five times at intervals of 10 to 15 minutes than by running 3000 meters or 5000 meters at moderate pace." The runner of the 1920s ran "ins and outs," "windsprints," and "speedwork". The great Polish runner Kusociński (1932 Olympic 10,000-meter gold medalist) would run 15 × 200 meter stride-outs after a cross-country run. Paavo Nurmi, before the 1924 Olympics, occasionally ran repeated sprints from 200 to 600 meters, but the system was not perfected until Germany's Waldemar Gershler and physiologist Dr. Herbert Reindell got scientific while training Rudolf Harbig in the late 1930s.

The research of Reindell and Dr. Joseph Nocker showed that, from a cardiovascular viewpoint, the fast sections should not last more than 60 seconds, the pulse should reach 180, its highest efficient rate, and the next fast run should not begin until the pulse returns to about 120. Reindell further found that since the heart undergoes its greatest stress and presumably its greatest development during the first 30 seconds *following* each fast run, the rest interval should last between 45 and 90 seconds in a well-trained athlete. When the pulse fails to return to between 120 and 140 within about 90 seconds, the runner has had enough. (When fast repeats are run with more than 1½ minutes of recovery, it's technically known as repetition training.)

In 1939 Harbig smashed the world record for 800 meters, running 1:46.6 (The time survived until 1955 when Roger Moens, also Gershler-trained, broke it.) A month later, Harbig ran 400 meters in a world-record 46.0.

After the outbreak of World War II in 1939, interval training was all but forgotten by the athletic world. America, for example, heard little of it until 1953. But in Europe and Britain, a number of new, if not eccentric, runners rediscovered the interval principle that sparked dramatic drops in times during the 1950s. The first to use the principle of repeating fast, short bursts to enhance distance running was Czechoslovokia's Emil Zátopek in the late 1940s. Harbig had demonstrated that repeated hard speed could benefit the quarter- and half-miler, which was not surprising, but the amazing Zátopek proved it would work just as well for distance events.

It must be said that if Gershler and Reindell fathered interval training, then Zátopek was its most forceful proponent. History must bestow upon Zátopek a different title, for with his bold and severe application of interval training, he must be known as The Father of Hard Work.

Anything but the epitome of style and grace, the antithesis of Nurmi in movement and temperament, Zátopek destroyed the picture-book running styles of the 1930s and 1940s and rewrote the standards of human capabilities. Whereas Nurmi and his followers tamed the track with graceful strides, Zátopek stomped it to death. He thrashed his way along "as a man who has just been stabbed in the chest," head bobbing, hands clawing the air, his bared teeth flashing like a rabid animal in pain.

From the beginning Zátopek was a man apart. By age 21 he became suspect of the training methods he and his teammates were following. Whatever it was that drove Zátopek, it impelled him to undertake a regime that was staggering in its mental and physical proportions. He drew his inspiration from Nurmi and founded his training concepts upon the Finn's logic, but he extended them beyond anything Nurmi envisioned. As Zátopek tells it, "I didn't know much. It wasn't possible to buy a book about Nurmi. But I found out that in order to be faster over 10,000 meters, he ran 5000 meters many times in training. And to be faster at 5000 meters, he ran 1500 meters many times. And to be better at 1500 meters, he ran 4 × 400 meters in training. Maybe this isn't true because I never spoke with Paavo Nurmi, but running is easily understandable. You must be fast enough—you must have endurance. So you run fast for speed and you repeat it many times for endurance."

In 1943, he ran 10 × 400s with a 200-meter jog and began to set records. By 1948 he was running 10 × 200 and 10 × 400.

Zátopek was astute enough to realize that if "I trained . . . 5 × 200, 20 × 400, and 5 × 200, this is 10,000 meters divided into short distances, each run faster than the 10,000-meter pace." Zátopek says that at that time in Czechoslovakia, "Runners were only repeating the event. The 5000-meter runners came, warmed up, and ran 5000 meters. They were running long and slow for stamina." But Zátopek says, "Why should I practice running slow? I already know how to run slow. I want to learn how to run fast. Everyone said, 'Emil, you are a fool.' But in Oslo when I first won the European championship, they said, 'Emil, you are a genius.'"

After Viljo Heino broke Zátopek's 10,000-meter record in 1949, Zátopek decided that if he was to run faster, he must run more in training. He worked up to 5 × 200, 40 × 400, 5 × 200. Following this he cut 19 seconds off Heino's record. Finally, Zátopek increased the training to 5 × 200, 50 × 400, 5 × 200, "but it was no good. I was not able to recover the next day. I was ex-

The last 100 meters of the 1952 Olympic 5000 meters. The irrepressible Emil Zátopek has galvanized his last reserves of energy to come from fourth place and take the lead from Chris Chataway (fallen), Herbert Schade, and Alain Mimoun.

hausted for two days. So I stayed with 5 × 200, 40 × 400, 5 × 200, and I decided to run all three distances at Helsinki."

Years later Zátopek realized he had tried to run too far in training. "It would have been better," he concluded, "if I had decided to run faster." This is what the runners who eventually dethroned him (primarily Vladimir Kuts and Gordon Pirie) did. They decreased the volume of work and increased the speed. Eventually by the late 1950s and early 1960s, runners emphasized speed and reliance on interval training so heavily that the pendulum swung too far in the other direction, and performances began to suffer.

What seems to be forgotten about Zátopek's training was that he often ran his repeats so slow that the workout was almost like a distance run with moderate pace changes. Hardly ever did he have the pressures of the watch, and because he often ran on trails, he avoided much of the monotony of the track. As Zátopek insisted, "You must *feel* hard and *feel* easy, and you must run that way."

OVERCOMPLICATING INTERVAL TRAINING _____

As you can imagine, when you have a system of training based on several timed runs over a measured distance with controlled rests, a lot of theory occurred concerning the number of repeats to do, at what speeds, and with how much rest. It thoroughly boggled minds and spread confusion.

A plethora of scientific-looking interval workout programs emerged such as repeat runs in sets (for example 5 × 400, rest, 5 × 400, rest, and so on), "ladder" workouts (for example, 200, 400, 600, 800, 600, 400, 200), repeated sprints with short rests, and long repeats with long rests (repetition training). Intricate tables were constructed controlling and varying every conceivable aspect of these workouts, singly and in progression throughout the season. In some countries, interval training became the mainstay of conditioning. Coaches like Austria's Franz Stampfl and Hungary's Mahali Igloi ran their athletes to variations of it nearly every day. Race times improved because it was the best method yet to appear.

But there were problems. The Finns and Germans, especially, began to rely upon ever-faster interval training until they had become "interval slaves." In Finland, for example, during the 1960s, runners were struggling in vain to get inside 14:00 and 30:00 for 5000 and 10,000 meters. No distance records had been broken there between 1960 and 1967. Once leaders in training, the situation became something of a joke to the rest of the world and a national disgrace to the Finns.

THE LYDIARD SYSTEM

Picture this: A few aspiring kids approach a neighborhood shoemaker to teach them to run. The shoemaker is a high-school dropout and retired distance runner whose own brand of torturous training methods have so far earned him little more than scorn and ridicule from the coaching community. He agrees to help, and although the runners are not the country's best, not even the city's best—just eager kids from the neighborhood—the shoemaker promises them world records and Olympic medals if they can endure the workouts. The boy the shoemaker first publicly predicts will set a world record is crippled in one arm, and another runner, who the shoemaker says will be the best middle-distance runner ever, looks muscle-bound and awkward. A few years later, the country's entire contingent of distance runners to the Olympics is coached by the former shoemaker. Thirty minutes apart the crippled one and the awkward one win gold medals; a day later another of his runners, seemingly athletically nondescript, takes a bronze. From these and other of the shoemaker's pupils come most of the world records from 800 meters to the one-hour run, and two more golds and a bronze in the next Olympics.

Wild dreams? A fairy tale? Hardly. I'm just recounting the emergence of New Zealand's Arthur Lydiard, guru of distance runners, father of the jogging craze, prime mover and motivator of Olympians worldwide. During the last 25 years Lydiard has either directly coached or influenced more world-record holders and Olympic medalists than anyone. With seemingly endless energy he has lectured up one country and down another, pausing periodically to serve as national coach in Finland, Denmark, Mexico, and Venezuela. Ironically, he is, like many prophets, largely ignored in official circles in his own country.

When Peter Snell and Murray Halberg sprinted off with the gold in the 1500 and 5000, and Barry Magee won the marathon bronze at the 1960 Rome Olympics, the rest of the world was full swing into interval training. So ingrained is the Lydiard philosophy now, we almost have to force ourselves to recall that before him, the coaching of distance runners was aimed 180 degrees in the other direction. Lydiard was the beginning of a magic era: jogging became acceptable, if not godlike. The realization that middle-distance runners could run better if first conditioned like marathoners eventually opened the door to their success as marathoners. No longer did these misfits from other sports need to reach out for public acceptance, the public began to reach out and embrace them—and then joined them en-masse.

Lydiard was the keystone of all this, and he never let us forget that, as an unschooled layman, he did what physiologists, theorists, and professional coaches hadn't been able to do. He was unsophisticated, but he was smart, and he had the tenacity of a bulldog. His method of training developed from 15 years of experimentation on himself when, as an aspiring runner in the 1940s and 1950s, he couldn't learn much from available literature.

Lydiard says of his experimenting, "I realized that a lot of people had theories, and had tried for years to prove them. They were playing around with hard anaerobic training without understanding it, and in many ways doing more harm than good. They didn't understand the athlete's reaction to 25 or 30 hard 400 meters, but I did because I did it myself. And I knew how I felt several days later. So I began to experiment, varying the distance each day and trying to find out what mileage I could run while still improving. For one six-week period I was doing between 200 and 250 miles a week—I'd get up at 4 in the morning and run a marathon before breakfast. . . . After six weeks I'd had enough—I was so damn tired I just couldn't go on."

But with 100 miles a week he became fitter, and said that even middle-distance runners, who at this time were running 30 to 50 miles a week, would benefit from it. His rationale was that runners do not primarily lack speed. Even average runners can run a 440 in 60 seconds, four-minute mile pace. Besides, speed and the ability to run while in oxygen debt (anaerobically) can be developed in four to five weeks, so why waste a lot of time running intervals and speed work when performance is governed by the oxygen uptake level (aerobic capacity)? Additionally, extended hard anaerobic training upsets the metabolism and the runner's performance worsens.

Lydiard faced a stiff challenge in convincing runners, especially half-milers and milers, that a large volume of relatively slow training could eventually result in fast racing. But Lydiard gained their confidence by training with them. He said that besides cover-

ing the distance, they were to run as much of that mileage as possible at fast aerobic speeds, roughly marathon race-pace, which he
claimed was necessary to fully develop cardio-respiratory efficiency. After about three months of this, he took them to a half-
mile hill and had them spring up with exaggerated kangaroo-like
bounds, rest, stride down, and run stride-outs at the bottom. This
developed power and stamina. It was a transition between the
long road work and the sharper training and racing coming up.

So far they had not done any interval or speed work. But now
they were ready. Carefully, he began to develop their speed using
a mixture of fartlek, interval work, sprints, time-trials, and finally
races. Lydiard says now, "Because we did lots of running, they developed such very fine endurance and high oxygen-uptake levels
that they could do more speedwork, in volume, faster than anyone
else at that time." In response to the criticism that he emphasized
quantity rather than quality, Lydiard counters with, "Snell and
Davies could run twenty 400 meters in 60 seconds or under in
reps. . . . These people don't know what they're talking about."

It was the Lydiard approach that turned my career around,
and it is the basis for my concept of efficient training. Before Lydiard's system became popular (and even now for many runners),
conditioning was based upon interval training to build endurance
and speed.

Lydiard's program, essentially, is the creation of stamina as
the foundation of speed. In other words, whereas interval training
conditions by repeating speed to produce stamina, Lydiard
stressed endurance and stamina as the prerequisites to which
speed was later added. Within that concept Lydiard insists that
you maintain several critical balances. Foremost is the balance
between stamina and speed training, and nearly as important are
the balancing of racing and training, hard and easy days, long and
short runs, and developmental and critical races. And, as Viren so
impressively demonstrated, with the building-block approach to
training and racing, timing one's peak sharpness is far easier.

Unfortunately, much of the world identified Lydiard's system
with marathon training. It was said he "has no use for interval
training." He does, but he uses it sparingly and efficiently. Twenty
years ago runners thought Lydiard's athletes jogged or ran big
mileage all the time, and even today that notion lingers.

The person invited to Finland to straighten out the mess described earlier was Arthur Lydiard. The outcome of that 19-month

visit came into focus when in 1972 Olavi Suomalainen won the Boston Marathon, and then at the Munich Olympics, Viren got up after falling in the 10,000 meters to stun the world by galloping off with the gold medal and a world record. Viren won again in the 5000, Pekka Vasala won the 1500, and Taki Kantanen took the bronze medal in the steeplechase. According to Matti Hannus, author of *Finnish Running Secrets* (World Publications, 1973), "the [Finnish] renaissance began in 1967, when Arthur Lydiard arrived in Finland."

Ron Clarke says that the disadvantage of Lydiard's approach is that "the schedule is completely upset by interruption. It presupposed that all athletes need a similar balance between speed and endurance work. Concentration on road running [during] ... the build-up can promote injuries, especially to the tendons and knees."

I don't agree. Neither did Rolf Haikkola, who asked Lydiard to come to Finland to teach coaches there how to produce Olympic champions. Haikkola says, "Lydiard's ideas of how to bring runners to the best shape at the right time seemed ideal for us with our long winters and short racing seasons." Haikkola knew how to balance Viren's workouts within the framework of the system. The build-up does not promote injuries. In fact, it minimized them because it keeps the stresses of fast running to a minimum until the athlete is ready.

Lydiard's methods are not geared toward immediate results. He speaks of progressing over several years and sacrificing early success to lay the groundwork for bigger victories later. Even within each season you would not reach your peak until the last possible moment. Both of these concepts are implied when Lydiard wrote: "You will come to your peak slower than many others, and you will be running last when they are running first. But when it is really important to run first, you will be passing them."

8.

AEROBICS AND ANAEROBICS

*I*n New Zealand the story is told of how Lydiard first tried to explain the physiology of aerobic and anaerobic training to Bill Baillie, who broke the world records at 20,000 meters and the one-hour run in 1962. Originally, Lydiard had discussed training in terms of hard and easy efforts. Then Dr. Kenneth Cooper got everyone talking about aerobics, and Lydiard, quick to impart scientific credibility to his system, began using phrases like oxygen uptake level, liters of anaerobic debt, and blood pH. Baillie, a practical man, listened patiently and then in that fast Munchkin-like voice of his, asked innocently, "Aerobics? Anaerobics? You mean slow stuff and fast stuff, coach?"

To runners, aerobic work is the slow stuff, and anaerobic is the fast. I could, as Lydiard did originally, speak of training in terms of fast and slow running, but because the concepts of aerobic and anaerobic metabolism are so ingrained in the running jargon, and at the very root of proficient training, I think it will be worth your effort to understand these concepts if you already don't. In the introduction I promised "no complex physiology."

Fortunately, in order to run, it is no more necessary to ponder intricate physiological mechanisms than it is to memorize which muscles to contract and relax in order to walk. It is important to know how fast and slow training affect conditioning, and then to structure your training accordingly.

RELATIVE IMPORTANCE OF AEROBIC AND ANAEROBIC METABOLISM

Endurance is associated with aerobic metabolism. At relatively slow speeds a runner can absorb, transport, and utilize enough oxygen in the muscles to economically split the chemical which is the source of our energy—adenosine triphosphate, mercifully abreviated to ATP. The ATP stored in the working muscles is limited to only a few second's work, but fortunately creatine phosphate (CP) is also there for rebuilding ATP. But CP is also limited and runs out after about 15 to 20 seconds of heavy exercise.

So how are milers able to race for four minutes and marathoners for over two hours? Enter aerobics and anaerobics. If the rate of work is moderate, as in a marathon, a runner can get enough oxygen to economically burn fat and glycogen. This enables ATP to be rebuilt as fast as it is being broken down, and a trained runner can continue for several hours at least. This is *aerobic* metabolism. If the rate of work is very rapid, as in the sprints, oxygen cannot be absorbed fast enough for the breakdown of fat and glycogen. The body is able to cheat chemically for a short while and breaks down glycogen *without* oxygen. This is *anaerobic* metabolism. Unlike aerobic metabolism, with its innocent waste products of water and carbon dioxide, the nasty waste produce of anaerobic work is lactic acid which, as it accumulates, ultimately prevents the muscles from contracting.

Pure anaerobic running means, just for a start, that you can continue for only 15 to 20 seconds. In the sprints you can't begin to breathe in, transport, and utilize enough oxygen to enable you to run flat out. But that doesn't matter to a sprinter. The 100 and 200 take only about 10 or 20 seconds, and a sprinter can suck in enough oxygen after finishing to get rid of the lactic acid. The oxygen debt that is incurred while sprinting is paid back with high interest when the sprinter gasps after the race, but it is a welcome trade-off for one interested in speed at any cost.

The anaerobic system always functions to some small degree,

but only really kicks in when a quick source of energy is needed for a burst of speed, a tough hill, or when the pace becomes so fast aerobic metabolism cannot meet all your energy needs. Surprisingly, even when you begin a run slowly you start out anaerobically because it takes a minute for the aerobic mechanism to completely react. That's why you pant and can't seem to get going at first. This has implications for warming up before a fast workout or race, and against going out too fast at the gun.

For races longer than about half a mile, physiologists agree that aerobic metabolism is the primary producer of energy, so the bulk of training for any endurance runner should be to improve the speed at which he or she can run aerobically.

The limit on the amount of oxygen your muscles can use no matter how hard you breathe is known as your maximal aerobic capacity or maximal oxygen consumption, or in physiological shorthand, VO_2 max. It is a measure of how much oxygen you can consume per minute divided by your weight to compensate for the fact that, other things being equal, a large person can use more oxygen than a small one. If, say, you can use four liters of oxygen per minute and weigh 65 kg., your VO_2 max would be 4000 ml/65kg or, 61.5 ml/kg.*

VO_2 max varies considerably among runners and the general population. A normally active 25-year-old male can utilize roughly 44 to 47 milliliters of oxygen per kilogram of body weight per minute. Top male endurance athletes commonly consume over 70 ml/kg/minute. Women, on average, score lower than men. The male distance runner with the highest measured VO_2 max was Steve Prefontaine, with 84.4, and the top woman so far measured is Joan Benoit, with 79, which is exceptionally high. Women score lower mainly because pound for pound they have less muscle mass than men. Their red blood cell counts are lower, but this seems to be only a slight disadvantage. Now that social constraints are being lifted from athletic women, many more will emerge to reduce the difference.

Physiologists used to say that you couldn't raise your VO_2 max much by training. You basically got what was dished out at birth. Now they admit that it may be possible to raise it by 10 to 20 percent as a result of training and weight loss. Unfortunately, no one has measurements on world-class runners before they began train-

* See chart on p. 144.

ing, but the fact that one top runner's VO_2 max dropped from 72.4 to 47.6 three years after he quit running implies that it responds quite impressively to training (or lack of it), since 72.4 is a 52 percent increase over 47.6.

What is important is that you get your VO_2 max as high as you can, because other things being equal, the faster you can run before dipping into anaerobic metabolism, the longer (much longer) you will perform at any racing speed. This is the main reason Salazar, de Castella, and Steve Jones have run 26 consecutive miles in 4:53 while the rank and file run their marathons several minutes per mile slower. At 4:53s Salazar, de Castella, Lopes, Steve Jones and the like are still aerobic. Joe Jogger at 4:53 pace is flat out, completely anaerobic, and can't come close to completing one mile.

That's because anaerobic work is so costly in glycogen expenditure and lactic acid build-up. Whereas in aerobic exercise, one molecule of glycogen forms 38 molecules of ATP, anaerobic exercise yields only two. So with aerobic metabolism you get more "miles per gallon." Additionally, as Lawrence Moorehouse asserts, very severe anaerobic work may be as little as 40 percent efficient as aerobic work.

Another reason the world-class can run so far at fast speeds is because as long as the pace remains aerobic, the muscles are able to break down and release fat from the fat cells and oxidize it as a fuel.

Fat is the main, but not exclusive, fuel during sub-maximal work. But when your muscles metabolize mainly fat, there's a greater demand for oxygen than when burning glycogen, so you either have to take in more air or slow down. Fat is not a preferred fuel at fast paces. In races shorter than 10km, runners burn glycogen almost exclusively. When a marathoner efficiently burns fat, that means he or she conserves glycogen, which will be there to be burned with devastating effect on the competition during the last 10km. David Costill found that the gastrocnemius (calf) muscle becomes seven times more capable of burning fat after marathon training (prolonged endurance runs) than normally occurs in untrained muscle. He concludes, "Thus, we have evidence to substantiate why it is essential for the endurance runner to perform extremely long runs in training, and to log 80 to 120 miles per week." Furthermore, West German physiologists at Cologne University found that if muscle groups are exercised *continually* for long periods, especially two or more hours, dormant capillary beds are reactivated and new ones are formed. This means more blood flow, more oxygen to the muscles. That raises one's VO_2 max, which in turn, makes it easier for the muscles to burn fat.

What training doesn't seem to affect is the ratio of fast-twitch to slow-twitch muscle we were born with. Slow-twitch fibers are best for aerobic metabolism, whereas explosive and powerful fast-twitch fibers are anaerobically oriented. You've observed this distinction yourself, probably without realizing it, when at Thanksgiving you opted for white or dark meat. If the turkey had an abundance of white meat, which is fast-twitch muscle, it probably was able to impress the axman with some quick evasive tactics.

Physiologists, by inserting a special needle-like instrument in the muscle, snipping out a cross-section of muscle and looking at it under the microscope, have found that the proportion of fast- to slow-twitch fibers in various people can go as much as 90 percent or more one way or the other. Distance runners are typically lop-sided with slow-twitch (high endurance) fibers.

But there is a sub-type of fast-twitch muscle that will improve its aerobic capabilities after endurance training. This implies that even fast-twitch muscle fiber, which is associated with sprinting, can be recruited and taught to behave like slow-twitch fiber. Perhaps that's why Don Kardong, with only 53 percent slow-twitch fibers, and Jeff Galloway, with 96 percent, could perform about evenly in a marathon. Paradoxically, and somewhat inexplicably, with only four percent sprint fibers, Galloway was dangerous in the finishing kick.

ANAEROBIC THRESHOLD

There's more to racing fast than just raising your VO_2 max. Herein lies a vital paradox: On the one hand, a high oxygen uptake is the very source of distance running potential, while on the other, a distance runner with a VO_2 max of 60 could consistently out-run another scoring 70. The solution to this apparent contradiction is one you should understand because it has profound implications for training.

What most runners do not understand is that if you run hard enough to be working at your VO_2 max, you are also producing a lot of your energy anaerobically (you would have to run two miles flat out). You VO_2 max, therefore, *is not* the maximum pace you

WHEN THE O_2 CONSUMPTION REMAINS CONSTANT EVEN THOUGH THE WORKLOAD INCREASES, VO_2 MAX HAS BEEN REACHED

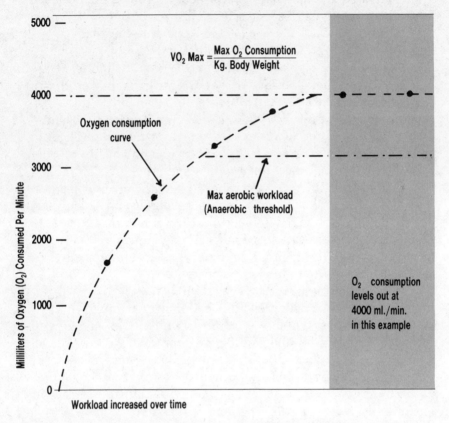

The best way to measure a runner's VO_2 max is with an all-out treadmill run. The runner wears a nose clip and mouth mask, which enable the expired air to be collected and the amount of oxygen consumed per minute to be monitored. Oxygen consumption will rise with the workload until the VO_2 max is approached. Then it will level off no matter how difficult the workload (See the chart above). The maximum amount of oxygen consumed per minute (shaded area) is divided by the runner's weight in kilograms to determine the VO_2 max.

An accurate measurement can be obtained only be performing the activity one is trained to do. Therefore, runners should be tested while running, cyclists while pedaling an ergometer (stationary bike), etc. A runner tested on an ergometer would post a lower VO_2 max.

can run before dipping into anaerobic work. This is important because, as you will see, it is around this concept your training should be structured.

Let's say your VO_2 max is 60 ml/kg/min. and the marathon is raced at one's maximum aerobic pace. This doesn't mean you consume 60 ml. of oxygen per minute per kilogram of body weight during the race. No one can run a marathon at their VO_2 max because the cardiovascular system can't deliver enough oxygen to the working muscles. Also, the muscles are limited in their ability to extract oxygen from the blood. Therefore, even though the muscles are capable of utilizing more oxygen, they can't get it at aerobic efforts.

Most good runners tolerate working at only 75 to 80 percent of their aerobic capacity during a marathon. Running faster means accumulating lactic acid, and that means disaster later in the race. Derek Clayton and Shorter seemed able to run at around 90 percent of their VO_2 max for 26 miles, but unexplainably, they didn't build up lactic acid. Some physiologists believe that this critical advantage is a function of muscular adaption to endurance training, but also important I think, is your adaptation to anaerobic training.

The highest percentage of your aerobic capacity you can run at without producing lactic acid is known as your anaerobic threshold. Stated another way, it is the fastest pace you can run at without dipping into anaerobic metabolism. The table below shows the approximate percent of you VO_2 max you use in racing various distances (It varies among runners). Notice that when most runners begin to use more than 75 to 80 percent of their maximal oxygen consumption, they begin to supplement their energy needs anaerobically.

**ESTIMATED PERCENT VO$_2$ USED RACING DIFFERENT
DISTANCES AND RATIO OF AEROBIC TO ANAEROBIC WORK**

Distance	% of VO$_2$ Max Used	Ratio: Aerobic to Anaerobic
1 mile	115–130%	60% aerobic, 40% anaerobic
2 mile	95–100	70% aerobic, 30% anaerobic
5 km	90–95	80% aerobic, 20% anaerobic
6m–10km	85–90	90% aerobic, 10% anaerobic
15km–10m	80–85	95% aerobic, 5% anaerobic
Marathon	75–80	100% aerobic

The difference in technique between elite runners (the first three) and those back in the pack (last two). Note the excellent rear leg extension, knee lift, and erect to near-erect body carriage of the elite. The fourth-place runner has tilted his head back at the expense of overall relaxation. The last runner rotates her shoulders, which hinders forward progress.

You can see that even after putting aside the mental aspects of performance, racing well involves more than a high VO_2 max. Otherwise Clayton, with his 69.7, couldn't have run a 2.08:36 marathon, and Shorter, with 71.4, couldn't have won an Olympic gold and silver. It also depends on how close to your VO_2 max you can run at and remain completely aerobic.

BIOCHEMICAL EFFICIENCY

My own VO_2 max was measured at 70.6 in 1969 by David Costill at the Ball State University Human Performance Laboratory. In 1973 I raced a marathon wearing an EKG monitor that showed something that astounded physiologists: I ran close to 95 percent minimal heart rate, which means I was consuming oxygen at close to 90 percent of my VO_2 max for nearly 2½ hours. At first the physiologists said that couldn't be done, but later a few other runners with similar abilities were discovered. To know I had a high VO_2 max and could operate at 90 percent output was both elating and depressing. If my VO_2 max was so high, and I could run so damn hard, why were my race times so slow compared with others with comparable credentials?

Insight is gained when you watch Carlos Lopes, de Castella, and the like running, and then get a look at me. You easily see that

I'm not as mechanically efficient. You can observe this difference even more dramatically yourself by watching joggers and then superimposing an image of Lopes cruising along at two or three minutes a mile faster. He *still* looks easier. Dr. Mike Pollock found that long-distance runners use three to four milliliters of oxygen per minute less than even comparably good middle-distance runners at all speeds. Shorter, with his 71.4 VO_2 max was able to run alongside Steve Prefontaine with his 84.4 VO_2 max using 16 percent less oxygen than Prefontaine. Obviously efficiency of some sort is involved, but physiologists aren't sure how. Either Shorter gets more work out of the oxygen he does take in, or his style uses less energy. It'a synthesis of chemical and biochemical efficiency. Either the training distance runners do enables them to be more efficient, or those who are naturally more efficent gravitate into the distances. It's the chicken and the egg all over again, but I believe that both answers are reasonable. If so, distance training can affect metabolic efficiency and should be an ingredient in any training program.

While muscle-cell efficiency is still a mystery, Peter Cavanagh at Penn State found that some runners move consistently more symmetrically and with superior stride and foot-plant characteristics, but even that's difficult to correlate with performance. More recent studies have shown that the most efficient-*looking* runners are not necessarily the most economical, undoubtedly of some comfort to Salazar and Rod Dixon, who run "sitting down."

Later I will explore the mechanical side of running fast—to show that when you practice running fast you learn to make more efficient movements which enable you to feel smoother and more comfortable at racing speeds. But for now, let's move on to find out how all this relates to training.

IMPLICATIONS FOR TRAINING

RAISING YOUR VO_2 MAX _____

The best way to begin raising your VO_2 max is with slow aerobic training over fairly long distances (long depending upon your capabilities). There are many advantages to starting out slowly. One is you keep mechanical stresses low and greatly reduce the risk of injury. Easy efforts give you a chance to adjust to the workload. It makes sense to try to build gradually to two hours or more of continuous running every seven to 10 days. This won't happen

The unorthodox "sitting down" running style of Alberto Salazar. While economical for a marathon, his inability to get good rear leg extension probably hinders his speed in track races.

overnight. It will take several seasons or years. If you break this run into two workouts, its value is diminished. As you become fitter and have reached a high but endurable weekly mileage, you shouldn't try to run more miles, but more at or near the fastest pace you can without becoming anaerobic (your anaerobic threshold).

Many runners use the "talk test" to determine this limit. If they can carry on a conversation during the run, it is aerobic. When they can't squeeze words between breaths, it is anaerobic. I can always tell when I'm approaching my anaerobic threshold when running with someone because the chatter stops.

Or look at it this way. Since a marathon is raced on the edge of your anaerobic threshold, your marathon pace, or a little slower, is about as fast as you can run completely aerobically. If you don't race marathons, use your average mile pace in the 10km plus 30 seconds. During training it's not necessary to check your splits; it's done according to effort, but remember that your maximum aerobic pace is quite fast. For world-class men, it's about 5:00 per mile. For a 2.37-marathoner or someone who races 10km in 34:10, it's roughly 6:00 per mile. When translating that into workout speeds, allow for wearing slower training shoes and possibly sweatclothes by focusing on effort rather than pace.

Regardless of what Lydiard says about running near your best aerobic speed almost all the time during your build-up, it can't be done if you are running much mileage. That would be like going through various stages of a marathon race each day. What you can do is on some days, run fast steady aerobic pace or sections of hard aerobic effort during a continuous run in what becomes a form of aerobic fartlek. So during a 10-mile run, for example, you might begin with 1½ to 2 miles easy, then fast sections of one to three miles the next seven miles, with slower recoveries between them, and then ease off the last mile or so. The following day you would run easier to recover before the next such workout. All totaled, allowing for warmups, cooldowns, recovery intervals and recovery days, its difficult to log much more than 30 to 40 percent of your mileage near your fastest aerobic pace.

It has been found that after you complete your aerobic training, by dipping into anaerobic work, you can develop your VO_2 max even further. Scandinavian research indicates that this is best accomplished with short interval runs of 60 to 90 seconds with jog recoveries of one-third to one-half that *time*. Translated into an

actual workout, that would be something like repeat 400s at
10,000-meter race pace with 80- to 120-meter jog recoveries. The
important point is that the intensity need not be great, but that
the recoveries are short enough to keep the conditioning stimuli
present even during the recovery. This same research also mentions "short-short" repetitions (about 100 meters) with 5 to 15 seconds recovery jogging repeated 20 to 60 times (perhaps in two or
three sections with a few minutes of jogging between sections).
These 100s are not fast, roughly two-mile race pace but the recoveries must be short to keep the conditioning stimuli ever present.
Apparently the key to improving both your VO_2 max and anaerobic threshold with either continous or interval workouts is *constant movement.*

New Zealand's Peter Snell, three-time Olympic gold medalist
and former holder of several world records, went on to get a Ph.D.
in physiology after retiring from running. Armed with science to
evaluate the training he did under Lydiard, he says, "I now have a
good rationale for running the longer distances at the pace we did.
To get the proper benefit from these workouts hinges on running
at a speed that is hard enough, or at a distance that is far enough to
exhaust the glycogen in the slow-twitch muscle fibers. . . . Only if
the exercise level is hard enough or long enough will the fast
twitch fibers be recruited. This recruitment of the fast-twitch
fibers is what was happening during the later stages of our long
runs.

"With one exception I wouldn't have changed my training
program if I had known then what I do now about physiology. I
spent too much time plodding along at seven minutes a mile.
Long, slow distance is good for cardiovascular development, but
to really develop your maximum oxidative capacity, [VO_2 max]
you've got to do a bit of faster running. The higher the oxidative
capacity of your muscles, the later you'll see the rise of lactic acid,
which is associated with one onset of muscular fatigue."

RAISING YOUR ANAEROBIC THRESHOLD _____
After you have progressed as far as you can with aerobic work, the
addition of anaerobic training increases the percentage of your
VO_2 max you can operate at when racing. In other words, if your
VO_2 max is 60 ml/kg per minute, and aerobic training has brought
your anaerobic threshold to within 75 percent of that, anaerobic
training might allow you to race at 80 percent. While part of this

is physiological tolerance to anaerobic fatigue, much is also mental because during anaerobic work you learn to accept a different kind of discomfort than you encounter during a long, hard, steady effort. The sensation of fatigue experienced after 10 fast 400s is worlds apart from that felt after a fast 20-miler, even though both workouts could be rated equally difficult.

There is considerable circumstantial evidence for using uphill running, stair running, and stationary biking to fully develop your VO_2 max and your anaerobic threshold. Generally, the highest VO_2 maxs recorded have belonged to cross-country skiers because they heavily recruit almost every major muscle group—legs, abdomen, back and arms—into the action. Some female cross-country skiers have VO_2 maxs of over 80ml/kg per minute. But the highest oxygen uptake ever recorded belonged to Belgium's bicyclist, Eddy Merckx, who posed a phenomenal 95 ml/kg/mn. How Merckx's VO_2 max came to be this high is probably the result of two factors. One is that successful cycling is a product of efficient and powerful quadricep (thigh) muscles, the body's largest, and therefore potentially able to gobble up the most oxygen. Secondly, since a VO_2 max of 95 is about nine to ten standard deviations above the mean, Merckx must have been born a physiological freak even among physiological freaks.

Because running uphill, stairs, and stationary biking all heavily work the quads, it is my belief that these exercises are valuable in not only developing your capacity to use oxygen efficiently, but because they are physically and mentally demanding compared with fast aerobic running on the flat, they would also raise your anaerobic threshold. This perhaps explains why many coaches intuitively stress hill training. It also provides logic for Jack Foster's marathon capabilities, since Foster began his athletic career as a bike racer and still bikes at least one day a week. It perhaps partially explains why the year I used a nine-floor spiral staircase for my morning workouts, I won the National Marathon championship and made the Pan-American Games team, and why the next year, running my morning workouts uphill on a treadmill, I made the Olympic team. I now doubt that stair climbing and cycling are the poor cousins to running that most runners think they are.

ANAEROBIC TRAINING

We have seen that for middle-distance and distance runners, aerobic training is the primary concern. But anaerobic training is also valuable, although it doesn't require as much time to develop as many coaches and runners allot. Lydiard, using empirical methods, guessed that it requires five weeks to develop your anaerobic systems. He also says that East German research indicates it can be done in four. In any case, it depends upon how fast and how often it is performed. From a physiological standpoint, the value of anaerobic training is that you not only learn to tolerate the lactic acid produced during anaerobic work, you develop the ability to neutralize, or buffer it, thus enabling you to continue longer at fast speeds.

Interval training makes sense for any distance runner because it enables you to do a lot more work at relatively fast paces than if you did a fast continuous run. Your heart rate and blood lactate will be far lower during interval work because during the aerobic rests you partially oxidize the lactates your muscles are accumulation.

When first beginning anaerobic training, ease into it because you never want to make sudden changes in your training. With introductory workouts like 20 × 400 at about 10km race pace between 100-meter jog rests, you don't run particularly fast, but you also don't get much rest. With this *kind* of work you still raise your VO_2 max while beginning to deal with anaerobic fatigue.

But to fully develop your aerobic and anaerobic capabilities, your workouts should eventually (over the remaining four to five weeks of training) involve hard-effort runs that last between two and five minutes with nearly complete rests in between. The idea here is that the highest degree on anaerobic work occurs when you begin the fast run. Because your heart is not yet pumping enough blood, you rely heavily on anaerobically produced energy. With hard efforts lasting between two and five minutes, you can run far and fast enough to accumulate the most lactic acid in your muscles. If your fast sections are shorter, say 400s, you don't run long enough to produce high lactate levels. With runs lasting longer than five minutes, the pace is basically aerobic.

Complete rests between fast repeats in the form of *walking* and *slow* jogging are required in order to run the next hard section fast enough to maximally stimulate you anaerobic system. If you jog your recoveries, you maintain good circulation, which lowers your muscle-lactate levels—great for recovering, but not good for building to your highest possible acid levels during the workout.

And this is what you need to do in order to fully train the anaerobic system.

Sprints, while very anaerobic, do not last long enough to heavily tax the anaerobic system. Sprints and fast 400s, however, develop good leg-speed, and therefore, are valuable for putting the final touches on your race preparations.

Translated into practice, a basic workout maximizing your anaerobic capabilities might be something like 3 to 5 × 1200 meters, each run at two- to three-mile race pace with enough walking between each to bring your pulse down to 100 before running the next one. As you can see, this is a tough workout, and it should not occur more than once during any week.

Developing your anaerobic capabilities gives you a quick source of energy to get going at the beginning of a race, for tactical bursts en-route, and, of course, for a finishing kick. By recruiting your fast-twitch muscle fibers, you enable them to help out with the workload as well as improving their strength and quickness. Obviously you can then run with more power and speed.

And then there are all the mental and mechanical aspects of anaerobic training that I don't want to address at this point, except to say that you won't be able to mentally or physically accept the kind of fatigue produced in a race (especially the finishing kick) unless you encounter anaerobic work during training, some of it faster than race pace.

I need to mention one of the physiological problems of scheduling hard anaerobic workouts for prolonged periods. Because lactic acid is produced, the blood pH is progressively lowered during these workouts. In fact, one of the goals is to learn to run with lactic acid. That's what the final stages of races are all about. On recovery days the blood pH returns to near normal (between 7.46 and 7.48) and then one to three days later you lower it again. However, eventually—especially if racing is added to hard interval training—there is a great risk that the blood pH may not return to normal. When that happens, it can upset your ability to get nutrients out of food, upset the central nervous system, and manifest itself in loss of performance and interest in running. In the end, excessive anaerobic training pulls down your VO_2 max, and you can't even run the slow stuff very well. It is what many runners call going stale.

Haikkola makes this very point in describing how the Finnish

runners began to replace time spent running with speed in the
1950s and 1960s. "The idea is that by running a little faster, we get
the same load as by running long and steady. But this is anaerobic
training, and we are in continual oxygen debt. The body does not
develop as it should. It is not being built up, it is being torn apart."

TO SUM UP

We now have a rationale for dividing a season's training into three
periods, which accomplish three physiological goals. There's a lot
of overlap, however, because just as anaerobic training continues
to develop your aerobic capacity, and fast aerobic training helps
push back your anaerobic threshold, most quality workouts contribute, in varying degrees, to your endurance, stamina, and speed.
But by stressing certain types of work at specific times, you build
strength upon strength, which minimizes injuries and allows you
to be at your best when the training is finished.

The first goal is to raise your VO_2 max, and that is best accomplished with long runs that increasingly approach your fastest
aerobic pace at that time (it rises as you get fitter). Interval work,
fartlek, and sprinting will also raise your VO_2 max, but are not the
best way to begin.

Secondly, you want to push back your anaerobic threshold,
and that is accomplished best at that time by dipping into anaerobic work. So you add faster up- and downhill runs, easy striding,
and more running at five to 10km race pace.

Finally, you want to develop your ability to run anaerobically
because you will have to do that in races, plus be mechanically efficient at fast speeds. This is accomplished with sprints and making
yourself run while "out of breath" during hard repeats lasting two
to five minutes.

Now let's move on to see how we apply all this to actual
training.

9.

LAYING OUT A SEASON'S TRAINING

*M*any runners train without considering how workouts fit together. Purposeful training is a balancing act embracing
three basic considerations. The first is the sequencing of, and time
spent on, the various phases of training. The second recognizes
that as you mature, the ratio of aerobic to anaerobic work shifts as
you gain running maturity. The third is the day-to-day balancing
of hard and easy efforts, long and short runs, and fast and slow
training.

Unbalanced training often looks amazingly like good training.
Until something goes drastically wrong with hit-and-miss training,
the differences in results often are not apparent. For one thing,
you aren't aware of how well you could have performed. What if
better training netted you only one percent improvement? For a
miler that's about three seconds. It's nine seconds off a 35-minute
10km. A three-hour marathoner runs 2:58:12. Considering that the
first four in the 1976 Olympic 5000 were separated by less than a
second, and that for Bill Rodgers, Alberto Salazar, and Rob de
Castella, a mere two seconds have meant the difference between

winning and second place in major marathons, statistically insignificant differences can have monumental effect on the placings and medal distribution. And it can be just as true for someone trying to place in their age group or defeat a rival for the first time. As Fred Wilt has said, "There is no thread of life as narrow as that which separates those who win from those who lose."

You must be organized in your training and racing. Each day there is a type of workout that is better than any other. The difference may be slight, but differences accumulate over time and seriously affect your performance. If you just train, although you will be working hard and mixing workouts, you won't go as far as when you approach individual workouts as components of a larger plan. My own running took a dramatic leap when I discovered this because I then saw the necessity of doing workouts I otherwise wouldn't have.

After winning the 1977 Boston Marathon, Jerome Drayton, a 2:10 marathoner and three-time winner of Japan's Eukoka Marathon, summarized the key elements of a season's training in a way that enables any aspiring distance runner to grasp the basic concept. It is, in a nutshell, the approach I'm advocating in here.

"Basically, you have all these different types of workouts. You've got general distance running, you've got fartlek, you've got hill work, you've got anaerobic training sessions, and then you've got the rest phase. You take these phases and you arrange them in the right order. You have to work in time frames. You attach so many weeks to each phase.

"What most runners do . . . is try to incorporate any number of these different types of training in a typical week. They will do distance one day, and track another time, and maybe a little hill work. They're sort of fishing in the dark. That's the biggest mistake.

"You can get fit no matter what you do, but the idea is to get the best out of yourself. So you should take each of these phases, arrange them in the right order in degree of difficulty, attach so many weeks to each phase, and stick with it. If you are doing hill work, don't introduce track workouts at all. If you are doing general distance, don't introduce hill work.

"What I'm saying essentially is that you have to be very organized with your training. You work in time frames. You work in units. The order would be general distance, hill work, aerobic track, anaerobic track and then the rest phase. The rest phase is a drastic taper. . . . It's a combination of aerobic and anaerobic, high quality and low quality. And the general principle that can be applied to each phase is one day of rest followed by one hard day, depending on your state of fitness."

Drayton makes several valuable points. One is you don't go for everything at once. Decide what you are trying to accomplish during each phase and then select workouts that do it best. I knew a high-school runner who felt he should run one speed or interval workout a week during his aerobic base. This, I discovered, had messed up his program in the past. When I said running hard intervals during his build-up was not good, he probably thought "big deal," but it showed that he neither understood what he was trying to accomplish during the base period, nor the purpose of speed training. Intervals were increasing his odds of getting injured because, starting out, he wasn't ready for that kind of stress. But the real issue was that he didn't need leg-speed or anaerobic tolerance at the beginning, and by training for it, he was neglecting what he did need.

An improper workout hurts you because it does not contribute as much as another. What happened to this runner was that when he needed fast work, he was sick of it. So much of training is mental. A good schedule recognizes that. If you hold off on intervals and speed work, you can't wait to do them later.

BASE TRAINING

Whether you are a 4-minute or 5-minute miler, a 2:15 or 3:15 marathoner, the order of training is roughly the same. Everyone begins easily, getting used to running, strengthening tendons and muscles, raising the VO_2 max and increasing biochemical efficiency.

After a two- or three-week break from training, begin with aerobic distance runs. Keep the stresses light for a while; don't run hard until you can run easily. That means no kicking in at the end of runs. You want endurance, and how fast you run later depends upon keeping your head and having patience. Go for as much mileage as is *comfortable.* Try to run every day, with more or less the *same* efforts and distances. You need miles, so sacrifice whatever else for that.

When beginning a session, listen more to your body than the schedule. Target a mileage that you (experienced runners) can

work up to in three or four weeks, going slowly. Relative beginners should take more time. This minimizes stresses until you are
ready. After you reach your target weekly mileage, repeat it at the
same intensity for another week or so to be sure you can live with
it during the weeks to come. If you can't hold it the second week,
cut back or try again.

Once you can handle your target mileage at slow speeds, to
become fitter *don't go further* each week, pick up the pace on
some runs or parts of them, gradually running more at or near your
maximum aerobic pace. This will require that you ease into a
hard-day easy-day, long-day, short-day approach. Now a schedule
helps you balance efforts and distances.

The importance of mileage as the primary concern during
base training is alluded to in what Pat Clohessy tells de Castella:
"If you've got to cut back, try to avoid reducing your long runs, as
the strength you get from these is vital." Clohessy speaks in context of a marathoner who must cut a workout and has to choose
between the distance or the speed run, but the implication is that
without the distance base, speed training isn't effective.

The mileage of a typical week of base training should consist
of the following ratios:

One continuous long run (20 to 25%)
Two faster moderate distance runs (each about 15%)
One aerobic fartlek workout (about 10%)
One steady hard run (about 10%)

The other days (25 to 30 percent of the mileage) should be
reserved for slow recovery runs.

Moderately hilly routes force you to vary the efforts and pace.
They expose your legs to a greater range of motion, and inject a
touch of fartlek to an otherwise steady run. Hills add variety and
begin to prepare you for the hill workouts that follow. Castill says
that "When runners [run] at 70 percent of VO_2 max for two hours
. . . it was found that the [thigh] muscle was metabolically more
active during uphill and downhill effort than during level running.
This would suggest the need for including grade running in training to compensate for these specific demands of road and cross-
country competition."

Base training isn't just a lot of jogging. This is where many
Lydiard followers get it wrong. They become stuck on mileage at
the expense of effort. Slow mileage will improve your endurance,

but it won't fully develop your VO_2 max or prepare you mechanically and emotionally for hard efforts. On the other hand, *don't race workouts.* Always finish knowing you could have run a little further or faster.

BASE TRAINING CONSISTS OF THE FOLLOWING TYPES OF RUNS:

EARLY-SEASON DISTANCE RUNS _____

Begin the season with these easy- to medium-effort steady runs that get you used to training. Mileage, or time spent running, is the main concern. These runs are used exclusively during the first few weeks to extend your mileage. Each day's effort is roughly the same. The purpose is to raise your VO_2 max, and get your body used to regular training. Never finish feeling that you couldn't have gone further and faster. Later these kinds of runs become recovery efforts.

FAST AEROBIC RUNS _____

These are what some of the easy-distance runs gradually evolve into. They create endurance, stamina (the ability to run relatively fast, relatively far), extend your VO_2 max, develop mechanical efficiency at faster speeds, and prepare you for anaerobic work. The simplest way to do this training is to gradually work into a steady fast aerobic effort and hold it for as long as you can without feeling like you are racing. Run this way, a 10-mile begins with one to two easy miles and concludes with eight to nine miles at steady hard effort. Aerobic fartlek breaks a run into segments of fast aerobic pace with short recoveries in between. You can combine the two, running hard steady pace the first half of the workout, and faster and slower sections the second.

Another variation is to break distance runs into two or three fast sections with four- to seven-minute easy running between them. I often do this on my 14-mile course, i.e., run it as three 4⅓ fairly hard mile sections, with half-mile recoveries between them. It's still a continuous 14-miler, and even with partial recoveries, I run as fast as during a steady hard effort. By changing gears, 90 percent of the run is faster than I could run with a comparably difficult steady effort. Someone running 8½ miles might do

2 × 4 miles with an easier half-mile between them. These runs are most valuable near the end of the base period when you are trying to increase your speed during relatively long sessions.

Lydiard says to do base work "for as long as possible," but because that could be all season, let's consider other options. During a season, balance the weeks required for this type of work against the time required *and available* for other kinds of training. To do this, lay out your program in reverse from the first serious road race, or if you are a track or cross-country competitor, the *last half* of the racing season.

If you have 20 weeks to train, and sharpening takes four, anaerobic training four, and hill work another four, that leaves eight weeks for base work. Often, however, you won't have 20 weeks. There may be only 10, which means something gets shortchanged. A rule of thumb is to trim thinly on base work. If you don't run that properly and rush into anaerobic work, there's a great risk of running out of gas before the season's end. Much, however, depends on your maturity as a runner.

A reasonable solution to parceling out 10 weeks' work might be (working backward) two weeks of sharpening (relying upon races to finish the job), four weeks of combination hill and interval-type work, and four weeks for aerobic base work. Although not ideal, it's a good compromise under the circumstances. Stated simply, you should base train until you can run your fastest without getting out of breath, because after you cross over into speeds that leave you breathless, the distance you can cover drops dramatically. If you don't believe that, calculate how far Rob de Castella could run at 4:50 pace, or how far Joan Benoit could go at 5:20 pace, and how far you can go.

HILL (RESISTANCE) TRAINING

Probably the three major weaknesses of distance training are:

1. The fast-twitch muscle fibers aren't recruited and trained.
2. Because it slows the contractual speed of fast-twitch muscles, you get slower over distances from 100 yards to a mile.
3. It doesn't enable you to generate much anaerobic energy, a drawback especially in races of 10km and less.

What most runners do after base training is interval training. It's a reasonable next step. But there is another that's better, so much better, in fact, it may be that shortcut or gimmick every runner wants. It's hill training.

It was Lydiard who refined the application of hill training and provided logic for not only running fast up and down them, but using them for special exercises—uphill springing and bounding. Although no one wants to bounce up a hill during a race, these exercises, practiced in training, ultimately enhance one's ability to both run uphill *and* fast on the flat. And as Lydiard promised and I've repeatedly verified, hills are a great shortcut to sharpening for races. You can accomplish in four weeks of hill work what would take six on the track—without the pressure and boredom.

Hill workouts saved Lorraine Moller's 1980–81 track season in New Zealand. She had concluded the U.S. season with a marathon in Rio de Janeiro in November on the way to New Zealand where she rested until December. Although the break was necessary, it left only eight weeks to prepare for the track races. I drew up a schedule with four weeks of base conditioning and four weeks of hill training (which I'll explain shortly). She ran only three track workouts before competing, using early races for her main sharpening efforts. To make a short story shorter, she ran each week's race faster, eventually winning the Pacific Conference Games 3000 meters with a personal best by seven seconds. The year before, after spending two months on the track to get faster, she actually ran slower, taking over 60 seconds to complete the last 200 meters of the National Champs 3000 after the "bear" jumped on her back.

THE CASE FOR RUNNING HILLS _____

Just running over hilly routes isn't hill training. Hill training involves difficult repeats with rests in between. It's resistance work, in the category with hill bounding and springing, running in water, stair running, running in sand, snow, or up a treadmill. Resistance develops strength, works the fast-twitch muscles, and conditions the anaerobic system without the mechanical and mental stresses associated with anaerobic work on the flat. Getting up hills with exaggerated knee lift or spring redevelops resiliency in the legs that distance running destroys.

Although distance training produces excellent cardiovascular development, it does nothing to develop explosive power necessary for speed. A rest will revitalize "dead" legs, but during the season hill bounding and springing help restore and maintain that resiliency. Hill training also strengthens the drive from the ankle and foot, and prepares you not only for hilly races, but also the track. As for strengthening, de Castella says, "I don't believe in weights. My strength comes from running the hills."

Seb Coe relies on hill work to perfect his drives to the tape. George Gandy says, "Virtually any runner can do uphill/downslope work and repetitions to develop speed potential for the kick." David Costill adds that uphill running develops powerful thigh and hamstring muscles which are essential to running fast. Marti Liquori says that in distance training your stride shortens, so your muscles are not extending and do not become strong. On the uphills you extend your stride by bounding, exaggerating knee lift and armswing, pushing off with the toes and calves. This strengthens your quads and buttock muscles. "Hills may be the wave of the future," he contends. Pat Clohessy emphatically stresses that "hills are ideal for developing sustained speed."

DOWNHILL TRAINING

Jogging downhill wastes half the workout. Gravity will do much of your work down a hill if you know how to relax and let go. As a transition from relatively slow base work to fast sharpening, downhill striding allows you to run fast with relatively little effort. When you are not used to running fast, there's a tendency to strain when trying to sprint on the flat. Peter Snell, says, "[Fast] downhill work enables running with increased stride length and frequency, which should develop new neuromuscular patterns of speed." Bill Dellinger says that "Downhill running, if done properly, can dramatically increase your leg-speed and lengthen your stride." Bill Rodgers, one of the best downhill runners ever, trained up and down Heartbreak Hill in Boston.

Some, such as Grete Waitz, have misjudged the value of downhill training and regretted it. In the 1982 Boston Marathon, Waitz ran with authority until cresting Heartbreak, only to cramp so badly on the descent she had to drop out. "To train on the downhill seems not to be really training," she told the press afterward. "To run uphill, that is training. But I learned today that to run downhill well can be as difficult as running uphill."

LYDIARD'S CLASSIC HILL WORKOUT _____

While there are numerous ways to run a hill workout, I like Lydiard's original version best: Locate a 400- to 800-meter hill. Lydiard says it should be a 1:3 grade, but that's too steep. A 10 to 15 percent grade is fine, and best is a loop with a steep uphill and gentler downhill. The uphill should be tough enough to make you work, and the downhill not so steep you can't relax with the brakes off. Grass is ideal for downhills, but because there's so little leg shock on uphills, roads or walks are okay. When hill training *always* wear well-cushioned training shoes. If you wear racing flats you risk injury.

The main ingredients of Lydiard's hill workout are: 1) uphill running, bounding or springing, 2) recovery, 3) fast relaxed downhill striding, *and* 4) relaxed stride-outs of about 200 meters. An actual workout might be: 1½ to 2-mile warmup, hard uphill running, bounding, or springing (to be explained), an equal distance recovery jog, downhill striding, a 200-meter jog and then 2 to 3 × 200 meter striding on the flat with 200-meter jogs in between, and a 1½- to 2-mile cooldown. The uphill, recovery, downhill, and 200s comprise one "set." Lydiard recommends that elite runners using a half-mile hill do four sets. If warming up and down covers two miles each, the total distance is about 14 miles, the maximum *anyone* should do. Unless you are damn tough, run fewer sets or use a shorter hill. If you think, for example, that eight miles is enough for you, structure your warmup, cooldown, number of hills, and stride-outs accordingly. Mileage is no longer a priority. If you make this workout too long, either you will poop out before finishing, or there won't be enough intensity on the hills and 200s. You are finished with easy running up and down hills and aerobic striding. Hill training is a major transition from basic road work. The physical demands can be strenuous in the extreme and taxing enough to be the making or breaking of the athlete. This training almost seems to be what Nietzsche had in mind when he said, "What doesn't destroy me makes me strong."

SPRINGING AND BOUNDING _____

This is a good place to pause and describe hill bounding and springing. *Hill bounding* resembles running through deep snow; you get the knees and head up, drive with exaggerated arm action and grossly overdo everything including vertical height and stride length. *Hill springing* works the calves, Achilles tendon, and ankles. The knees don't come up as high as with bounding, but there's greater vertical lift because the drive is from the ball of the foot and nearly straight up, similar to a basketball player making a one-legged jump shot. Executed properly, each stride nets only a foot or two of forward progress. At this rate, with even moderately vigorous springing, you can't (or at least shouldn't) complete a 400- to 800-meter hill without breaking it into alternate segments of running and bounding. After you are used to springing, do it until fatigue prevents you from getting good lift (perhaps 50 to 100 yards), break into a run or semi-bounding, and then revert back to springing until you've had enough again. You might run the first and last hills and spring parts of the middle one depending upon your reaction to this type of work.

Relative beginners, marathoners, and those susceptible to tendon problems should run the uphills with slightly exaggerated armswing, knee lift and bounce. In general, the shorter your races, the more valuable springing and bounding are. That's why 400-, 800-, and 1500-meter runners drill various jumping, bounding, and high knee lift exercises, and distance runner frequently don't. But even marathoners benefit from these exercises.

Starting out, go easy on the springing and bounding, monitoring the reaction of your Achilles tendon and what I call the "lifters"—the tops of the quads in the groin area. If you spring every hill on day one, you probably will end up too stiff or injured to run the next day's recovery, or to repeat this workout in a few days. Concentrate on the movements, not on how fast you can reach the top. Try to move symmetrically. If one leg is stronger, you may have to work the other a little harder to get the same action on both sides. This requires that both arms move identically, vigorously forward and back along the line of travel, not crossing the body's center line (which causes rotation). When you run with others, trade leads to watch and correct each other.

200 METER STRIDE-OUTS

Don't omit these from this workout. Use them to practice the technique used in running fast. Start them a notch faster than you've been running, but not yet sprinting. Picture yourself sprinting smoothly: knees up, good arm carriage, getting good drive from your ankles and toes, staying relaxed. Think about technique rather than speed. Master speed technique at moderate ef-

forts in order to stay smooth later at fast efforts. Otherwise, you'll
lose control and teach yourself bad habits. Furthermore, you'll risk
injury.

These 200s, either at the top or bottom of the hill, teach you
to stride smoothly as fatigue builds. You learn to change gears,
switching from fast striding to uphill running or springing, to
downhill striding, and to striding again. There's never much rest,
but each hard section uses a different muscle group. In races you'll
respond to an opponent's tactics, or initiate a move of your own
when the opposition least wants it.

If I were limited to using the type of training for every workout, I'd pick the hill workout. Because it covers up to 14 miles
nonstop, it's a distance run. There are uphills, downhills, and fast
striding on the flat. It teaches technique and builds stamina and
speed. It can be run at any level of difficulty and still works the different muscle groups.

Don't get suckered into timing uphills and 200s. When

*Practicing hill bounding under the critical eye of Lydiard. No-
tice the exaggerated knee lift, stride length, and arm action.*

bounding or springing uphill, you don't derive as much benefit by racing to the top. Timing an uphill run has meaning, but don't introduce this kind of pressure yet. You'll get enough of that later. Instead, think about effort.

Because a hill workout crosses over into anaerobic work and introduces new mechanical stresses two or three times a week, drop the week's mileage by at least 10 percent from what you were averaging during base training. Increased effort has to be compensated for by reduced mileage. One long run each week is enough to maintain your endurance base during the four weeks or so you'll spend in this phase.

Don't be surprised if during the first week or two of hill training you feel worse rather than stronger. You've made a substantial break with base running; power is being developed for the hills, there's leg shock on the downhills, and on the 200s you're trying to get your knees up and a sprinter's foot action. It takes a while to adjust. Start out easy the first week and apply the pressure gradually thereafter. Otherwise, all will seem well, and then, presto, injury. By the third week, you should be strong and more injury-resistant. By the fourth week you should be able to take the brakes off down the hills as well as move well on the 200s. When you begin track (type) workouts and races, you'll be ready for them.

I have portrayed hill training as a well-defined period lasting about a month. In practice, however, the edges between hill work and other training are not that distinct. During the last two weeks of base training, it's often smart to run one easy hill workout each week to get ready for what's coming up—especially if the time available for hill training is short. Also, if you will be racing on hills, carry forward one hill workout per week into your sharpening, working with greater intensity on shorter steeper hills, or using fewer repetitions.

Although I don't recommend racing during base training, it's OK to have a race or two during hill training. The danger with racing at this point lies not in the racing itself, but in that it interrupts training. If you can, don't sacrifice workouts to rest for unimportant races, and don't race each week. The training you lose won't be worth it when it's time for the really important races. Hill training may be the one true shortcut in training, so don't get sidetracked. When you do your homework on the hills, not only will you be tougher in important races, you will be tougher sooner.

No hills? If your area is without hills, does that mean you skip this phase?

No, because there are good substitutes. There's springing up stairs and bounding through calf-deep water, snow, or sand. One guy I corresponded with in New York used a freeway overpass for his hill. It was short, but he made it work for him. If there are no hills around, review Chapter 3 on supplementary training for ways to integrate other forms of work into your program.

SHARPENING

Until now, milers could have trained alongside marathoners. Now they split company. Not only are their training needs different, milers often race more frequently over a shorter, more intense season. Marathoners and road racers compete less frequently over longer periods. Therefore, rather than talk about specific workouts—that's covered in the schedules—I'll summarize what any runner, miler to marathoner, beginner to elite, should be aiming to accomplish in the final weeks.

In short, sharpening involves preparing for the *specific* demands of your race(s). Milers, at the short end of the spectrum, need a high VO_2 max, good speed, extreme tolerance to anaerobic fatigue, and quick tactical reflexes. In training it may have taken an hour or two to become fatigued, but in a race you must be able to exhaust all your energy in four to five minutes. Since most of your work has been less intense than that and spread out, quantity has to give way to quality.

Marathoners also need a high VO_2 max, but they don't require as much speed, anaerobic tolerance, or quick tactical reflexes. Base training has developed good endurance, and hill training has introduced anaerobic hills and stride-outs. Sharpening becomes a refinement and blending of speed and endurance. So some runs become even longer and harder, and some faster. Some are a combination of the two, slightly faster than race pace for less than the racing distance.

When I helped Lorraine Moller get ready for her first competitive marathon, she was so used to sharpening for track races she had trouble accepting that besides track-type work, sharpening also included tough three-hour runs and sustained efforts between 12 and 15 miles. Rather than cut most of the distance work, marathoners extend and intensify it while also building speed.

As an example of how seriously the Japanese take these long runs, coach Kiyoshi Nakamura says that Toshibo Seko covers "up to 70 km [43 miles] sometimes. But the Soh brothers run much more sometimes." Nakamura is referring to the Soh brothers' six-hour runs.

Marathoners also need to get moving once or twice a week, as evidenced by Joan Benoit's experience. Benoit was an impressive, but not phenomenal runner prior to 1982. She reviewed her training logs and decided that between 1980 and early 1982 there was an almost complete lack of track work. "Track work and pace work," Benoit now says, "are necessary for the developing runner if he or she is going to survive in the competitive circle of marathoning and road racing."

That's a different attitude than she originally had toward marathon training. She used to think that the main goal was to log as many miles as possible. In order to keep near 100 miles a week, she cut almost all track work from her training. When Allison Roe lowered the women's marathon record to 2:25, Benoit decided that "the only way to get stronger and faster was to vary the speeds of my workouts and get on the track at least once a week." The result was a 2:26:11 at the 1982 Nike Marathon, followed by her 2:22:43 world best at Boston in 1983, and an Olympic victory in 1984.

The point being that for each competitive distance there exists an optimum blend of quality and quantity. If a marathoner trains solely on mileage, he or she will go the distance, but not fast. Conversely, all the speed in the world is useless if you can't make it to the finish. Milers, on the other hand, don't worry about lasting four laps, but rather holding their speed. Whether your event is the mile, marathon, or 10km, establish a speed-distance balance that works for you.

The sharpening phase is less defined than the other two. Base and hill training are prerequisites to sharpening and racing, but once you are sharp, it evolves into that gray area of *maintaining* while racing, and then as the final race(s) approach, sharpening becomes a *drastic drop* in the training workload, which is the "rest phase" alluded to by Jerome Drayton at the beginning of this chapter.

If racing were simple, a year's work would involve something like a big build-up during the winter, sharpening and racing until summer, backing off during the summer to recharge the mental and physical batteries, briefly rebuilding and racing again through late summer and fall, resting, and then starting the whole process over. The advantages are 1) the main mileage training is done in winter when you aren't (or shouldn't be) racing, 2) you are in peak condition in spring and fall when the weather is right for fast times, and 3) you get to back off during the summer heat.

That's the ideal. But there are big exceptions. Your big race may fall on the 4th of July or at any time you normally would be at less than peak shape. Traditionally, I'd be flat during late summers after indoor track and the spring races. Mentally it was hard to get "up" for low-key races in the heat. So guess how I felt in 1968 when I learned that the Olympic trial would be held on a southern Colorado desert in August. Like it or not, not only couldn't I slump that summer, I'd have to be sharper than ever. Summer slumps, I decided were motivational. The Olympic goal would correct that. I guessed that with an oxygen problem at 7640 feet, I should do some anaerobic running before I got there, and once there, not panic and jump into hard training.

Having a strategy provided a sense of direction. Even easy workouts had their purpose, and as I worked harder each week, I had a terrific feeling of reaching a new plateau. A lot of the other participants there seemed to be training willy-nilly and trying to cram as many hard workouts as they could into the time available.

Physical sharpening must also be coordinated with its mental counterparts. Gritty Herb Elliott warns that "What [is often neglected in training] is the spiritual and mental side. . . . If you emphasize the physical . . . you may become superbly conditioned, but mentally not advanced at all. On the other hand, if you concentrate on the mental aspect, it is inevitable that the physical side will follow." As an example, Elliott describes a session where he and opponent Merve Lincoln were sprinting and jogging, and Elliott noticed "that I was sprinting into this howling wind. On the other hand, Merve was sprinting with the wind. That was where I realized that in terms of mental toughness I would always have it over Merve."

As the big races draw nearer, sharpening should be geared to the problems faced in races. Road racers learn to hold the pace and respond to tactics when several miles remain. Track racers must maintain speed when tired, even throw in tactical burners to get into position for the finishing drive. Interval and fartlek training, which permits rests, will increasingly be replaced by time-trials, sprint-float sessions (like Viren's 5000 meters of 50/50s) and tune-up races—all of which don't allow many, if any, rests.

On long runs, road runners practice tactics, surging and easing, pushing the hills toward the end, drinking on the run, learning pace. Both Salazar and Beardsley include pick-ups of between three quarters of a mile and five miles during their long runs. Both use them tactically in races. Mentally and physically they've done it in training, so it isn't as frightening in the race. Salazar says, "I can pick it up and run three miles [in a marathon] in 4:43 average. . . ." Coach Dellinger taught him that. "You don't go into a race and try to do something you aren't calloused to," Dellinger says.

Dellinger also puts 5 × 3/4 miles at race pace or progressively faster efforts into his runner's fartlek workouts. They practice "dominating" during hard 300 to 500s, throwing in 90 percent effort bursts for 100 to 200 meters while imagining trying to open up on a competitor. Perhaps his most awesome race simulator is the 30th Avenue drill, a hard, hilly 11-mile run that includes a fast 3/4 mile at the beginning, middle and end. "It combines a little of everything that could happen to you in a race," Dellinger says.

The progression with anaerobic training, be you miler or marathoner, is from a fair amount of volume at relatively slow speeds with short rests (such as 20 × 400/100s), to less volume at faster speeds with longer rests (such as hard 1000-meter repeats with enough walking between to drop your pulse to 100), to even less volume at faster speeds with *less* rest. Finally, interval training should be fast with very little resting between (such as stride-float 50s or 100s).

Rob de Castella explains how he uses this principle in his weekly training for the marathon: "I rarely run faster than 30-second 200-meter pace. . . . The hardest session I do is of 8 × 400s with a 200-meter float. . . . When I'm running well, I'm doing the 400s in 62–63 seconds, maybe one or two at 61, but rarely any faster. But the 200 recovery is usually only at about 40 to 45 seconds, so it's really a three-mile sprint-float session."

There is another kind of anaerobic training that is *not* for developing anaerobic tolerance, but for developing leg-speed. It's running nearly flat out over 80 to 200 meters with almost complete rests in between. Obviously this is the training of those at the short end of the racing spectrum, but since even marathoners should occasionally become milers (or at least track competitors), it's applicable to almost everyone at some time.

When combining sprinting with serious racing, make sure there are nearly complete rests in between sprints. Many runners mistakenly continue to keep the recoveries short. Once you begin racing seriously and frequently, you shouldn't run many lactic acid-accumulating workouts. You'll get enough of that racing. If you add racing to hard anaerobic work, you risk breaking down. Road racers with time enough between races to recover keep in touch with this kind of work, but not just before a race. Races take the place of hard sustained efforts. They are the hardest training you'll ever do.

In your training, don't run just the workouts mentioned above. They are illustrative examples. Actual training is varied because as Haikkola warned, "Monotony is poison to a runner." Once you know a workout's main attributes and purpose, you can construct many workouts along the same lines.

In sum, the purposes and examples of the three kinds of anaerobic training are:

PRELIMINARY ANAEROBIC _____

Purposes: A transition between aerobic base work and hard anaerobic work. To extend your VO_2 max past what aerobic training can accomplish. To push back your anaerobic threshold and get mechanically, physically, and mentally used to race speeds.

Kinds of workouts: Medium-effort uphills. Moderate-effort fartlek. High-volume intervals with short rests such as 20 × 400/100, or other repeats of a mile or less with quick recoveries.

HARD ANAEROBIC _____

Purposes: Push back the anaerobic threshold. Build buffers against lactic acid to tolerate fast paces. Biomechanical efficiency, strength, and power. Drive from the feet and ankles.

Kinds of workouts: Two- to five-minute hard repetitions with near complete rests. Time-trials over 600 meters to a mile. Stride-float 50s or 100s. Sharp fartlek. Hard uphill runs.

LEG SPEED _____

Purposes: Increase mechanical efficiency at fast speeds. Handle tactical burners in races. Strength and power.

Kinds of workouts: Alternate stride-float 50s or 100s, sprints, and fast striding with complete rests. Downhill sprints.

HINTS ON RUNNING SHARPENING WORKOUTS _____

1. Stay off the track for most of your interval and speed work. Lydiard says, "I'm a great believer in keeping track athletes off the track." Herb Lindsay says, "I do most of my training as if I were on a track, on the roadway. The same loops that I used for my long runs, I use for my interval training."
2. Use fartlek for much of your track-type work. The track is repetitious, mentally demanding, and the curves are a potential source of injury. The track can be deceiving; exciting and stimulating at first, and then one day that's it! You hate it, and don't want to run that kind of work anywhere.
3. Run most of your intervals on trails or in a park. Measure out various distances if you want to. It's much more exhilarating than making quarter-mile circuits where the scenery never changes
4. Different runners need and tolerate different amount of anaerobic training. Too little is better than too much. Try to find your own balance.
5. Wear racing flats for fast anaerobic sessions. The rhythm is different when wearing racing flats, and so are the stresses on your feet, which you should get used to before racing.
6. Schedule aerobic recovery days between hard anaerobic workouts.
7. Interval training is easier when run with others. But keep competitive pride out of it. Run what you are supposed to whether it's out in front, alongside, or way behind.
8. Timing and patience are vital. Don't try to develop your speed and anaerobic tolerance all at once unless you want to feel burned out later. On your first interval workouts concentrate on running smoothly rather than hard. Always leave room for progess the next week. If you start peaking too soon, hold back on speed work; if you lack stamina (a strong second-half workout or race), emhasize long repeats and distance runs.

9. Don't become discouraged if you are slow at first and it seems as though you'll never run fast. Be patient, stay on schedule, and you'll be surprised at how soon you come around.
10. It takes only four to five weeks to develop your anaerobic capacity. After that you are maintaining. Track and cross-country runners racing frequently should cut back or eliminate hard intervals, and road racers should consider one race worth two hard workouts.
11. On workouts like 15 to 20 × 400/100, don't time the 400s. Time the entire workout if you need a measure.

REST PHASE

If you are a track or cross-country competitor with an intensive racing season, when the important races begin, training all but stops. There are two excellent reasons: 1) training is (or should be) finished, and 2) regular racing added to hard training exhausts rather than improves. Road racers competing once or twice a month for several months should generally maintain mileage, cutting back only before important races.

The rest phase is most important and least understood among high-school and college track and cross-country athletes. Once racing begins, they compete up to three times a week. Most of these runners mistakenly continue to train on the days they're not racing, right up to the State Meet or Nationals, when they could perform better by dropping all hard training during the last month. They or their coaches, however, think they have to get in those last licks. Like the favorite in the Minnesota High School State Meet 2-mile some years ago who, just two days before the race, time-trialed his best 660. Then he ran his flattest race all season. Which wasn't surprising. He was already fit and sharp. The 660 became his State Meet.

John Walker, first to crack the 3:50 mile, and Olympic gold medalist, once told me, "Most runners are too damn stupid to rest before competition." At that time he was racing mid-week, weekends, and training 30 miles a week. You must break away from hard training in order to bring out those big races. Hard interval training between weekly races can ruin your performance.

In order to stop training when racing, the training must, of course, be completed. If it is not, and because many high-school and college runners begin training too late, it's often not, then there's no alternative other than to train between races.

If you use the training approach just outlined and begin training early enough to be ready before the last half of the competitive season, then with just leg-speed work and easy recovery runs between races, you will be fit and sharp for the important competition. You won't get out of shape racing frequently, jogging, and sprinting. You'll become even faster.

How long can a middle-distance runner stay in top condition after training stops and regular racing begins? Depending upon the runner and his or her fitness level, it could be between four and six weeks. After a track runner is raced out or the season ends, he or she backs off, resharpens if another series of races awaits, or ends the season with a complete rest. Road racers customarily have longer competitive seasons, sometimes the better part of a year, but the period of peak conditioning is usually far shorter. When a road racer is raced out or ends the season, he or she does the same as a track competitor: backs off and resharpens, or takes a compelete rest.

This brings us to the final part of the rest phase. The first part was resting between frequent or important races. The second is a two- or three-week complete or near complete break from running each year.

Many athletes resist taking a break because it means losing conditioning and having to start over. But, paradoxically, this also works in your favor. When a season ends, you still might feel eager to go into the next season's build-up. The drive's there, and besides, you'd lose all that shape. But there's a big risk that without rest, you'll lose enthusiasm later when you cannot afford a break. Craig Virgin advises runners to "Take a break from running once a year involuntarily before your body forces you to." Ron Clarke, who had difficulty staying fresh for the Olympics and other championships, finally admitted, "I have always been a devotee of training all year round, but quite frankly, I think a month off each year freshens you up so much, it's worth it."

Joan Benoit even sees her injuries as blessings in disguise because they have forced her to rest. "I hate to say it," she said after having her Achilles tendon surgically repaired, and then setting the women's marathon record, "but maybe people should just tie me down once a year for about two months just to stop me. Every time I come back from an injury I come back stronger. I don't know why. Maybe because I take a forced break I wouldn't ordinarily have taken, and get that much more primed."

That's the essence of breaks: What you momentarily lose physically, you more than gain mentally. Your batteries recharge, and you are excited to embark on a fresh mission where there's constant improvement.

EXAMPLES OF BALANCING A SEASON'S TRAINING

Below are two sets of examples for balancing a season's training. In the first set of examples there are 20 weeks from the beginning of the season (which follows a two- to three-week break) until the first important competition. Some preliminary racing would take place during the sharpening (anaerobic) phase.

The second set of examples shows possible solutions for someone having only 12 weeks before the important races. Actually, this schedule could work quite well for someone who is raced out, needs to back off momentarily and resharpen. If the break preceding this training were a week or two of easy maintenance runs every second to third day, and the runner began it still fairly fit (and rested), the time required to go through the training phases could be fairly short.

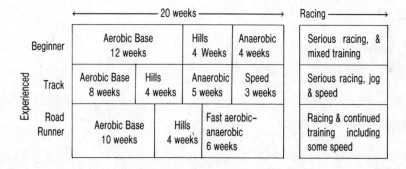

	← 20 weeks →			Racing →
Beginner	Aerobic Base 12 weeks	Hills 4 Weeks	Anaerobic 4 weeks	Serious racing, & mixed training
Experienced Track	Aerobic Base 8 weeks	Hills 4 weeks	Anaerobic 5 weeks	Speed 3 weeks → Serious racing, jog & speed
Road Runner	Aerobic Base 10 weeks	Hills 4 weeks	Fast aerobic– anaerobic 6 weeks	Racing & continued training including some speed

Experienced		←————— 20 weeks —————→			Racing ————————→
	Beginner	Aerobic Base 8 weeks	Hills & anaero-bic 4 weeks		Race every 2nd or 3rd week plus mixed training
	Track	Aerobic Base 6 weeks	Hills 3 weeks	Anaer-obic 3 weeks	Serious racing & anaerobic repeats
	Road Racer	Aerobic Base 8 weeks	Hills 4 weeks		Begin racing & anaerobic repeats

10.

BALANCING DAY-TO-DAY TRAINING

LONG RUNS—SHORT RUNS

During base training, all the running is aerobic. At first, when you are just running easy with the emphasis on mileage, vary the distance covered if you need to ease up. Gradually, however, as the target mileage is reached and you begin to run at faster aerobic speeds during some workouts, it is necessary to very both the distances covered and the efforts. The example below shows one solution to balancing a week's work after you've reached your target mileage and are running some workouts at fast aerobic efforts.

BALANCING A WEEK'S AEROBIC BASE TRAINING

Sun	Mon	Tues	Wed	Thurs	Fri	Sat
Long Relatively slow	Recovery (Shorter, easy aerobic)	Fast aerobic (Med-long distance)	Recovery (Shorter, aerobic)	Fast aerobic (Med-long distance)	Recovery (Shorter, easy aerobic)	Fast aerobic fartlek

EASY DAYS—HARD DAYS

When you get into hill training and sharpening, which involve anaerobic metabolism and leg-speed work, your training pattern
should ensure that after fatiguing one set of muscles or metabolic
system, you allow it to recover before working it again.

Stress with no letup always spells trouble. Therefore, never
run the same type of workouts consecutively; in fact, hard workouts of any kind are usually followed by a recovery day. This
means if you raced 10km on Saturday (hard aerobic—anaerobic),
and ran long on Sunday (long, slow aerobic), you would recover on
Monday (shorter, slower aerobic). Hard anaerobic intervals on
Tuesday would not be followed by hard anaerobic work on
Wednesday, and not even on Thursday if you weren't ready.
Thursday's workout could be another recovery day or a medium-
effort aerobic workout. When sharpening, a short-sprint workout with full recoveries could also provide recovery after a hard
aerobic or anaerobic day because there's little mileage or lactic
acid build-up.

Today's run depends upon what you ran previously as well as
what you plan to run tomorrow. Some runners habitually violate
this simple yet profound rule because they don't know better. In
others, the work ethic is so ingrained, they are reluctant to back
off long enough to recover. While there must be some pain (discomfort) for gain—no rest, and you don't run your best—to maul
two clichés.

Some runners should work on a one-day-hard—*two*-days-easy
pattern. If the hard run is especially strenuous, three easy days
may be required. Physiologists Jack Daniels and Bob Fitts amplify
this warning, advising that "you should never run hard on a day
when you feel fatigued. Fatigue is a sign that your body is not
ready to be stressed. . . . The purpose of the easy day of running is
to allow your body to recover from the previous hard training
while still allowing you to maintain at least a minimal training
stimulus. Three to five miles of moderate running is enough on an
easy day."

To heed that properly, you have to put it into context. During
the base period, mileage is the primary goal, so you wouldn't run
far or fast enough in any workout to warrant cutting back to three
to five miles (unless you are a beginner and three to five miles is
reasonably far). But when sharpening for races, this advice often

applies. The essence of easy and hard days is that the harder the hard days become, the easier the rests becomes. Whether you rest two days, as Viren and Kenny Moore have, or one day is an individual matter based upon how difficult the hard workout was, and how long it takes to recover. Bill Bowerman says that after a hard workout a runner has to say, " When am I ready to go?' instead of saying, 'Let's go out for another 20-mile run today.' If you do that two days in a row and your name isn't Frank Shorter, you're in deep trouble."

Viren says, "during the competitive season I also employ very slow runs in the forest, 60 to 90 minutes. . . . In this type of training the stress is not heavy. It is the opposite of exhausting interval sessions. . . ." This was Viren's pattern during his competitive season, but it could govern hard and easy days in general.

Grete Waitz also performed better with recovery days between difficult sessions. "I have been resting more in recent seasons," she reported in 1980. "Many middle-distance and long-distance runners are afraid to rest because they think they may lose their form. I used to think like that. I always had to train, and I was always exhausted."

Cliff Temple, British sportswriter and top coach, concludes, "A simple rule of thumb for getting fitter is: Hard work plus rest equals success. Hard work, plus hard work, minus rest, equals injury."

This brings me to an interesting, however annoying, oddity with respect to hard and easy days. There's a Catch-22. In Joseph Heller's superb novel of that name, Yossarian, a flyer during World War II, discovers Catch-22 when he pleads with Doc Daneka to ground him from flying more B-25 combat missions on the grounds that he (Yossarian) is crazy. Doc Daneka agrees that Yossarian would indeed be crazy to fly more missions, but concern for one's own safety in the face of danger is the process of a rational mind. If Yossarian is crazy he can be grounded, and all he has to do is ask, but as soon as he asks, it means he is no longer crazy and has to fly.

The hard days are easy to run and the easy days are hard. You probably are thinking that statement is not the product of a rational mind, but it is quite reasonable. A hard day is preceded by recovery, so you are usually relatively fresh and mentally up. You run the workout, a hard steady run, intervals or whatever, and although it's demanding, there's exhilaration and a sense of performing well. You finish tired, but it's okay; it was quality stuff. You feel uplifted and can't wait to record it in your log.

The next day is an easy run. Short and slow. You're tired. There's nothing exciting about recovering; you're trudging, just serving time, and it hurts. Boring. You can't believe the difference; how you were so tenacious and swift yesterday, and now this. You resist recording the run, and dread tomorrow's run, which is another zinger. But because you're recovered, you run it hard, and it's really quite easy.

The following examples show how a track competitor and a road racer could lay out a week's sharpening work. These examples illustrate only a couple of ways the pattern could be worked out. The actual workouts run are not important so long as they fit the pattern of stress and rest. "Fast anaerobic or speed," Thursday's workout for track competitors, in the example, could be fartlek, fast repetition 400s, a combination of quick 800s, 400s, and 200s, or a 100/100 sprint-float session, or any workout that involves hard anaerobic repeats lasting roughly two minutes or less. Although perhaps on paper 20 × 400s with 100-meter quick-jog recoveries looks like a fast anaerobic workout, the emphasis is on repeated relatively slow runs with very short rests. This type of 20 × 400 workout does not fit Thursday's definition. But it fits Tuesday's. And obviously, the two workouts could be switched.

EXAMPLES OF LAYING OUT A WEEK'S SHARPENING TRAINING

	Sun	Mon	Tues	Wed	Thurs	Fri	Sat
Track	Moderately long	Recovery (Short, easy aerobic)	Longer slower intervals with short rests	Recovery (Easy aerobic)	Fast anaerobic and/or leg-speed	Recovery (Easy aerobic)	Time-trial and/or leg-speed
Road Racer	Long run (Further than important race)	Recovery (Easy aerobic)	Anaerobic repeats	Recovery (Easy aerobic)	Fast aerobic (Med–long distance)	Recovery (Easy aerobic)	Fast aerobic-slightly anaerobic

11.

CONSIDERATIONS FOR CHILDREN AND OLDER RUNNERS

*I*n this third chapter on balancing your training, I am concerned with the effect of the maturing and aging process on one's approach to a season's work. Junior and senior high-school students and most masters runners cannot train as those at their peak competitive years do. Young runners, especially, should view their training over the long term, realizing that if they lay a good foundation at the expense of early results, they will reap bigger benefits later.

That children should try many physical activities before specializing is almost universally supported by successful runners, coaches, and physiologists. Herb Elliott says he "had a wide range of sports activities and enjoyed every single one of them (as a schoolboy). I think if I'd have become a specialist athlete at that particular stage I would have got awfully bored and never gone on to senior ranks." Nowadays Elliott tells kids, "For God's sake do what you enjoy doing and don't get too serious about it." Elliott says you can keep that attitude until about age 18 and still go on to become world-class.

Kids aren't as concerned with technique and tactics as with just running and getting a chance to have fun and experiment.

Rolf Haikkola says it's a mistake for children to do just distance running. "One should," he advises, "be as versatile as possible. By enjoying a variety of sports, a child can learn many things in play: a sense of rhythm, coordination, the mechanics of movement. Later all these things will be very important."

One of the best high-school coaches in the United States is my friend Rick Kleyman, who consistently has more than 100 runners out for cross-country at Armstrong High School in Plymouth, Minnesota, when some other schools have trouble recruiting the five to seven runners necessary for a team. Kleyman's approach is that sport should be fun, and if you also win, so much the better. His runners work hard and improve, but without pressure, and even though they claim a disproportionate share of championship wins and placings, Kleyman would rather see them peak several years later.

When Lasse Viren was once asked what he thought was the greatest fault of the Finnish distance-running system, he replied, "No doubt about that. Too much pressure is put on young athletes. When 10-year-olds are running 'records,' I feel like exploding. . . . They should be playing in sandlots. . . . The most dangerous people are fathers and mothers, coaching their offspring, often disappointed in their own endeavors. They burn out a lot of promising runners." Viren cites a father who asked him why his son ran fine the year before at age 10, but now after doing intervals was running worse. "Intervals," Viren exclaimed, "Let your son run as he likes, not as you like."

Frank Shorter thinks the Africans who learn distance running by trotting more miles to school and back than some kids train, and don't compete until they're physically and mentally mature, have the right approach. Steve Scott says it's just as well he didn't begin running till junior high, and wasn't that good at it.

Left to monitor their own efforts, young runners are naturals at coping with intense activity. Although they do not sweat as freely as adults, they tolerate heat well. Studies have shown their temperatures don't rise much racing 10km, probably because kids don't push as hard as adults.

Kids extract oxygen from the blood better than adults, but they don't tolerate prolonged anaerobic running well. Lydiard recommends that kid's races be either less than 300 meters or longer than a half-mile. Over short distances kids can run fast without getting into severe oxygen debt. Races longer than a half-mile are far enough that most kids begin aerobically. But the 400 is fast and far enough to be punishing, a factor that also has obvious implications for running hard repetitions 400s in training.

CHANGING YOUR TRAINING AS YOU MATURE

Beginners need to raise their VO_2 max more than mature athletes. Experienced runners already have high oxygen uptakes and can go through the build-up more quickly. All that is necessary is to re-establish basic fitness, and then concentrate on stamina and speed. Mature middle-distance runners like Seb Coe do not dwell on mileage, and do more quality work. But inexperienced milers trying to duplicate the training patterns Coe used when he was setting records would probably get into trouble. On the other hand, mature road runners can tolerate *more* mileage at comparatively greater efforts than novices. At each step of your career, as David Moorcroft points out, "Getting the balance between speed and endurance is very important. And it's a delicate balance. To overdo one is to the detriment of the other."

From the beginning it's important that you get experience training for and racing a wide range of events. Those with track and cross-country background may have used interval training to excess in high school or college, but at least they have experience with it. Those brought up on road races often deliberately keep anaerobic work out of their programs because when they tried it, it led to injury or took the fun out of training. Lack of training for and the racing of distances from 800 meters to 5km is especially evident among American women in their late 20s and older, because women's track and cross-country competition used to be unpopular or unavailable.

I'm often asked how New Zealand produces so many world-class women distance runners. What may not be realized is that New Zealand women such as Ann Audain, Mary O'Connor, and Lorraine Moller are just a few among the country's many, most of whom don't race abroad. These women began racing at age 13 or 14 with clubs that provided regular training and competition in track and cross-country. They had years of well-balanced training and racing before road racing. This is precisely what many U.S. women (and men) lack.

In summary, it is important both to increase the relative proportion of fast to slower mileage-oriented training as you mature and to develop a well-rounded background of training and racing. Don't, for example, start out by becoming a "marathoner" or "miler." Mix it up. Specialize at times in track, cross-country, and road racing. Eventually, you'll become better at whatever distances you gravitate toward.

AGING—TRAINING AND PERFORMANCE

Everyone who's lucky becomes an older runner sooner or later. The two questions of most concern as the years pass are how does aging affect training, and how much do race times slow? If you were a competitor at your prime and continue past your peak years, your training and racing times will eventually begin to slow. If you took up running in your 30s or 40s, as, say, Jack Foster and Alex Ratelle did, you can expect to improve for several years. Jack Foster didn't begin running until he was 32. At age 38 he set the world 20-mile track record and at 41 was the silver medalist in the '74 Commonwealth Games marathon with a 2:11:18. Ratelle began in his 40s and at age 56 ran his best marathon (2:31:56).

But what about those who continue past their 20s and into their 30s, 40s, 50s, and so on? Runners past their 20s used to be considered "old." The current trend is to continue competing at a serious level even after performances decline. Strong age-group competition gives the old blokes a chance to shine again. England's Joyce Smith, for example, ran her best marathon (2:29:43) at age 44 and finished 11th in the 1984 Olympic marathon in 2:32:48 at age 46. Carlos Lopes won the World Cross-Country Championship, turned in a 27:17.48 10,000 meters on the track, and then won the 1984 Olympic marathon at age 37. What do these older runners who excel have in common? Why aren't they slowing, or why do they slow so much later and less than one would expect?

As increasing numbers of athletes continue to train and compete past their prime, the factors governing aging become better understood. Genetics play a considerable part, but there are others more important. Perhaps the most important is body image. People slow when they perceive their body image changing. Perceiving themselves as less athletic, they become less active. Aging means "Use it or lose it." "Runners should never even *think* about aging," says Dan Conway of Wisconsin, who at age 45 ran a 2:23 marathon—an age-group record. "If they do, then their times are going to go up. Age is a state of mind."

Many physiologists, such as Dr. Michael Pollock, David Costill, and Ken Cooper, are examining the aging process and releasing many shocking findings. "I'm convinced," said Cooper in early 1983 after examining John A. Kelly, then 76 years old and about to run his 53rd Boston Marathon, "that the gerontology textbooks are perpetuating a myth. Most of the decline that comes with age isn't inevitable at all. It's caused by disuse."

The decline in physical ability due to aging in "normal" sedentary people is fairly well known. After about the early 20s (it varies), VO_2 max and cardiac output start to drop by about one percent per year. The breathing mechanism begins to deterioriate and there is a respiration loss. The ability to transport oxygen to the muscles declines more slowly. Peak cardiac output (max heart rate times the amount of blood ejected each beat) falls by about one percent per year. All these rates seem to accelerate after about age 60.

Those who remain active into their 30s and onward show far less deterioration. Their ability to consume oxygen often rises or levels off during their late 20s. Hal Higdon, for example, showed *no loss* in VO_2 max during the decade of his 40s. As the runners of the 1960s and the '70s running boom mature, they are rewriting

In the World Veteran Games cross-country the "old blokes" negotiate the same barriers as the younger runners do.

the record books almost daily, and there's no end in sight. At a clinic I gave in 1983, the audience was shocked to hear that at age 45 I ran a mile two seconds faster than I did in high school, and a marathon seven minutes faster than I had at age 26.

How much can a runner expect to slow *per year* after his or her peak years *if* a serious commitment to training and racing is maintained? For the marathon is seems to be 45 to 55 seconds, for the 10km about 10 seconds, and for the mile about one second. After age 60 the times might increase at an accelerated rate. Much depends upon genetics, how hungry you remain to run, and by what you truly believe is possible.

Jack Foster, who lost the urge to train during his late 40s, took several breaks for periods up to 10 weeks before getting serious about cracking 2:20:00 for the marathon when he turned 50. When he resumed consistent training he found he could go right out and run steadily for one hour or so without much difficulty. "What had disappeared almost completely," he admitted, "was the ability to run any kind of pace." Foster figured the answer was to incorporate repetition 440s into his program, but he dreaded the idea. Instead, he ran 50-meter sprints but "these just made my legs worse." What Foster finally settled for was interval 1000 meters at marathon race pace with 600-meter recoveries. My hunch is that after becoming proficient at repeat 1000s, Foster could, if he chose, ease into faster 400s and 50s.

I do not believe that aging in itself affects the training structure much except that it becomes increasingly difficult to run hard anaerobic work and sprints. Certainly caution must be observed when masters run speed work, but then everyone must be careful. If it causes injury, try to determine whether the problem is interval or fartlek work per se, and should be eliminated, or if you ran it before you were ready, went at it too fast, or had unrealistic expectations (such as duplicating the 400-meter times you ran 10 years ago).

Most older runners do not run the mileage they did in their 20s, but that's mainly a matter of motivation and priorities. The reason isn't so much they can't, as that they choose not to. Other interests and goals claim higher priority than testing the limits of their physical reserves.

12.

PEAKING

*F*rank Shorter, who won the 1972 Olympic marathon and placed second four years later at Montreal, was, nevertheless, in awe of Lasse Viren's ability to dominate the 5000- and 10,000-meter races at both Games. "He's something," Shorter says of Viren, "really something. I would love to be able to peak the way he does. He knows how to do it, psychologically as well as physically. It's nothing to do with anything else, no doping, drugs, or any of that stuff. The mere fact that everyone is so concerned about that shows what kind of control he has over his competitors."

Lasse Viren said of his ability to peak for the Olympics, "Some do well in other races, some run fast times, but they cannot do well in the ultimate, the Olympics. . . . The question is not why I run this way, but why so many others cannot."

Even many world-class athletes do not recognize the difference between fast times and excelling when it counts most. Viren learned it from Lydiard through Haikkola. Another runner who used the Lydiard peaking method after college to rise to first and second in the world 5000-meter rankings in 1977 and 1978 was Marty Liquori. "It was the Lydiard method that enabled me to drop from 13:40 for 5000 meters in May to 13:15 that July," Liquori says.

There is a difference in the way Viren and Liquori have applied peaking. Viren used it to win on a particular occasion, namely the Olympics. Liquori used it to set records. One involves achieving your best on a *specific day*, the other merely recognizes that training passes through stages, culminating in a period when you will be at your physical and competitive best. A small difference in purpose, but the one requires careful timing, and the other allows you to take your time, racing when training is finished. Both imply a definite completion of training.

The drawback with peaking, Liquori says, is that it is difficult to begin hard training in September for a first race in April. "Psychologically, most of us cannot put off gratification for six months or two years without some encouraging signs that we are doing the right thing."

But Liquori misses a few points, I believe. Your first race is not the Big One. Preliminary races are part of sharpening. They reveal strengths and weaknesses, enabling you to coordinate the remaining training. As for "encouraging signs," your training times and developmental racing—the last half of which can be quite serious—provides much of this.

The alternative to peaking is to simply train and race and hope things get better. This is often the case with runners who come to the Olympics (or any championship) with fast times, or even recent records, and then are flat. Whether you should peak depends upon your goals. Viren wanted Olympic victories and did not much care how he performed during the four years in between.

Viren believed that if he remained in top form during non-Olympic years, his strength would be squandered. Most world-class runners, however, are not willing to risk the rest of their races for a stab at an Olympic medal every four years. Peaking involves sacrifice. To be at your best on a particular occasion implies that you are less than that the remaining time. It's a trade-off: several fairly good races over many months, and perhaps a show of brilliance if you happen to get hot, versus gambling upon a superb performance when you really want it in exchange for doing what you can the rest of the time. Peaking means putting most of your

Portugal's Carlos Lopes is another elite marathoner who came up through the ranks of track and cross-country. Here, a few months before his Olympic marathon victory, Lopes clears the last hay barrier on his way to winning the World Cross-Country Championships.

eggs in one basket. Liquori, whom I used as an example of someone who went after fast times, recognized and endorsed this when
he said, "But whether the runner is going for the One Big Race, or
for a series of weekend victories, my recommendation is that he or
she picks one big race to be the ultimate test for the season."

MULTIPLE PEAKING

Multiple peaking is bringing yourself into peak condition, racing,
backing off to recharge your mental and physical batteries, then
resharpening for another race or races. The converse of multiple
peaking is not easing back during the interval between major
races.

Bill Baillie told me that in the early 1960s when Lydiard
coached him, Halberg, Snell, Magee, and Davies, they would all
get together at the beginning of each session to decide which of
the major upcoming races each would target. Rather than fight for

*Women's cross-country abroad. A background of cross-
country and track racing provides the foundation for road racing.*

every victory, each would pick two or three races he wanted to win. Since Lydiard's runners were the best in New Zealand, they shut everyone else out and split virtually all the titles among themselves. Because they could race hard, back off, recuperate, and then peak again, they were at their best in the races they wanted to win.

They recognized that instead of trying for everything, it was better to focus on a few races and make sure they won those. Baillie said he almost always won these he picked. But the problem with multiple peaking is deciding how to treat the training between major races. In blocking out a season it is rarely so simple as going through all the part of training till you peak, racing the big one, backing off, and then rebuilding and peaking again. Your important races may be a few weeks apart or a month or two apart. Another may occur a few weeks later. What then—try to hold your peak, or back off and repeak? The solution is sometimes tricky as Viren discovered before the 1972 Olympics.

Viren was not a shoo-in to make the team, and had to show the selectors he could run in July in order to run the Games in September. Haikkola describes the situation: "Lasse had to show Olympic form for the Finnish selectors, and he had to reach this form sooner than we really wanted him to. Originally we had planned the training schedule so that Lasse was ready to peak in late August and early September. But in July he had to run in the match against Great Britain and Spain. Lasse would not make the Olympic team if he ran badly in this race, and it would have been most difficult to go on after a terrible beating. . . . We had an alternate plan: two peaks, the first in June, the second for the Olympics."

But there wasn't enough time to slack off and resharpen. Consequently, Haikkola chose the steady approach and the only target was Munich. Fortunately, Viren won the 5000 in July in 13:19. Yet Viren claims that he reached his peak in July and August of 1972, prior to the Games in September. "I was better than my training was telling.' said Viren in 1980. "I had to peak earlier than we had been planning, because the Finnish Federation got impatient. I had to show I was worth going to Munich. During the games, I was already losing some of my best form."

America's marathoners usually face the same problem in qualifying for the Olympics. In 1984, for example, there were only

11 weeks between the trials and the Games, too long to hold a peak and not long enough to recover and then rebuild.

There is no standard formula for peaking. If, for example, short road or track races preceed a marathon, you could cut some leg-speed training before the marathon and stress endurance and stamina-oriented interval work. If you race exclusively from one to six miles, and don't have time to back off and resharpen, you must maintain speed throughout. Perhaps the most perplexing combination is a series of marathons, because it's difficult to recuperate (especially mentally) between them.

Contrary to popular notion that marathons must occur several months apart, I discovered that one could, if necessary, race three marathons a month apart. In 1967 I tried to qualify at Boston for expenses to the National Marathon Championship. It was hot and I missed by a minute. Three weeks later I raced another marathon, winning and bettering the qualifying standard. Four weeks later I won the Nationals.

But to race bang-bang-bang, I had to follow three simple rules. One is to be practically in top form by the first one. Another is to refrain from rushing into hard training after the race. Rest and then get a few sharp workouts before resting again, and you will be ready again quite quickly. Thirdly, one of the races should be less intense, perhaps one with an absence of tough competition or importance.

I used this strategy with Lorraine Moller in 1980 when she coasted through the Grandma's Marathon in Duluth, Minnesota in June to win in 2:38:36, ran hard to win the Avon women's championship in London five weeks later, and then won the Nike Marathon in Eugene, Oregon in 2:31:42 in another five weeks. The next year, in June, she won the Grandma's in 2:29:34 (on two month's training), won easily in Rio de Janeiro in August (2:34:52), and then ran hard four weeks later in 84-degree heat to win the Nike Marathon in 3:31:15. That combination of performances earned her second place in the world rankings that year.

TIMING AND HOLDING A PEAK

Haikkola says it takes no more than four weeks for a basically fit runner to reach a peak. "In itself," he claims, "it is quite easy . . . to reach the peak. All one needs is a faster pace in training, short enough intervals, and constant pressure in repetition training. However, Haikkola, is speaking of track races requiring speed over relatively short distances. For short races, hard distance work is behind you when you sharpen to a peak. As Haikkola says of Viren's final preparations for the Games: "Before Munich and Montreal, we aimed at the same goal: to create as tough a base as possible, then peak at the last possible moment. . . ."

Peaking is perhaps even more mental than physical. It's no good being in top physical condition if you aren't hungry to dig deep when races get competitive. After the 1968 Olympics, for example, I decided to race the City of Lakes Marathon in the Twin Cities a few weeks later. I didn't really have to train, and no doubt could win. Yet, back home and 100 yards into my first run, I stoped, said, "That's it!" and walked back. Emotionally I'd had it. Running was revolting. I had emotionally peaked for the Games, and now it was gone. But, after a three-week layoff, I was chomping at the bit to get ready for the indoor season and next year's Boston Marathon, nearly five months away.

As the big race approaches, your resolve can sometimes evaporate. Suddenly the race doesn't seem to matter. This may be a defense mechanism which isolates you from the unbearable pressures of those last couple of weeks or days when the enormity of what you are in for evolves from heroic fantasy to imminent reality. If it happens to you, it will be a difficult period requiring the tenacity to continue without panicking and the courage to stick to your goals. Unless you are unflappable, you either give up or else train so hard you ruin your chances.

Relative beginners may find the concept and application of peaking difficult. But I believe it is imortant to recognize that at various times one races better than at others. As you progress through the stages of training, be aware of when you raced best before, and try to isolate the factors responsible. Questions to ask are:

1. How many anaerobic workouts can I optimally handle a week?
2. How fast should I lower my training times when sharpening?
3. How far back do I have to ease up in training in order to race fresh and rested?

4. How many weeks after I began sharpening did I race best?
5. How long did the peak last?

That way, when you set up the next season's program, you will be better able to structure and fine-tune your preparations.

13.
THE SCHEDULES

*T*he schedules that follow represent a stylized approach for runners possessing an "average" blend of endurance, stamina, and speed, who have no special problems and who have enough weeks available for all the training. If you are injury-prone, recover slowly, have exceptionally good or below-average speed, are short on time before the big race, or get sick during the season, modifications will have to be made.

If you are basically fit when deciding to target a major race, you will be able to dispense with much of the base conditioning and allot more time to sharpening, especially if you are one who needs to exercise caution when developing speed. Some runners sharpen easily and don't require much fast running. Amby Burfoot was one of these; he could train at seven to eight minutes per mile and then, after two or three track races, run 13:45 for three miles. Most others capable of 13:45, however, would require a lot more fast training.

Are you prone to back or knee injuries? Then you must either carefully monitor your hill running, or perhaps eliminate it altogether. You also might have to pass up hilly races. If you can't run hills, you will have to get that kind of training effect with other work, perhaps running up stairs, uphill on a treadmill (which means you never have to run back down), running in water, or with machines such as the Nautilus.

SCHEDULE ORGANIZATION _____

It doesn't make sense to me to design separate programs for girls, women, boys, men, masters, and so on. Many young runners outrun mature runners in their late 20s. Many old-timers run the pants off those 20 to 30 years younger. If a woman and man are relatively fast, why shouldn't they train along the same lines? If a master can run a 2:30 marathon, why shouldn't he (or she if it was Britain's Joyce Smith when she was 44), train at roughly the same level as someone 25 who runs 2:30?

Adjustments *do* have to be made between young runners and masters who race at the same level, because their bodies are different. The young are *generally* more supple and quicker, while older runners generally can't tolerate as much fast repetition work and are more injury-prone. But masters are not as homogenous a group as runners with similar backgrounds and talents. Thus, a 40-year-old, inactive for 20 years and now running, would not resemble another 40-year-old who has been at it for 20 years. The beginning master may have more in common with a beginning 20-year-old, and would approach training similarly. Consequently, I've designed training programs according to *performance* level for those running their *major* competitive efforts in one of three distance ranges. Equivalent male and female performances differ by about 30 seconds *per mile* across all distances. In other words, a 5:20 mile for a female is roughly equivalent to a male clocking 4:50. A woman's 2:38 marathon is about equivalent to a male's 2:25. This is the rationale for the male-female time differences at each performance level in the table on page 198. To select the schedule you should be using, use your race times to determine your performance level.

PERFORMANCE LEVEL		PRIMARY RACING RANGE AND TIMES				
		Mile to 5km		10km to 30km		Marathon
Relative Beginner		Those training ≅ 35 MPW Those training ≅ 50 MPW		Those training ≅ 35 MPW Those training ≅ 50 MPW		Those training ≅ 50 MPW
		Mile	5km	10km	30km	Marathon
Intermediate Level	Male	5:30–4:50	20:00–17:00	40:00–35:00	2:20–1:59	3:30–2:50
	Female	6:00–5:20	21:30–18:30	43:00–38:10	2:30–2:08	3:43–3:03
Advanced Level	Male	4:50–4:15	17:00–14:45	35:00–31:00	1:59–1:40	2:50–2:25
	Female	5:20–4:45	18:30–16:15	38:10–33:10	2:08–1:49	3:03–2:38
Elite Level	Male	Sub 4:15	Sub 14:45	Sub 31:00	Sub 1:40	Sub 2:25
	Female	Sub 4:45	Sub 16:15	Sub 33:10	Sub 1:49	Sub 2:38

Those racing 5km one week and a 10km or marathon another, would blend the 5km, 10km, and marathon schedules. But usually, although racing a wide range of distances, one spends a period of time or session competing over a relatively narrow range, say 5 to 15km, and then builds for a major mile or marathon. A reasonable approach then would be to first use the program for 10km competitors, and then come in midway through the marathon or mile to 5km schedule. But a lot depends upon how races are scheduled, and time available. Realize that the schedules are designed for someone starting the season who has roughly 20 weeks to prepare for the major race(s). Often, however, you will not be faced with so simple a situation.

DEFINITION OF EFFORTS USED IN THE SCHEDULES

RECOVERY (R)

The main consideration is that the effort and distance are easy enough that you are not stressed afterward. It's just an active rest that warms and loosens you. Often during these workouts there is an anxiousness to get going or a feeling that the run is too slow to be worthwhile. This is what you want.

EASY (E)

A notch harder than recovery effort, but upon finishing you should feel as though it wouldn't be difficult to run more (unless it's the long Sunday run, which, upon finishing, you are almost always willing to stop).

MODERATE (M)

Now you are conscious of working. When you finish a moderate effort workout you should be able to do more, but feel fairly content not to have to. If running fartlek or intervals, some of the fast sections could be fairly hard, but the overall workout would not.

HARD (H)

Requires concentration and perseverance to hold the pace. Try to use as little "competitive energy" as possible, especially when with others. You should be quite tired afterward but not exhausted. Going faster would have been racing or nonproductive as a workout.

TIME-TRIAL (T-T)

These are *controlled* efforts over a particular distance in a specific time. They are not unsanctioned races. They need not be all-out efforts. They are used to provide a tough sustained workout and/or gauge your current condition. The goal may be even splits, or pace variations such as a 3-mile with the first mile in 6:00, the second in 5:50 and the third in 5:40. Or it may be two miles every other week at the same speed, checking your pulse to see if you can repeat the performance doing less work.

INTERVAL TRAINING SHORTHAND

A workout such as "15 × 400/100" means to alternate 15 faster 400-meter runs with 15 100-meter jogs. "4 × 1200/pulse 100" means to run four hard 1200-meter (¾ mile) runs, walking and jogging in between each until your pulse drops to about 100.

SCHEDULE LAYOUT

The first tier in the weekly schedules that follow indicates the type of workout, the middle tier the effort, and the bottom tier gives examples of the kinds of workouts you could do.

RELATIVE BEGINNERS*

Be patient. Like dieters, now that the spirit has moved you, you either want to drop 20 pounds a week or race a marathon in two months. Hold off on marathoning, develop a varied background, and begin with modest goals. You'll perform better with fewer injuries. Although I recommend that relative beginners hold off on running a marathon for a few years, for those who want to anyway, I'm providing a schedule for those training about 50 miles per week.

When beginning a season, cardiovascular development gets ahead of muscular, skeletal, and tendon development. After a few weeks you will be able to run farther and faster than your muscles and connective tissue can stand. Then, with little warning, you get injured. Instead, hold back at the beginning. Know you could do more. Better to be slightly undertrained and healthy, than having been fit, but now laid up.

My schedules have you running almost every day. But some days will be little more than a warmup. If you begin easily, you won't need days off. Structure your season's schedule to include all the phases of training. The emphasis the first few seasons is on aerobic training, but also experience some anaerobic and sharpening work. As Liquori warns, "The womb-like serenity of [base training] has trapped many a runner. Hypnotized by the simplicity and relative ease of the long, easy runs, they put off [fast training]. They become . . . 'training rats' or 'distance bums' destined to eke out glory . . . not from races but . . . mileage."

I worked with a woman capable of running the qualifying standard for the Olympic marathon trials, who had never run an interval workout and didn't know the distance around an outdoor track. When I asked for her best 100, 200, mile and 2-mile times, she confessed she had never raced or time-trialed these distances. When I took her to the track to time-trial 200 meters to gauge her basic speed, it became apparent she didn't know how to warm up to run the 6 × 800s scheduled afterward. This is typical of road runners who have never run track or cross-country.

* Someone who has run recreationally, but has not seriously trained or raced.

MILE–5km _____

1. BUILDING TO YOUR TARGET MILEAGE. Run easily each day, gradually building your target weekly mileage. Take as long as you need. Few beginners should tackle more than 50 miles per week. Much less than 35 isn't training. If signs of impending injury develop, back off. Speed is not important; mileage and/or time on your feet is. Tackle one goal at a time. Trying to improve your distance *and* speed at the same time increases the risk of overwork and injury. When you can run 35 to 50 miles per week for two consecutive weeks without straining, go to 2 below.

2. AEROBIC BASE. The goal is to raise your VO$_2$ max and general fitness level by varying daily mileages and efforts and placing recovery days between harder ones. Hold the same weekly mileage, but run increasingly more of it at faster aerobic speeds. Pick rolling terrain when not recovering. Don't run on the track. Don't kick in on the ends of runs. Begin easily the first five to ten minutes of any run. Wear good running shoes, not tennis or cheap "training shoes" from discount stores. Good shoes cost much less than a good foot doctor. Ideally, you should spend about six weeks on either of the following schedules:

35 MILES PER WEEK

Sun	Mon	Tues	Wed	Thurs	Fri	Sat
Week's longest	Recovery	Faster aerobic	Recover	Steady aerobic	Recovery	Steady aerobic
E	E	E—M	R	E—M	R	E—M
9 miles	3 miles	6 miles aerobic fartlek	3 miles	5 miles	3 miles	6 miles

50 MILES PER WEEK

Sun	Mon	Tues	Wed	Thurs	Fri	Sat
Week's longest	Recovery	Faster aerobic	Recovery	Steady aerobic	Recovery	Steady aerobic
E	E	M	E	M	E	M
11 miles	4 miles	7 miles	6 miles	8 miles aerobic fartlek	6 miles	8 miles

3. INTRODUCTORY ANAEROBIC. (For 4 weeks)

35 MILES PER WEEK

Sun	Mon	Tues	Wed	Thurs	Fri	Sat
Week's longest	Recovery	Resistance	Recovery	Fast aerobic	Recovery	Resistance
E	R	M	R	M	R	M
10 miles	3 miles	Run up 100- to 200-meter hill, jog 200 downhill easy stride. Repeat 10 times. 5 miles total	3 miles	6 miles aerobic fartlek	3 miles	Repeat Tues workout

50 MILES PER WEEK

Sun	Mon	Tues	Wed	Thurs	Fri	Sat
Week's longest	Recovery	Resistance	Recovery	Fast aerobic	Recovery	Resistance
E	E	M	E	M	E	M
12 miles	6 miles	Same as above. 6 miles total	8 miles	6 miles fartlek or intervals like 12 × 400/100	6 miles	Repeat Tues workout

Comments: The hill workout involves warming up, running a 100- to 200-meter hill at a moderate effort, jogging an equal distance recovery, and relaxed running down the hill. Run on grass or trails if at all possible. Jog warmdown.

Aerobic fartlek should also be on rolling soft surfaces. Because the aerobic stride-outs are not fast, keep the rests fairly quick and short. Just enough to recover.

The interval 200s, 400s or 600s are not particularly fast, but again the rests should be quick and short, about ¼ the distance of the faster sections.

4. SHARPENING. (For 4 weeks)

35 MILES PER WEEK

Sun	Mon	Tues	Wed	Thurs	Fri	Sat
Week's longest	Recovery	Aerobic-anaerobic	Recovery	Easy anaerobic	Recovery	Fast aerobic and leg-speed
M	E	H	R	M	R	H
8 miles	4 miles	6 miles fartlek with 100–2000 meter sections	3 miles	Intervals. 200–600 meter 6 miles total	3 miles	T-T. 1½ × race distance. Jog. 10 × 100/200 stride-outs

50 MILES PER WEEK

Sun	Mon	Tues	Wed	Thurs	Fri	Sat
Week's longest	Recovery	Anaerobic	Recovery	Anaerobic	Recovery	Fast aerobic and leg-speed
E—M	E	H	E	M	R	M—H
10 miles	5 miles	8 miles fartlek with 100–2000 meter sections	6 miles	Intervals. 200–600 meter. 8 miles total	5 miles	T-T. 1½ × race distance. Jog. 2 sets 10 × 100/100

Comments: The fartlek and intervals should be somewhat anaerobic with longer rests. Use Saturday's T-T to run a little faster each week *without* increasing the effort.(Don't race).

5. RACING. (During the racing season)

35 MILES PER WEEK

Sun	Mon	Tues	Wed	Thurs	Fri	Sat
Long aerobic	Recovery	Leg-speed	Recovery	Fast aerobic	Recovery	Race, or T-T.
E	R	Brief H	R	M	R	H—All out
6 miles	4 miles	3-mile warmup, 2 miles of 100/100, mile jog	3 miles	4–6 miles fartlek	3 miles	Race, or T-T. ¾ normal race distance

50 MILES PER WEEK
(Same as above)

6. WEEK OF THE BIG RACE.

35 MILES PER WEEK

Sun	Mon	Tues	Wed	Thurs	Fri	Sat
Recovery	Fast aerobic	Leg-speed	Recovery	Leg-speed	Recovery	Race
E	M	H	E	M—H	R	All out
6 miles	6 miles fun fartlek	2 × 400/400 2 × 200/200	5 miles	3-mile warmup 4 × 100/200, mile easy	3 miles	Big Race

Comments: It's important that there is no sensation of racing on the leg-speed or fartlek workouts. Run fairly hard, but try not to conjure up any competitive emotion. If running with others and someone takes off, let him or her go unless you can accelerate gradually with no feeling of racing.

50 MILES PER WEEK
(Same as above)

10KM–30KM (35 MILES PER WEEK) _____
1. BUILD TO YOUR TARGET MILEAGE. Same as Mile–5km.
2. AEROBIC BASE. Same as Mile–5km.
3. HILL (RESISTANCE) RUNNING. (For 4 weeks).

Sun	Mon	Tues	Wed	Thurs	Fri	Sat
Week's longest	Recovery	Resistance	Aerobic	Recovery	Resistance	Recovery
E	R	M	E—M	R	M	E
10–12 miles	3 miles	200-meter hills, up and down with jog rests. 4 miles total	6 miles	3 miles	Same as Tues, except 5 miles	4 miles

Comments: See 3. Introductory Anaerobic, Mile–5km.

4. SHARPENING. (During the racing season)

Sun	Mon	Tues	Wed	Thurs	Fri	Sat
Week's longest	Recovery	Anaerobic	Recovery	Anaerobic	Recovery	Race or T-Ts
E	E	H	R	M	R	H—All out
10–15 miles	4 miles	Repetitions lasting 3–5 minutes, or fartlek, or 2 sets 5 × 400/100. Total 6 miles	3 miles	Shorter, sharper fartlek, or interval 1200s, or up and down hills. 4–5 miles total	3 miles	Race or hard 10km, or 2 × 5km/800

RELATIVE BEGINNERS
10KM–30KM

5. WEEK OF THE BIG RACE.

Sun	Mon	Tues	Wed	Thurs	Fri	Sat
Aerobic	Recovery	Anaerobic	Leg-speed	Recovery	Recovery	Race
E	E	H	M	R—E	R	All out
6 miles	3 miles	Mile fast, mile jog, 800 fast	6 × 100/100	4 miles or no running	3 miles	Big Race

Comments: See comments for Week of the Big Race, 35 miles per week.

10KM–30KM (50 MILES PER WEEK) _____

1. BUILD TO YOUR TARGET MILEAGE. Same as Mile–5km.
2. AEROBIC BASE. Same as Mile–5km.
3. HILL (RESISTANCE) TRAINING. (For 4 weeks)

Sun	Mon	Tues	Wed	Thurs	Fri	Sat
Week's longest	Recovery	Resistance	Recovery	Resistance	Recovery	Aerobic
E	E	M	E	M	E	M
15 miles	6 miles	Up and down 200-meter hills with jog rests. 7 miles total	4 miles	Same as Tues	4 miles	7 miles

Comments: See comments for Introductory Anaerobic, Mile–5km.

4. SHARPENING. (During the racing season)

Sun	Mon	Tues	Wed	Thurs	Fri	Sat
Week's longest	Recovery	Anaerobic	Recovery	Anaerobic	Recovery	Race or hard aerobic
E	E	H	E	M	R	H or All out
10–15 miles	4 miles	Up and down 200-meter hills with jog rests. 9 miles total	6 miles	Short, sharp fartlek or interval 1200s or up and down hills. 8 miles total	3 miles	Race or 10km–10 miles hard, or 2 × 5km hard

5. WEEK OF THE BIG RACE.

Sun	Mon	Tues	Wed	Thurs	Fri	Sat
Aerobic	Recovery	Anaerobic	Leg-speed	Recovery	Recovery	Race
E	E	H	E	R—E	R	All out
10 miles	3 miles	2 × 800/400, 2 × 400/200, 2 × 200/200	6 miles	6 miles or no running	3 miles	Big Race

Comments: See comments for 6. Week of the Big Race, Mile–5km.

MARATHONERS—50 MILES PER WEEK _____

1. BUILD TO YOUR TARGET MILEAGE. Same as Mile–5km.
2. HILL (RESISTANCE) TRAINING. Same as 10km–30km.
3. PRELIMINARY ANAEROBIC. (For 4 weeks)

Sun	Mon	Tues	Wed	Thurs	Fri	Sat
Week's longest	Recovery	Recovery	Easy anaerobic	Recovery	Fast aerobic	Recovery
E	R	E	M—H	R	M—H	E
15–20 miles	3 miles	4 miles	10 miles or repeat 800s-mile	3 miles	2 x 2 mile/800 or 6 miles	4 miles

Comments: The 10 miles hard on Wednesday could be steady pace or aerobic fartlek. If you choose repeat 800s to miles, the actual distances run don't matter as much as that they dip into the anaerobic, and the recoveries are relatively quick, short jogs, say 200s between 800s, and 400s between repeat miles. The same holds for Friday's workout.

4. MARATHON SHARPENING. (For 4 weeks)

Sun	Mon	Tues	Wed	Thurs	Fri	Sat
Week's longest	Recovery	Aerobic–anaerobic	Recovery	Aerobic–anaerobic	Aerobic	Recovery
E	R	M	E	M—H	M	E
Alternate 18- and 22-milers each week	3 miles	6 miles fartlek	4 miles	8 miles fartlek or 20 x 400/100	10 miles	3 miles

Comments: Eighteen to 22 miles may seem far for Sunday, but if you can't jog 18 to 22, how can you compete for 26? Thursday's fartlek or 20 x 400/100 should be sharper than the running done on Wednesdays and Fridays in 3 above.

RELATIVE BEGINNERS
MARATHON

5. RACING. (During the racing season)

Sun	Mon	Tues	Wed	Thurs	Fri	Sat
Week's longest	Recovery	Aerobic	Aerobic	Anerobic	Recovery	Race or leg-speed
E	R	M	E	M if race. Otherwise H	R	All out if race, or M
15 miles if race last Sat. Otherwise 18	3 miles	10–12 miles	4 miles	If race Sat, 45 min. fartlek. Or 3–4 × mile/400	3–4 miles	Non marathon race or 12 × 200/200

Comments: If you are racing on Saturday, just run 45 minutes of fartlek with a few sharp stride-outs on Thursday. Keep it fun and not too difficult. If not racing, then run 3 to 4 × one mile hard. Saturday's workout (if not racing) should include short sharp stride-outs of the type shown in the example. Don't run so fast that you are sore for Sunday's run.

6. WEEK OF THE MARATHON.

Sun	Mon	Tues	Wed	Thurs	Fri	Sat
Week's longest	Recovery	Faster aerobic and leg-speed	Recovery	Recovery	Recovery	Race
E	R	H	—	E	R	All out
12–14 miles	3 miles	5km T-T., jog mile, 4 × 100/100	No run	6 miles	2–3 miles	Marathon

Comments: Keep Tuesday's 5km T-T non-competitive. Run hard, but don't use your "competitive energy." You'll be tired afterward, but after a mile jog recovery, you should be able to work into four 100-meter stride-outs. You'll resist starting the first one, but by the 3rd and 4th, they'll be fun. This is a short, sharp workout. You'll get tired, but you'll also recover fast.

Take Wednesday off. Go for a hike, or walk and just relax. Think about the race you want to run on Saturday.

INTERMEDIATE LEVEL PERFORMANCES

MILE—5KM. _____

1. BUILD TO TARGET MILEAGE as quickly and comfortably as possible, keeping the daily efforts roughly the same and not too difficult. Perhaps 60 to 70 miles per week (7–11 miles per day).

2. AEROBIC TRAINING. Hold target mileage. (For 5-6 weeks).

Sun	Mon	Tues	Wed	Thurs	Fri	Sat
Week's longest	Recovery	Aerobic	Fast aerobic	Aerobic	Recovery	Hard aerobic
E	E	M	E	M	E	M—H
14–17 miles	6 miles	8 miles aerobic fartlek	6–7 miles	10–12 miles	6 miles	8 miles

Comments: Review the definition of aerobic fartlek in Chapter 7 if you have any doubts about how to run Wednesday's workout.

3. HILL TRAINING. Drop the week's mileage by 10 percent. (For 4 weeks)

Sun	Mon	Tues	Wed	Thurs	Fri	Sat
Week's longest	Recovery	Hills	Recovery	Hills, easy anaerobic	Recovery	Hills
E	E	M—H	E	M—H	E	M—H
15 miles	5 miles	Hill workout totaling 9 miles	5 miles	9-mile hill workout or 9 miles of hilly fartlek	5 miles	9-mile hill workout

Comments: Review the description of hill training in Chapter 9 if there is any doubt about how to set up this workout. The hill workout, including warmup and cooldown, should cover about nine miles. Back off if you develop soreness.

INTERMEDIATE LEVEL PERFORMANCES
MILE–5KM

4. ANAEROBIC TRAINING. Raise the week's mileage by 10 percent. (For 4 weeks)

Sun	Mon	Tues	Wed	Thurs	Fri	Sat
Week's longest	Recovery	Beginning anaerobic	Recovery	Fast aerobic	Recovery	Striding
M	E	M—H	E	M	E	M
10 miles	5 miles	20 × 400/100 or 9 miles fartlek, short rests plus skipping and bounding exercises	5 miles	Hill workout or 6 miles plus skipping exercises	5 miles	Interval 100s, and/or 200s with equal dist. jog recovery or 3–4 × 600–800/ pulse 100

Comments: See the comments on the 20 × 400/100 workout in 4 of the Relative Beginner Schedule. When doing Saturday's interval 100s to 200s, do them until you feel you've had enough. Don't go on until you lose control or end up sore.

5. SHARPENING. Drop the week's mileage by 10 percent. (For 4 weeks)

Sun	Mon	Tues	Wed	Thurs	Fri	Sat
Week's longest	Recovery	Anaerobic	Recovery	Anaerobic or Hard aerobic	Recovery	Time-trial & Leg-speed
M	E	H	E	H	R	H
10 miles	5 miles	3 × 800–1200/ pulse 100 plus 6 × 200/200	5 miles	6–8 miles sharp fartlek or 8 miles hard aerobic pace	3–5 miles	Time-trial 800–3000 meters plus 30-min, leg-speed fartlek

6. RACING. Drop the week's mileage by 20 to 30 percent.

Sun	Mon	Tues	Wed	Thurs	Fri	Sat
Long relaxed	Leg-speed	Recovery	Relaxed fast	Long recovery	Recovery	Race
E—M	M—H	R	M	E—M	R	All out
6–8 miles	1–2 miles of 50/50 or 100s, 200s fast with complete rests	3 miles	Easy fartlek (If high school, perhaps race)	8 miles	3 miles	Race

Comments: High-schoolers should use this pattern during the racing season. If you have Wednesday races, try to enter distances above or below your primary racing distance and take it less seriously than Saturday's competition.

10KM—30KM

1. BUILDING TO YOUR TARGET MILEAGE. Same as for Mile–5km
2. AEROBIC BASE. Same as Mile–5km
3. BEGINNING ANAEROBIC. (For 4–5 weeks)

Sun	Mon	Tues	Wed	Thurs	Fri	Sat
Week's longest	Recovery	Anaerobic–anaerobic	Recovery	Aerobic–anaerobic	Recovery	Beginning anaerobic
E	E	M—H	E	M	E	H
15–17 miles	6–8 miles	Hill workout or 5–10km T-T or 9 miles fartlek	6–8 miles	8–9 miles fartlek	5–6 miles	20 × 400/100

Comments: For an explanation of the 20 × 400/100 workout, see the comments in 4. Relative Beginner Marathon Sharpening.

INTERMEDIATE LEVEL PERFORMANCES
10KM–30KM

4. SHARPENING. (For 4 weeks)

Sun	Mon	Tues	Wed	Thurs	Fri	Sat
Week's longest	Recovery	Anaerobic	Recovery	Aerobic	Recovery	Race or anaerobic
E	E	M—H	E	M	R	H
15–17 miles	6–8 miles	Faster 400/200s to 800/400s or sharp fartlek	8–10 miles	12 miles	3 miles	3-4 × ¾-mile/pulse 100

5. RACING. (During a race week—otherwise use 4)

Sun	Mon	Tues	Wed	Thurs	Fri	Sat
Aerobic	Leg-speed	Aerobic	Aerobic-anaerobic	Rest	Rest	Race
E	M	E	M	R	R	All out
10–15 miles	Sharp 100s and 200s with complete rests	8 miles	5–8 miles with stride-outs en route	No run	3 miles	Race

Comments: Monday's leg-speed should consist of something like 8 × 100s or 6 × 200s. Wednesday's workout should be a fun, basically easy run with 4 to 5 quick accelerations of 100 to 200 meters. Take Thursday off. Go for a hike or walk and just relax.

MARATHON _____

1. BUILDING TO YOUR TARGET MILEAGE. Same as Mile–5km
2. AEROBIC BASE. Same as Mile–5km
3. HILL TRAINING. Same as 10km–30km
4. AEROBIC-ANAEROBIC. (For 4 weeks)

Sun	Mon	Tues	Wed	Thurs	Fri	Sat
Week's longest	Recovery	Aerobic-anaerobic	Recovery	Steady aerobic	Recovery	Anaerobic
E	E	M—H	E	M	E	M—H
20 miles	6 miles	Hill workout or 10km T-T or 8 miles fartlek	8 miles	12 miles	6 miles	Interval 200s to 800s, the fast sections totaling to 3 miles

5. SHARPENING AND RACING. (During the racing season)

Sun	Mon	Tues	Wed	Thurs	Fri	Sat
Week's longest	Recovery	aerobic	recovery	Aerobic-anaerobic	Recovery	Race or fast aerobic
E	E	M—H	E	M	R—E	All out or H
18 miles E when race day before. Otherwise, 22 miles (perhaps with a few mile surges)	6-8 miles	12-14 miles (perhaps in 3 faster parts)	6-8 miles	8-10 miles fartlek with some sharp hills	3-8 miles	Race, T-T, 2×5km/800, 6× mile/400 or 10 × 400/200 quick jog

Comments: If you run Tuesday's 12- to 14-miler in three faster sections, have two 3/4-mile rest sections (about a minute per mile slower than the fast sections). Don't race more frequently

INTERMEDIATE LEVEL PERFORMANCES
MARATHON

than every other week. Good race distances are from 5km to 20km. If you can, race 25km 3 to 4 weeks before the marathon.

6. WEEK OF THE MARATHON.

Sun	Mon	Tues	Wed	Thurs	Fri	Sat
Aerobic	Aerobic	Fast aerobic and leg-speed	Rest	Recovery	Rest	Race
E	E	H	—	E	R	All out
12–14 miles	8–10 miles	5km T-T., jog mile, 4–6 × 100/100	No run	6 miles	3 miles	Marathon

Comments: See the comments for 6. Relative Beginner, Week of the Marathon, for an explanation of this week's work.

ADVANCED LEVEL PERFORMANCES

MILE—5KM _____

1. BUILD TO TARGET MILEAGE as quickly and comfortable as possible, keeping the daily efforts roughly the same and not too difficult. Perhaps 70 to 90 miles per week.

2. AEROBIC BASE. Hold target mileage. (For 5–6 weeks)

Sun	Mon	Tues	Wed	Thurs	Fri	Sat
Week's longest	Recovery	Faster aerobic	Aerobic	Sustained aerobic	Recovery	Fast aerobic
E	E	M—H	E	M	E	M—H
15–20 miles	8–12 miles	10–12 miles aerobic fartlek plus skipping and bounding exercises	10 miles	15 miles	8 miles	10 miles aerobic fartlek or 15 × 400/100 or 15–20 × 200/100 or 10 miles steady

Comments: If you have any doubts about how to run aerobic fartlek, review that section in Chapter 7. If you have any doubts about how to run 15 × 400/100, or 15 × 200/100, see the comments in 4, Relative Beginner Marathon schedule.

3. HILL TRAINING. Cut mileage about 10 percent. (For 4 weeks)

Sun	Mon	Tues	Wed	Thurs	Fri	Sat
Week's longest	Aerobic	Resistance	Aerobic	Resistance	Aerobic	Resistance and/or anaerobic
E	E	M—H	E	M—H	E	M—H
15 miles	10 miles	Hill workout totaling 10–14 miles	10 miles	Hill workout totaling 10–14 miles	10 miles	Hill workout or 10 miles of hilly fartlek

Comments: If there are any doubts about how to run this hill workout, review that section in Chapter 9.

ADVANCED LEVEL PERFORMANCES
MILE–5KM

4. PRELIMINARY ANAEROBIC. (For 4 weeks)

Sun	Mon	Tues	Wed	Thurs	Fri	Sat
Week's longest	Recovery	Resistance-anaerobic	Recovery	Anaerobic-anaerobic	Recovery	T.-T. and leg-speed
E	E	M—H	E	M—H	E	M—H
15 miles	10 miles	Hill workout or sharp fartlek or 10 × 400/200 plus skipping and bounding exercises if no hill workout	8 miles	2 × mile/600, 2 × 800/400, 2 × 400/200, 2 × 200/100 plus skip and bounding exercises	8 miles	T-T over or under normal race distance plus 8–10 × 100/100

5. SHARPENING. (For 4 weeks)

Sun	Mon	Tues	Wed	Thurs	Fri	Sat
Week's longest	Recovery	T-Ts and anaerobic	Recovery	Anaerobic-anaerobic	Recovery	T-T, and anaerobic
E	E	M—H	E	M	E	H
15 miles	6–8 miles	T-T 1½ mile, T-T 800 plus 10 × 200/200, plus skipping and bounding exercises	6–8 miles	8–10 miles fartlek plus skipping and bounding exercises	8 miles	T-T or 3 × 800 fast/600 plus 10 × 100/100 plus skipping and bounding exercises

Comments: After Tuesday's T-Ts, recover with about a mile of jogging before the 10 × 200/200s. Jog another mile before the skipping and bounding.

ADVANCED LEVEL PERFORMANCES
MILE–5KM

6. RACING. (During the racing season)

Sun	Mon	Tues	Wed	Thurs	Fri	Sat
Recovery	Leg-speed	Fast aerobic	T-T.	Recovery	Recovery	Race
E	H	E—M	M	E	R	All out
10 miles	2–3 miles of 50/50 sprint-float. plus skipping and bounding exercises	45 minutes fun fartlek	T-T 300 and 600 to mile plus 4-6 × 100/200	8 miles	3 miles	Race

Comments: If you have any doubts about how to run the 50-meter stride/50-meter float workout, see the comments in the Intermediate Level, Mile–5km section. In Wednesday's workout, milers should T-T a 300 and 600, and 5km racers a mile and 2-mile. Jog full recoveries. If you feel stiff coming into the 4–6 × 100 meter striding, work into them carefully.

7. WEEK OF THE BIG RACE.

Sun	Mon	Tues	Wed	Thurs	Fri	Sat
Recovery	Leg-speed	Aerobic	No run	Recovery	Recovery	Big Race
E	H	E—M	R	E	R	All out
10 miles	2 miles 50/50 or 100/100 plus skipping and bounding exercises	45 min. fun aerobic fartlek	No run	6 miles	3 miles	Big Race

10KM–30KM _____

1. BUILDING TO YOUR TARGET MILEAGE. Same as Mile–5km except 70-100 miles per week.
2. AEROBIC BASE. Same as Mile–5km
3. HILL TRAINING. Same as Mile–5km
4. ANAEROBIC. (For 4 weeks)

Sun	Mon	Tues	Wed	Thurs	Fri	Sat
Week's longest	Recovery	Fast aerobic and anaerobic	Recovery	Fast aerobic	Recovery	Leg-speed
E	E	M—H	E	M	E	M—H
15–20 miles	10 miles	Hill workout or 10 miles fartlek or 15 × 400/200 or 15 × 200/100 plus skipping and bounding exercises	8 miles	2 × 5km/800 or 10–12 miles	8 miles	3-mile M, 8 × 100/100, 3-mile M, 8 × 100/100, 3-mile M

Comments: Saturday's leg-speed work is combined with fast aerobic. Work into a 3-mile run at about marathon race pace, then immediately into 8 alternate stride-float 100s (on the track or elsewhere), then right into another 3-mile, etc. This workout teaches you to use "burners" during fast aerobic pace.

ADVANCED LEVEL PERFORMANCES
10KM–30KM

5. SHARPENING. (For 4 weeks)

Sun	Mon	Tues	Wed	Thurs	Fri	Sat
Week's longest	Recovery	Fast aerobic & anaerobic	Recovery	Long aerobic	Recovery	Race or anaerobic
E—M	E	M—H	E	M	E	H
18 miles E if a race the day before. Otherwise, 22 miles with 1–3 mile surges	8 miles	Hill workout or 10 miles hilly fartlek, or interval 800s-miles. Skipping & bounding exercises	8–10 miles	12–15 miles (Perhaps with 3×3½–4½ mile faster sections)	3–6 miles	Race or 15 × 200/200, or 15 × 400/200, or 3–5 × 1200/pulse to 100 You may want to T-T 2-miles every other week taking pulse

Comments: If Tuesday's workout is interval 800s to miles, the fast repeats should total to 34 miles. Use about half the distance to recover. If you break Thursday's 12 to 15 miles into three parts, see the comments for 5, Sharpening and Racing for Intermediate Level marathoners. You may want to T-T roughly two miles every other week to evaluate your training by running the same course in the same time and taking your pulse as described in the section on evaluating training in Chapter 6. If you run this T-T, supplement it with 80 percent of the regularly scheduled workout.

ADVANCED LEVEL PERFORMANCES
10KM–30KM

6. RACING. (Use 5 above for minor races or when not racing)

Sun	Mon	Tues	Wed	Thurs	Fri	Sat
Long aerobic	Recovery	Leg-speed	Recovery	Leg-speed	Recovery	Race or fast aerobic
E—M	E	M—H	E	M	R	M to All out
15 miles	8 miles	2–3 miles of 50/50s or 100/100s plus skipping and bounding exercises	8–10 miles	6 × 400/400 sharp plus 10 × 100/100	3 miles	Race

Comments: If you have any doubts about how to run the 50 meter stride/50 meter float workout, see the comments in 5, Sharpening, Intermediate level Mile—5km. Generally, you should not race more than once every two weeks. On Thursday's workout, except for warming up and down, don't do more than the leg-speed work shown.

ADVANCED LEVEL PERFORMANCES
MARATHON

7. WEEK OF THE BIG RACE. Same as Mile–5km.

MARATHON _____

1. BUILDING TO YOUR TARGET MILEAGE. Same as for Mile–5km, except 70 to 100 miles per week.
2. AEROBIC BASE. Same as for Mile–5km
3. HILL TRAINING. Same as for Mile–5km
4. AEROBIC-ANAEROBIC. (For 4 weeks)

Sun	Mon	Tues	Wed	Thurs	Fri	Sat
Week's longest	Recovery ·	Resistance or hard aerobic	Recovery	Long aerobic	Recovery	Aerobic-anaerobic
E—M	E	M—H	E	E—M	E	M—H
20 miles	8 miles	Hill workout or 10–25km T-T	8 miles	18 miles	6 miles	20 × 400/100 or similar work with short rests

Comments: If you have any doubts about how to run Friday's 20 × 400/100 workout, see the comments in 4, of the Relative Beginner Marathon schedule.

ADVANCED LEVEL PERFORMANCES
MARATHON

5. SHARPENING. (For 4 weeks)

Sun	Mon	Tues	Wed	Thurs	Fri	Sat
Week's longest	Recovery	Resistance or aerobic-anaerobic	Recovery	Aerobic	Recovery	Fast aerobic
E—M	E	M—H	E	M	E	H—All out
20 miles if a race the day before. Or 24 miles with 1–4 mile surges the last 12 miles	8 miles	Hill workout or 6-8 × mile/400	8 miles	15 miles (3 × 4½ miles)	6 miles	Non-marathon race or 2 × 10km/800 or 3 × 5km/800

Comments: If you don't understand Thursday's workout, see the comments for 5, Sharpening and Racing for Intermediate level marathoners.

6. SERIOUS RACING. Use for important races. (For minor races use 5 above)

Sun	Mon	Tues	Wed	Thurs	Fri	Sat
Week's longest	Recovery	Anaerobic	Aerobic	Recovery	Recovery	Race
E—M	E	M—H	E	E	E	H
20 miles	8 miles	3-5 × 1200/pulse 100	6 miles	10 miles	3 miles	Non-marathon race

Comments: Don't race more than every other weekend.

ADVANCED LEVEL PERFORMANCES
MARATHON

7. WEEK OF THE MARATHON RACE.

Sun	Mon	Tues	Wed	Thurs	Fri	Sat
Aerobic	Recovery	Fast aerobic and leg-speed	Recovery	Recovery	Recovery	Race
E	E	H	R	E	R	All out
12–18 miles	6 miles	5km T-T, jog mile, 8 X 100/100, jog mile	No run or easy fun run	6 miles	3 miles	Marathon

Comments: See the comments for Relative Beginner, Week of the marathon for an explanation of how to approach this week's work.

ELITE-LEVEL PERFORMANCES

MILE–5KM _____

1. BUILD TO TARGET MILEAGE as quickly as comfortably possible, keeping the daily efforts roughly the same and not too difficult. Perhaps 80 to 100 miles per week.

2. AEROBIC. (For 4–6 weeks)

Sun	Mon	Tues	Wed	Thurs	Fri	Sat
Week's longest	Recovery	Fast aerobic	Recovery	Fast aerobic	Recovery	Fast aerobic
E	E	M—H	E	M	E	M—H
15–20 miles	8–12 miles	10–12 miles of aerobic fartlek	10 miles	15 miles	8 miles	15–20 × 400/100, or 15–20 × 200/50 or 10 miles steady

Comments: If you have any doubts about how to run the 20 × 400/100 workout, see the comments in 4, Relative Beginner Marathon schedule.

3. HILL TRAINING. Drop the week's mileage by 10 percent. (For 4 weeks)

Sun	Mon	Tues	Wed	Thurs	Fri	Sat
Week's longest	Recovery	Resistance	Recovery	Resistance	Recovery	Resistance-fast aerobic
E	E	M—H	E	M—H	E	M—H
15 miles	10 miles	Hill workout totaling 14 miles	10 miles	Hill workout totaling 14 miles	10 miles	Hill workout or 10 miles hilly fartlek

4. PRELIMINARY ANAEROBIC. Raise the week's mileage by 10 percent. (For 4 weeks)

Sun	Mon	Tues	Wed	Thurs	Fri	Sat
Week's longest	Aerobic-anaerobic	Recovery	Fast aerobic-anaerobic	Resistance	Leg-speed	Fast aerobic
E	M—H	E	M—H	E	M	M—H
15 miles	15 X 400/200 or 15 X 200/100 plus skipping and bounding exercises	10 miles	2 X 3000/800 or 4 X mile/600 or 6 X 800/400 plus skipping and bounding exercises	8 miles	2 sets of 10 X 100/100 plus skipping and bounding exercises	10 miles

Comments: For Wednesday's workout run the 2 × 3000s the first week, the 4 × mile the second and the 6 × 800s the remaining weeks.

5. SHARPENING. Drop the week's mileage by 20 percent. (For 4 weeks)

Sun	Mon	Tues	Wed	Thurs	Fri	Sat
Week's longest	Anaerobic	Recovery	Leg-speed	Recovery	Recovery	Anaerobic
E	M—H	E	H	E	E	H
15 miles	T-T 1½ mile, T-T 800, plus 15 X 200/200, plus skipping and bounding exercises	8 miles	2-3 miles of 50/50s or 100/100s, plus skipping exercises	One hour fun fartlek	8 miles	4 X 800/600 or 3-5 X 1200/pulse 100, plus skipping and bounding exercises

Comments: On Monday, jog 1 to 1½ miles between the T-Ts, and a mile to recover for the 15 × 200s.

6. WEEKLY RACING. Drop the week's mileage by another 20 percent. (During the racing season)

Sun	Mon	Tues	Wed	Thurs	Fri	Sat
Week's longest	Leg-speed	Recovery	Anaerobic	Recovery	Recovery	Race
E	M—H	E	M—H	E	R	All out
10 miles	1½–2 miles of 50/50s or 100/100s, plus skipping and bounding exercises	Fun fartlek 45 minutes	T-T 300 and 600 to mile and 2-mile, plus 6 × 100/200	8 miles	3 miles	Race

Comments: On Wednesday's workout, milers should T-T a 300 and 600 with about 800 meters jog in between, and 5km racers should T-T a mile and 2-mile with a mile jog rest. Jog a mile before the 6 × 100/100s.

7. WEEK OF THE BIG RACE.

Sun	Mon	Tues	Wed	Thurs	Fri	Sat
Aerobic	Recovery	Leg-speed	Recovery	Recovery	Recovery	Race
E	E	M—H	—	E	R	All out
10 miles	6–8 miles	45 minutes fartlek or T-T 200 and 400 to 1200 and 3000	no run	6 miles	3 miles	Big Race

10KM–30KM _____

1. BUILDING TO YOUR TARGET MILEAGE. Same as for Mile–5km except 80 to 120 miles per week.
2. AEROBIC BASE. Same as for Mile–5km
3. HILL TRAINING. Same as for Mile–5km
4. PRELIMINARY ANAEROBIC. (For 4 weeks)

Sun	Mon	Tues	Wed	Thurs	Fri	Sat
Week's longest	Recovery	Resistance or prelim anaerobic	Recovery	Fast aerobic	Leg-speed	Fast aerobic
E	E	M—H	E	M	M	H
15–22 miles	10 miles	Hill workout or 12 miles fartlek or 20 × 400/100 or 20 × 200/50 plus skipping and bounding exercises	10 miles	2 × 5km/800 or 6 × mile/400 or 8 × 800/400	2 sets of 10 × 100/100 plus skipping and bounding	10–12 miles

Comments: If you have any doubts about how to run Thursday's 20 × 400/100 workout, see the comments for 4, Relative Beginner Marathon schedule.

ELITE LEVEL PERFORMANCES
10KM–30KM

5. SHARPENING. (For 4 weeks)

Sun	Mon	Tues	Wed	Thurs	Fri	Sat
Week's longest	Recovery	Resistance or anaerobic	Recovery	Fast aerobic	Recovery	Hard aerobic or anaerobic
E—M	E	M—H	E	M	E	H or All out
18 miles E if tired from Sat, or 22 miles with 1–3 mile surges the last 10	10 miles	Hill workout or 4 × mile/pulse 120 plus 10 × 200/200	8–10 miles	12–15 miles (3 × 3½–4½ miles)	3–6 miles	Race or 3–5 × 1200/pulse 100 ___ You may want to T-T. 2-mile every other week taking pulse

Comments: If you want to break Thursday's 12- to 15-miler into three faster parts, see the comments for 5, Intermediate Level Marathoners.

6. RACING. Use for important races. Use 5 above for minor races.

Sun	Mon	Tues	Wed	Thurs	Fri	Sat
Week's longest	Recovery	Aerobic–anaerobic	Recovery	Leg-speed	Recovery	Race or Fast aerobic
E—M	E	M	E	M	R	All out
18 miles E if race last Sat. Or 20 miles with surges the last 10	8–10 miles	12 miles fartlek	10 miles	6 × 400/400	3 miles	Race

ELITE LEVEL PERFORMANCES
MARATHON

7. WEEK OF THE BIG RACE.

Sun	Mon	Tues	Wed	Thurs	Fri	Sat
Recovery	Recovery	Anaerobic and leg-speed	Recovery	Recovery	Recovery	Race
E	E	M—H	—	E	R	All out
10 miles	6–8 miles	Sharp fartlek 45 minutes or 2 miles of 50/50s	No Run	6 miles	3 miles	Race

Comments: On Tuesday's workout, avoid using "competitive energy." On Wednesday don't run; walk or hike instead. Relax, have fun and picture the race you'd like to run.

MARATHON _____

1. BUILD TO YOUR TARGET MILEAGE. Same as for Mile–5km, except perhaps 90 to 120 miles per week.
2. AEROBIC BASE. (For 4–6 weeks)

Sun	Mon	Tues	Wed	Thurs	Fri	Sat
Week's longest	Recovery	Fast aerobic	Recovery	Long aerobic	Recovery	Fast aerobic
E	E	M—H	E	M	E	M—H
20 miles	12 miles	12 miles aerobic fartlek	10 miles	15–17 miles	8–10 miles	12 miles aerobic fartlek or 20 × 400/100 or 12 miles steady

Comments: If you have any doubts about how to run Tuesday's and Saturday's workouts, review the definition of aerobic fartlek in Chapter 8.

ELITE LEVEL PERFORMANCES
MARATHON

3. HILL TRAINING. (For 4 weeks)

Sun	Mon	Tues	Wed	Thurs	Fri	Sat
Week's longest	Recovery	Resistance	Recovery	Resistance	Recovery	Resistance
E	E	M—H	E	M—H	E	M—H
20 miles	10 miles	Hill workout totaling 14 miles	10 miles	Hill workout totaling 14 miles	8–10 miles	Either 14 miles hilly fartlek or Hill W.O.

Comments: Review the description of hill training in Chapter 10 if you have any doubt about how to set up this workout.

4. SHARPENING. Use during the early part of the racing season. (For 4–6 weeks)

Sun	Mon	Tues	Wed	Thurs	Fri	Sat
Week's longest	Recovery	Resistance or anaerobic	Recovery	Long aerobic	Recovery	Hard aerobic
E—M	E	M—H	E	M—H	E	H—All out
20 miles if race the day before, or 24 miles hilly with 1–5 mile surges	8 miles	Hill workout or 8 × mile/400 or 8 × 880/200	8 miles	15–18 miles	3–10 miles	Non marathon race or 2 × 10km/800, or 3 × 5km/800

Comments: Don't race more than every other week. Another good Saturday workout if not racing is Friday's workout for 4, Advanced level 10km–30km.

5. FINAL SHARPENING. Use during the later part of the racing season.

Sun	Mon	Tues	Wed	Thurs	Fri	Sat
Week's longest	Recovery	Resistance or anaerobic	Recovery	Aerobic	Recovery	Aerobic-anaerobic
E—M	E	M—H	E	M	E—R	H—All out
22 miles E if race the day before. Or up to 30 miles with tactics the last 10	10–12 miles	Hill workout or 3–6 × 2–5 minutes fast/pulse 100	10 miles	15 miles (3 × 4½ miles)	3–10 miles	Non-marathon race or 10 miles of fartlek or interval 400s–800s

Comments: If you want to break Thursday's 15-miler into three faster sections, see the comments for 5, Intermediate Marathoners.

6. WEEK OF THE MARATHON.

Sun	Mon	Tues	Wed	Thurs	Fri	Sat
Anerobic	Recovery	Anaerobic & leg-speed	Recovery	Recovery	Recovery	Race
E	E	M—H	—	E	R	All out
15–20 miles	6 miles	5km T-T, mile jog, 8 × 100/100	No run	6 miles	3 miles	Marathon

Comments: See the comments for Relative Beginner, Week of Marathon Race for an explanation of how to approach this week's work.

ALTERNATE TRAINING PATTERNS

There are two other basic patterns you may want to try after you have finished hill training. The first probably works best for those who recover quickly between workouts (most likely *not* those at the Relative Beginner or Intermediate level), and the second works best for those torn between cutting mileage to get quality, and maintaining mileage such as those racing 10km to the marathon who face a long season.

1. TWO DAYS HARD-ONE DAY EASY. Two consecutive hard days are separated by a complete recovery day before the process is repeated. On each of the consecutive hard days, different muscles groups and metabolisms are worked. The first hard day involves *anaerobic* repeats, and the second, fairly difficult *aerobic* speeds. It is essential that the third day be a complete recovery—three miles of jogging for less than Advanced Level athletes, and about five miles for the Advanced and Elite. The reason for running rather than taking off altogether is to loosen up and provide a minimum training effect. I've found that it's not difficult to work fairly hard for two days in a row when a *different type of work* is done, and you know that a complete recovery awaits you. If you haven't recovered from one day's rest, take another. To make this pattern work, you have to think on a two-week repeating cycle as follows:

Sun	Mon	Tues	Wed	Thurs	Fri	Sat
Week's Longest run	3-6 mile jog	Anaerobic	M—H aerobic	3-6 miles jog	Anaerobic	Long run (Same as Sun)
3-6 mile jog	Anaerobic	M—H aerobic	3-6 mile jog	Anaerobic	M—H aerobic	3-6 mile jog

2. HIGH MILEAGE WEEK-LOW MILEAGE, QUALITY WEEK. Here you alternate a high mileage week with a low mileage, high quality week. In a sense, the hard-easy, long-short pattern is woven into a weekly concept. Schedule races on low mileage weeks. The high mileage week should total about half again as many miles as

the low mileage week. (The first week in the example below is the low mileage week).

ALTERNATE TRAINING PATTERNS

Sun	Mon	Tues	Wed	Thurs	Fri	Sat
Fairly long run	Recovery 4 miles	Fast aerobic	Recovery 4 miles	Intervals (100s–800s)	Recovery 3–6 miles	Varied pace fast aerobic such as fartlek
Very long run	Recovery 6 miles	Fairly fast longer aerobic than above	Recovery 6 miles	Fairly fast longer aerobic as on Tues.	Recovery 3–6 miles	Varied aerobic pace such as fartlek

Yearly Pattern For High School and College Track and Cross-Country

December. Easy aerobic training.

January. Fast aerobic training.

February. Hill training.

March. Beginning anaerobic (slower intervals with short rests).

April. Sharpening and early races (fast anaerobic repeats with longer rests; leg-speed, sprint-float sessions).

May. Serious racing. (Training is basically finished. Just leg-speed and recovery runs).

June. Rest two weeks. Easy golf course running for two weeks.

July. Build mileage and fast aerobic.

August. Three weeks of hill training.

September. Two weeks of interval training and early races. Two weeks of sharper intervals and races.

October. Serious racing plus just leg-speed and recovery runs.

November. Two to three weeks off.

PART III
RACING

14.

PRE-RACE PREPARATIONS

*T*raining is well underway and now you are at least reasonably ready to begin testing yourself in races. What sort of races should you run first? How do you integrate racing with the rest of training? What race tactics should you use? How soon should you race again? This chapter explores what you need to know when approaching a race, and Chapter 15 guides you through the races.

WHEN AND WHAT TO RACE

It's easy to get seduced into racing before you are ready. Runners who do not acknowledge periodic layoffs will be racing when you're not (or shouldn't be). Unless you are physically prepared to race, you risk injury (as exemplified earlier by the miler who ran 4:19 during base training and wrecked his Achilles tendon). Premature racing also produces sub-par times which are valueless and often disheartening. If you want to see how far your conditioning has progressed, there are better ways.

That doesn't mean you couldn't use a 10-mile race as a hard

10-mile workout, just don't get caught up in premature racing. Shoot for a fast *workout* time are stick to that pace. Resist skipping workouts to rest beforehand, and don't run all out. As mentioned earlier, don't race seriously until at least midway through the hill training. On the other hand, don't think you can just train and race the big one without preliminary racing over and under your primary distance. If, during early season, you are short on speed, race over distance, and run faster, shorter repeats in training. Later, race under distance. Shorter races are excellent for sharpening your tactical skills and speed because everything happens so fast. Don't worry that you'll be beaten by the specialists at the distance. If you always race the same event, there's pressure to improve each time.

Most road runners racing from 10km on up rarely enter mile, 2-mile, and 5km events even though these races are excellent for developing speed. Often, short races are unjustly regarded as kids' or jogger's events. But any experienced runner knows that the 5000 meters is just as tough as the 10,000 meters. Both run you to a standstill.

RACING FREQUENCY

Four factors determine how often you race: 1) the distance raced, 2) how fast you recover mentally and physically, 3) the race schedule, and 4) how you train between races.

The longer the race, the longer the recovery time. Some say you need one day of recovery for each mile raced. That's probably not a bad rule of thumb, but much depends upon how mentally draining the race was. Although some runners seem to race successfully most every weekend, the majority do not recover that fast. If the week after racing 5km or more you don't feel competitive yet, wait until you are. Participation shouldn't be the main goal. A few fast races are better than several uninspired races. Usually you can't race fast and often for long.

Although I mentioned earlier how to race three marathons roughly four weeks apart, it's usually better to space them out and simply limit yourself to *two* or *three* a year even if you are primarily a marathoner. Apart from the stress of running marathons, it's tempting to abandon quality training in preference to mileage. You'll have better success marathoning if you alternate them with training for and racing shorter distances.

Championship track meets often requires qualifying for the final. Olympic 5000-meter runners, for example, must be trained and rested to survive two qualifying rounds. Similarly, you may find that your two main races fell within the same week, thus allowing less recovery than you'd like. In this case, don't run anything other than recovery and light leg-speed work between races.

PREDICTING RACE TIMES

It's often difficult to predict the pace you should aim for in the first few races. Comparing your time-trial and training times to previous sessions provides clues, but comparisons to training times are often misleading because competition almost always raises you to new heights. I've run 6 × 880s struggling for the pace needed for Saturday's 2-mile and then strung four of them together with no rest. Rob de Castella mentions running fairly difficult 10-milers in 60 minutes wondering how he will pass 10 miles in a marathon in under 50 minutes and continue for another 16 miles. Count on competition for that extra.

EQUATING PERFORMANCES ACROSS DIFFERENT DISTANCES

If a miler runs 4:00, a 10km runner performing equally well will average about 4:40 per mile to clock 29:00, and a marathoner will average about 5:10 per mile to run 2:15:00. At the 5:00 minute mile level the spread is wider, about 5:54 miling for a 36.45 10km and 6:34 miling for a 2:52:30 marathon.

Relationships such as these enable the construction and use of scoring tables (for example, Portuguese and Purdy Scoring tables) which allow one to equate performances across various distances. However, although you may be able to run at a certain level at your best racing distance, it does not necessarily follow that you can run at that level at all other distances. To exaggerate, a sprinter running 11 seconds for the 100 meters could not expect to run 32:07 for 10km or 2:30:10 for the marathon even though each performance is equally good. But if you run at a certain level at your best racing distance, say 10km, you could expect to perform similarly at other distances in that vicinity—for example at five and 15km. For shorter and longer races your performances would probably fall off somewhat.

By plotting your performance on semi-log graph paper, you

can construct a performance curve which enables you to determine your best performances and probably times for other distances (assuming roughly equal conditions). Simply join two sheets
of one cycle semi-log paper end to end as in the example below,
and mark distances on the X axis and pace on the Y. Put a dot at
the fastest pace at which you have raced each distance. Connect
the dots as shown by the dotted line, and then, using the topmost
dots, construct a smooth performance curve (the dashed line in the
example).

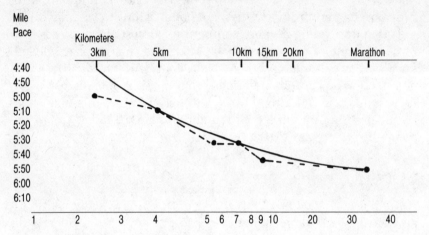

Performance Curve

In the example, the best performances were at 5km, 10km
and the marathon. This runner's 2-mile, 5-mile and 15km dots
should be where the dashed line falls above them. By reading
along the dashed line you get an idea of the pace to shoot for any
distance along that performance level.

USING RACES TO REVEAL STRENGTHS AND WEAKNESSES

Time-trials and race splits reveal whether you tend to go out fast,
sag in the middle, and then sprint in; go out fast and die; run even
pace throughout; or run a faster second half. Knowing this, you
can adjust your training and tactics. If it is revealed that you have
a good sustained kick, but not a good sprint kick, you will either
have to develop a better sprint, or leave your opponents before
you reach the point from which you can no longer outrun them. If

you habitually go out too fast or allow the pace to sag in the middle, you may have to practice pace in training, or run intervals and time-trials with faster middle halves.

PRE-RACE ROUTINE

MENTAL PREPARATIONS

In Chapter 6, "Mind Games," I've already described the necessity of combating pre-race tensions, getting emotion and excitement to work for you, and to visualize the race you want to run.

Before an important race, tell yourself you have done everything you could have. The training is finished, so there's nothing left to do but relax and conserve energy. I like to go to the movies the night before; I get absorbed in the film and temporarily forget the race.

CUTTING BACK ON TRAINING

Ever notice how many runners perform best after getting into top shape, picking up a small injury that costs them training, and then recovering in time to run a few good workouts before resting again? Two classic examples are Bikila, who won the 1964 Olympic marathon by four minutes after an appendectomy six weeks earlier, and Dave Wottle, who won the 1972 Olympic 800 after becoming injured after the Olympic trials and hardly training before the Games. Most of his training came from qualification heats of the 800.

Similarly, I had trained well until 10 days before the 1968 Olympic marathon trial, but then picked up an injury which, except for a few 15-minute miles, sidelined me for three days. My hard training was limited to one cautious 3-mile time-trial five days before the race. Thus, I came into the trial fit and rested, and the others competed fit and tired. Had the injury not forced me to lay off, I probably would have trained myself out of contention.

If you are not fit a week before a big race, it's too late. All you can do the last week is sharpen what you already have and stockpile mental and physical energy. With the reduced workload you may feel as though you're metamorphosing into a circus fat person, but I'll guarantee that's illusionary. Any weight gain is water retention.

Before minor races, however, sacrifice no more training than necessary to compete reasonably well, especially if the time before

Six weeks after an appendectomy, Ethiopia's Abebe Bikila pulverized the rest of the field in the 1964 Olympic Games marathon, winning by over four minutes.

important races is short. Don't expect to always run your best, and don't get discouraged when you don't. Sometimes, however, you will need to approach a minor race seriously in order to perform well and bolster your confidence. A mental boost when you're doubting your form is a good trade for a couple of workouts. It's delicate balance, trading training for a psychological lift.

SLEEP

Fortunately, racing well doesn't seem to require that you sleep well the night before. In fact, although I normally require eight hours of sleep, I limit myself to six the night before a race. On one occasion I set a course record after staying up all night. The main problem with lying awake the night before competition is the anguish you endure worrying about it. Deliberately stay up a little later the night before the race to make sure you are tired when you go to bed.

Extra sleep is far more critical two and three nights before the race. Although the experts say you can't store sleep, when I get extra sleep for one or two nights, I don't require as much the next night.

SHOES

It's a mystery to me why anyone would race wearing training shoes. Racing flats are far more responsive. With the current state of the art, they are comfortable and protective, and it doesn't cost more to own racing flats *and* training shoes. Mileage accumulated in your racing flats saves your training shoes, and over time it costs no more to split the wear between two shoes than to wear them out one at a time.

Contrary to what the shoe manufacturers claim, good shoes don't enable you to run faster, they just slow you down less. Ideally, barefooted is the best way to run, but few can take the pounding and scuffing. Zola Budd races shoeless, and Ron Hill and Abebe Bikila did. Bikila won the Olympic marathon on Rome's cobblestoned Appian Way running barefoot.

When I raced college cross-country, I ran barefoot when the course permitted, even once when it was snowing. But it requires checking out the course beforehand for glass and stones. And acorns. I found out about acorns while racing and yelping for six miles on an oak-infested golf course.

Danie Burger reports that "The protective plate in . . .

[spiked shoes] together with the sole of the shoe and the shoe itself limits toe drive drastically. The toes in a running shoe can only move minimally up and down past the plane of the ball of the foot. An analogy is a shot-putter who is prevented from giving a final flick before the shot leaves the hand."

The best shoe for you has little to do with ratings. It's a matter of personal preference. The essential qualities are good fit, flexibility at the ball of the foot, and protection from road shock. The shorter the race, the lighter and less protective the shoe can be.

Runners shelling out $50 to $100 for a pair of shoes are usually reluctant to perform corrective surgery on them even though the shoe may be cutting *their* feet. I have never hesitated to cut, rip apart, cement together, or rebuild any shoe I could improve or fix, and I cannot remember ever ruining a shoe. With contact cement, a sander, various rubber materials, patience, and practice, you can fit in lifts, add padding, rebuild heels, and repair almost any shoe sucessfully. If you want any shoe to keep its shape and last much longer, cement a plug of Eternal Sole to the wear area of the heel while the shoe is still new. Trace around the patch and notch it flush into the heel with a razor blade. Eternal Sole adheres much better if you first sand the cementing surfaces.

You may think it should be the manufacturer's responsibility to get the shoe right in the first place, but if he doesn't or your foot requires something extra, the time spent customizing a shoe will be well worth it. Running on chopped liver negates a lot of training, and orthopedic surgeons are more expensive than proper shoes.

TIME CHANGES

Foreign competition often means time changes. This interferes with our circadian clocks—our natural rhythms of sleep and other biological functions such as the hours at which we are most energetic. Rule of thumb has it that it takes roughly one day to adjust to each hour of time change. But there are exceptions and ways to cheat.

It's easier to adjust if, upon arrival, you have napped on the plane, and nighttime comes quickly. Departing in the morning and flying for eight to 12 hours to face another whole day is far more difficult even when the time difference is the same. Ron Clarke said he went for a light run immediately upon arrival, no matter how wiped out he was. A run loosens and relaxes you for a nap, which speeds adjustment. If you have several days between arrival and the race, schedule a hard workout just before leaving so that the trip coincides with your recovery day. If departing a day or two before competition, don't work out that day (except to loosen up after arriving). Traveling, with all its attendant pressures, is exhausting enough. The way to cheat the clock is to begin moving your bedtime forward or back an hour a day, depending upon the direction of time change, before you leave.

CHECKLIST

Ever arrive at a race and discover your forgot your racing flats or brought two left shoes? Because those last few hours before the race are hectic enough, prepare a list of the items you will need for the race beforehand, when your head is screwed on right. The items you might need include:

- lubricant for feet, crotch, and underarms
- adhesive bandages to protect your nipples (during a marathon)
- water and containers
- pencil and paper
- directions to the race

- entry fee
- safety pins
- sweatband, hat, mitts, or plastic bag for wet or cold conditions
- racing flats—a left and a right

LYING LOW

The bigger the race, the greater are the opportunities to become sidetracked into all sorts of fatiguing nonsense during the last few days. If you've raced the Boston Marathon when the headquarters was the Sheraton Hotel, you probably found it near impossible to get through the lobby without bumping into everyone you ever knew and being invited to wander about the running exposition, join someone's workout, or tour the town. Your most important move before competition, therefore, may be to make as few moves as possible and maintain your normal routine.

To maintain a low-key existence before the 1984 Olympic marathon, Joan Benoit escaped the Olympic village to Eugene, Oregon. Carlos Lopes said he wouldn't use Portugal's Olympic training camp if it was located beyond commuting distance of his family is Lisbon.

Before Lorraine Moller raced the 1980 women's marathon

championship in London, England, I cautioned that rather than stay at the hotel-headquarters, she accept an offer to hole up in a private home because the hotel would be a nightmare of photo sessions, interviews, clinics, and constant surveillance by competitors and the curious public. Moller agreed and visited the hotel but once, to register. She surfaced for the race relaxed and rested, and won handily.

Admittedly, before a mega-race it's difficult to resist scurrying around like the ever-late White Rabbit, but you can wipe out months of preparation in exchange for a few thrills that will pale against coming up flat at race time.

Constant preoccupation with running without the relief of diversions can also wear one down. When I trained for six weeks at the Colorado high altitude camp before the 1968 Olympic marathon trial, I decided to live with my family, apart from the other runners, and to get involved in other projects. The others shared special quarters where the conversation centered around running—who was training toughest, who ran what, and who would make the team. One runner, who awakened in the middle of the night and could not fall asleep, dressed and put in another session on the roads because he couldn't think of anything else to do. Little wonder most everyone there burned out before the trial.

Before your race, try to keep roughly the same meal times and hours. Schedule activities that aren't race related and don't involve a lot of walking or excitement. Even let yourself become bored. Then you'll face the starter's gun eager for something to do.

FINAL CALL

LAST MEAL _____

Years ago I told a reporter I ate six sweet rolls before a marathon. Some kid, upon reading this from an "expert," decided he'd run on them in a 2-mile race. Well, he did just that. After a few laps they came up and he ran on them. Which confirms an old cliché that what's one man's meat is another man's poison. Although I can eat sweet rolls a couple hours before a marathon and run well, you perhaps cannot. Neither of us would eat them before a 2-mile race. Eating before anaerobic races is a different ballgame.

Even world-class runners sometimes eat the wrong stuff before competition. I recall watching Wade Bell run the first qualifying heat of the 800 at the Mexico Olympics, where he was the favorite to win the gold medal. At the 400 he was last and fading. Later I learned that Bell had wolfed down bacon and eggs before the race.

Don't eat anything during the last four hours before short races because digestion slows when you are nervous. Before any race, avoid fats and other hard-to-digest foods. And sugar. Sugar stimulates the pancreas to release insulin to lower your blood sugar level. Low blood sugar levels produce a lethargic feeling, anxiety, and depression.

Three days before a marathon emphasize carbohydrates and starches such as potatoes, vegetables, grains, fruits, etc. The pre-evening meal should include simple carbohydrates derived from breads, pasta, and sugars that agree with you. Avoid large amounts of protein because it can cause ammonia and amino acids to be built up in your bloodstream, which will tire you quickly. That's why no one eats big steaks before competition anymore.

Make sure you've already raced or time-trialed off what you plan to eat before an important race and that it agrees with you. Never drastically change your eating habits before competition. No matter what the others eat.

Concerning carbo-loading before a marathon, the depletion phase (a long muscle-glycogen depleting run a week before the race followed by three days of eating mainly proteins and fats) is both unnecessary and potentially dangerous. In your depleted state you will be susceptible to infection and feel exhausted, a condition hardly conducive to self-confidence.

A long run will deplete your muscle glycogen, and reduced training enables your muscles to store all the glycogen they can. You don't have to pig out, but drink plenty of water and eat foods rich in potassium (fruits, vegetables, grains, and beans). Water stores in the muscle with the glycogen, and will be taken from other organs if you don't drink enough. When you are two percent dehydrated (a three-pint water loss for a 150-lb. person), your work capacity is reduced by 10 to 15 percent, so in long races stock up before the gun goes off (a final 8–10 ounces 10 to 15 minutes before the gun). The surest sign of enough water is clear urine. For anyone competing for less than two hours, carbo-loading is useless.

Diet in general, though a fascinating subject, is beyond the scope of this book. "Scientific" diets go unheeded by most athletes anyway. My approach to diet, condensed to 10 points is:

1. Avoid overly processed foods.
2. Choose fresh fruits and vegetables over canned and frozen ones.
3. Avoid preservatives.
4. Avoid artifical food coloring.
5. Restrict your intake of fats, particularly saturated fats.
6. Avoid foods and snacks high in refined sugar.
7. Eat a balanced combination of vegetables, fruits, whole grains and protein foods that supply the eight essential amino acids.
8. Avoid or go easy on red meats, especially fatty sausages, organs, and fatty cuts of beef or pork.
9. Drink lots of water.
10. Don't substitute "junk foods" for the basic foods.

Vitamin and mineral deficiencies should generally not be a problem with balanced diets, although individual requirements differ widely. Extra calcium speeds recovery from hard workouts and races and retards the leaching of calcium from the bones and teeth in older runners. Vitamin D, potassium and magnesium should accompany calcium. To play it safe, you may want to take other vitamins and mineral supplements. Women especially should ensure that they get enough iron and calcium.

RACE COUNTDOWN

The morning of the race go to a quiet place and visualize the race you want to run (review Chapter 6). Memorize or write on the back of your hand your splits and review your tactics. If the plan is to move hard at strategic places in a road race, or kick at a certain place in a track race, rehearse these moves in your hand.

Make sure you arrive at the race with enough time to check in, get your number and warmup (after checking when the race will start). Make sure you know where the race finishes. I recall turning a corner in a road race, and, bang!, I had finished before I started my kick. If you can warm up before the race in the finish area you'll get the "feel" of it. When you race, it won't seem like what you saw on a map or from a car.

Warm up in your training shoes, change into your racing flats 10 to 15 minutes before the start, run your stride-outs and jog until lining up. Just before the race, re-tie your shoes, and then double-knot them. Even Bill Rodgers forgot to do this before his 1975

American Record at the Boston Marathon. He became almost as famous for the photos of him redoing his shoes as for his 2:09:55. Although he got the record, the stop certainly cost him time.

Don't be surprised if you receive a helping hand with your warmup from your kidneys and stomach. It's not uncommon, before a race, to cover considerable distance on accumulated trips to the rest room. Because the satellites, service stations, and restaurant facilities near mega-races will most likely be overloaded, plan to make your last pit-stop at home or on the way to the race.

15.

AFTER THE GUN GOES OFF

*E*very sport has its tricks of the trade. I'll describe six of distance running's main ones. The first four apply both to road and track running; the last two concern track runners only.

1. *Keeping track of split times.* During the heat of competition it's often difficult to remember what your lap, kilometer, or mile splits should be during a long race. And it's difficult to determine what you ran for the last section because even the simplest arithmetic calculations can become a nightmare. Therefore, many runners write their intended splits in waterproof ink on the back of their hand and check them against those in the race.

2. *Slipstreaming.* Race car drivers do it. Bicyclists do it. Skaters do it. But runners often don't bother to tuck in behind other runners to lessen the air resistance created by their forward movement or a headwind. It has been estimated that when Olympic gold medalist Bob Hayes

was timed at over 27 mph in the last 25 yards of a 100-yard dash, it required 0.8 horsepower, or 40 percent of his mechanical work, just to overcome wind resistance. Although you will never go that fast, at about 5:00 mile pace 12 percent of your energy goes toward overcoming wind resistance on a calm day. If you tuck in three feet behind another runner you reduce that by 64 percent, at five feet back by 51 percent, and at 10 feet back by 31 percent.

Slipstreaming in a 1500-meter race could save you a second a lap. Into a headwind, it would be worth considerably more because wind resistance increases by the *square* of the speed, and energy consumption goes up by the *cube* of the speed. In crosswinds, try to find the wind shadow to the rear left or right of the lead runner.

3. *Contact*. High-school and college coaches often instruct their runners to "stay in contact" with the rival they went to beat. Usually, the coach intends that they follow a stride or two back, but contact actually means staying in range of passing before the finish. Obviously, depend-

Keeping contact. Running with the pack is psychologically easier than running at the same speed 20 yards ahead or behind.

ing upon the race and the runner, this gap could vary from staying within touching distance to merely keeping the other runner in sight.

Contact is a confidence issue. If you are a stride behind, but losing ground, contact has been broken. If you are 20 yards back, but on the hunt and confident of closing the gap, you are in contact. So on one hand, although contact is an abstract in the mind—the almost sixth-sense perception of whether you have the leading runner covered—on the other, it is concrete; almost as if the two of you were mentally tethered together. Almost always, it is easier to run with someone than run at the same pace 10 to 30 yards behind. If you find the gap between you and the runner ahead remains constant, move up and let him or her pull you along.

4. *Straightlining.* Even in the Boston Marathon, while slipstreaming behind the lead pack, I've temporarily relinquished my windbreak to straightline a curve while the others ran wide. This isn't cheating; when courses are measured and certified it's along the shortest route unless you are supposed to run on one side of the road. If you are running on the left side of the road approaching a right-handed turn, draw a diagonal to the turn and run *it* rather than cutting over abruptly. In twisty road races you can save considerable distance by staying alert and running the tangents.

5. *Running the pole lane.* The track corollary to straightlining is keeping in the first lane when possible. Running in the second lane adds about six yards per lap, in the third lane about 13 yards (look at the stagger marks for the 400 meters). Of course, it isn't always possible to run on the pole (the inside); in crowded fields you might have to run wide until you can either pass and tuck in or drop behind. Toward the end of a crowded race you may have to move out a lane or two in order to keep from getting boxed. It's useless to conserve distance if you wind up buried in the pack when the others kick.

Getting boxed nearly cost Peter Snell his second gold medal during the 1964 Olympic 1500. With 800 meters to go, teammate John Davies was supposed to take the lead (which he did) with Snell moving to his outside

Track races are often crowded with considerable potential for shoving, bumping, and boxing. Number 510 and the runner at his rear are "boxed" and would have to perform some quick maneuvering to cover a break by any other runner.

shoulder. But before Snell could get free and run up on Davies, another runner blocked his path. With runners surrounding Snell, he should have had to drop back and go around, but instead he stuck out his right arm to spear an opening, and with the gap Britain's John Whetton obligingly gave him, Snell got loose for a final killing sprint. But don't you count on most runners to be as sporting as Whetton.

6. *Track etiquette.* During track training, the first lane is for those running hard repeats or time-trials. On rest intervals keep to the second or third lanes, and when jogging, way to the outside. Likewise, when *you* are running fast repeats, you will not want joggers clogging your way. When a slower runner impedes your way, call out "Track!," the password that alerts the runner in front that you are coming through. Conversely, if you are running a fast repeat, but someone overtakes you, yield the inside. Every runner has the right to the inside lane when overtaking a slower runner (in practice, *not* during racing). If the others don't know what "Track!" means, explain it.

Whenever you pass another runner in a track race, you must be at least one stride ahead before you can cut in front. Likewise, insist upon the same clearance when you are passed. Often the passing runner does not know the gap and cuts prematurely in order to avoid running wide. When someone intentionally or unintentionally cuts me off, I yell, "One stride!" to remind him. If he still cuts, I may get my elbows out or put my hand on his shoulder to steer him. This is probably what Mary Decker should have done with Zola Budd in the 1984 Olympic 3000-meter final. Midway through the race barefoot Budd challenged Decker for the lead by cutting in with no more than a two-foot lead. Decker's foot clipped Budd's causing Decker to trip and sprawl onto the infield. Decker, the overwhelming favorite to win, twisted her hip and was unable to finish.

The leading runner has every right to surge and hold the challenger to the outside lane. It's a way to make him or her run wide on a curve. If the passing runner cannot cut without interference, it's a foul, although legalities didn't do Decker much good as she lay sprawled on the grass.

TACTICS

"Sex appeal," Sophia Loren has said, "is 50 percent what you've got, and 50 percent what they think you've got." I could say the same for tactics. When two or more competitors are evenly matched, the runner with the best tactic usually wins. A good tactic capitalizes on your strengths and your opponent's weaknesses. It requires adherence to Socrates' ancient admonition to "Know Thyself," as well as Knowing Thy Opponent. You mission in races, as is theirs, is to strike strongly at those moments when you are physically and mentally strong, and your opponent is off-guard or having trouble. The best physiological tactic is even pace because it requires the least amount of energy.

But races are not always won by running your best time.

Often they're won by causing your rivals to run below their potential by using a combination of unnerving psychological tricks and leg-deadening changes of pace. Years ago, when I first began winning road races, I was bested by a runner who I thought had no business beating me. He had shadowed me for four miles in a 10km, and when I waved him by so I could sit on him before kicking in, he became so enthralled at getting that lead that he seized the initiative, dug in, and won.

We were to meet again in a 10-mile track race, and I vowed not only to beat him, but to run him into the ground. At the gun I took the lead and pulled him around for 20 laps. Then at five miles I threw in a 100-meter surge that momentarily caught him off guard before he closed the gap. At the same place on every lap I surged for 100 meters. Gradually he realized he didn't have to hang on, but could pull up after I eased back. I let him do this for a few more laps to lure him into a false sense of security, and then changed the rules. The next time I took off I was determined to hammer until I dropped him.

I recall it with a smile now, but at the time it was nerve-racking. When I didn't let up at the end of the 100, I could hear him desperately galloping to close the 10 or so meters I had opened. Whenever I thought he was gaining, I ran furiously, more intent upon breaking him than finishing. I was near my limit before he finally cracked. By now I was so charged up I lapped him before the finish. My winning time was not particularly fast, but I had ruined his race altogether.

This was not an original tactic: Zátopek and Russia's Vladimir Kuts had used it in the 1950s with devastating effect on their competitors. Kuts won the 1956 Olympic 5000- and 10,000-meter gold medals. During the 1960s, repeated surging was largely abandoned in favor of more evenly paced races until a new breed of Africans—among them Kip Keino, Naftali Temu, Henry Rono, Mirits Yifter, Juma Ikangaa, and Gidamis Shahanga—again reduced races to a test of wills with seemingly crazy uncontrolled changes of pace.

The list of tactics is endless, and it's safe to say that there's no tactic that hasn't been tried. For every move there is a countermove. A slight hesitancy, or a minor miscalculation is often enough to turn a basically sound tactic into a misfire. A fast opening pace or midrace surges against an opponent who is hardened to sudden pace changes may kill you off rather than him or her. Likewise, allowing the race to be decided in the finishing sprint is foolhardy against faster kickers. When you have no chance of winning, the best tactic is to run your fastest steady effort and be content with where that places you, although a fiercely competitive struggle in which you cover an opponent's tactics can also be so absorbing you reach an emotional pitch that releases normally untapped power.

The basic tactical elements are even pace, going out slow and finishing strong, starting fast and hanging on, tactical burners enroute, long sustained kicks, sprint kicks, controlling the pace from the front, controlling from the leader's shoulder, and using the physical attributes of the course in your favor (for example, track competitors forcing opponents to run wide on curves, and road runners shifting gears on hills or turns). The permutations and combinations of ways in which you can use these tactics are, however, almost limitless.

CHOOSING A TACTIC

Your best race strategy is one that both defends against the tactics the opposition is likely to use on you, and hits them when they least want and expect it. Because the tactical possibilities in any race are numerous, it is essential that the game plan be tailored to fit the situation.

When I was coaching Lorraine Moller for the 1980–81 New Zealand track season, the ultimate goal was to win the Pacific Conference Games 3000 meters. During 1980 Moller had been primarily a marathoner, and as I've described earlier, had only eight weeks to train for this track season.

The week before the 3000 meters she raced a 1500 in which she was poised to kick with 300 meters to go, but because of a strong headwind up the backstraight, she hesitated until the final curve. The delay set the race up for the fast kickers. With 200 meters to go there was a big pushing match during which Moller was spiked and outsprinted into fifth place. Afterward she swore she'd never race another 1500, and began to doubt her chances in the 3000.

"Nonsense," I insisted. "This works right into our hands, because it reveals the tactic you must use to win." The situation was clear. Moller had great endurance and strength, but was short on speed. Her main rival, Cindy Bremser, was track-trained and fast, but I was convinced that Moller could survive a sustained kick better. In any race there is a point far enough out from the start that everyone is tired, and far enough from the finish that no one yet wants to kick. It was at this point Moller had to strike. Thus, the plan was this: To stay off the leaders and out of trouble the first two laps, and then move up to the leader's shoulder by the mile. Run as relaxed as possible and concentrate on what she'd have to do two laps from home, which was kick as hard as possible. I warned that it would take a supreme mental effort to make herself do it, but I guaranteed her it would catch the others off guard because they would want to jockey around until the last lap. "You are the only one in the field strong enough to kick from 800 meters out," I assured her, "and by the time the others get going, you'll have a lead they won't be able to close."

I nearly panicked when the first mile took just outside five minutes, because we had gambled on a fast start to soften up the sprinters. But Moller kept her poise and ran as planned. When she lit out, confusion spread behind with no one wanting to take the move seriously. Although the others gained on her over the last 400, she cruised home a relieved winner.

This tactic was not original. In the 1960 Olympic Games Herb Elliott used it to win the 1500, and Murray Halberg escaped with three laps to go in the 5000. As Moller had, both Elliott and Halberg dreaded changing gears when the time came. Elliott remembers thinking, "This pace is killing me! Surely I shouldn't feel as tired as this! Maybe I'd better not make my break where I thought I would. Maybe I ought to wait. No I *won't*. I'll *give it a go and see what happens.*"

New Zealand's Bill Baillie at times would get so caught up in tactics that the races took on a comical twist. Baillie was a great sitter, and in the National Championships one year was bent on beating Halberg, also a sitter. Baillie managed to trail Halberg until about three laps to go when Halberg stopped dead. Cheeky Baillie slammed on the brakes and the two of them stood there with the field streaming past, each waiting for the other to go first.

Ron Clarke tells of a tour when Baillie, who wasn't his fittest, raced Lutz Philipp of West Germany, who was very confident. Philipp prompty strode out with little Baillie tagging behind. Lutz would look back contemptuously while keeping a fairly hard pace. Toward halfway Philipp grew irritated, dropped his smirk and began to surge. Baillie surged with him. Philipp slowed and Baillie slowed. Philipp jogged, Baillie jogged. Philipp sprinted, Baillie sprinted. Two laps from home Baillie was still sitting on Lutz, seemingly untroubled, and Philipp was furious. In desperation, Lutz jogged the next to last lap in about 85 seconds, but Baillie played caboose. The bell sounded and still they jogged up the backstraight and into the final bend. Suddenly Baillie dashed for home. Philipp went after him, but Baillie won by three yards. "As soon as Lutz finished," Clark recalls, "he exploded into the most vehement torrent of what I assumed was abrasive German. Bill just smiled. Lutz no doubt learned a good lesson about the way New Zealanders could run virtually any kind of race."

TACTICAL MISTAKES

BLASTING OUT _____

The most common tactical blunder is going out fast at the gun in hopes of "putting money in the bank." Runners go out fast reasoning that they will create a "cushion" for later when they slow. Granted, if you get clear of the pack and carry a sizable lead near the finish, although you may be more tired than everyone else, you might appear to be unbeatable, thus causing fresh runners behind to lose heart and let up.

This often works in large championship cross-country races where you can get knocked about at the start. England's former cross-country great, Brendan Foster, says "To be realistic, the starting in many cross-country races abroad [Europe] is disgraceful [jumping the gun, pushing and shoving], but it's better to be at the front of a group of disgraceful runners than at the back saying 'how disgraceful.'"

Normally, unless you face inferior competition or are prepared to run yourself to a standstill at the finish, blasting out usually leads to disaster. Nine times out of ten you will be reduced to a slowing target for everyone else to shoot at later. Even so, some runners persist, waiting for that magic day when they'll keep going and uncork the performance of their life. However, if the race is begun at normal pace and you Have It, you can take off in the second half and still run faster than if you charged out at the gun. Understand, however, that the distance others get on you by blasting out will have to be gained back at some point. When they slow, you have to hold your pace. It requires a deliberate pre-planned effort to resist slowing once you settle in. Don't kid yourself that it doesn't matter how fast you go out; that you'll slow anyway. If you *are* doing that, it's because you fail to initiate a conscious drive later to win back the distance.

"I used to think you had to go out a little faster in a race so that when you naturally slowed down you'd still have a good time," says Salazar. "But I've started to notice I've had all my best 10,000s in Europe when I've gone out a little slower in the first half, or even on the first lap. . . . I think you get back more than you lose at the beginning."

Bill Dellinger adds, "If you know you can run for a [particular] pace all the way, start slower and run the second half faster . . . and if someone wants the lead early, let him have it. Let him make all the moves; the guy who makes the final move is the one who wins."

In a marathon, never begin faster than you can average all the way. The faster you take off, the more of your limited glycogen stores you burn relative to your nearly inexhaustible free fatty acids, and the sooner you'll hit "the wall." Even pace also keeps your core body temperature lower. Therefore, you'll run faster because you won't sweat as much, and not as much blood will be needed near the skin to cool you.

What appears to be a fine finishing kick in a marathon is often simply slowing less than the others. If you can maintain pace or pick it up at the end, you will get a tremendous psychological lift every time you pass. When I'm on the move at the end of a marathon, the runners in front are like magnets that pull me forward. I develop an insatiable appetite to pass and I go a little berserk. It's probably what a compulsive eater feels like after falling off a diet and beginning a food binge. But if you are coming apart at 20 miles, it's devastating to have scores of runners you should have beaten streaming by.

Even pace keeps your legs fresh longer. When your legs (quads) become traumatized early on, you have to run more of the race with less mechanical efficiency even though your energy stores may be relatively intact. But if your legs are responsive at 15 miles and you can *race*, you still have 11 miles in which to overtake the speed merchants who are beginning to pay for their sins. Going out fast in a marathon saves you *seconds* during the first miles, but costs you *minutes* at the end.

"What people don't understand," Pat Clohessy says, "is that the kick at the end of a marathon . . . [is] a product of your strength, timing the finish properly, and to some extent, your speed."

No man ever timed a finish with more composure and patience than did de Castella in the 1982 Commonwealth Games marathon in Brisbane. The favorite in front of a home crowd, de Castella nevertheless calmly allowed the impatient Tanzanians, Ikangaa and Shahanga, to build a lead then put them out of sight at 30km. "Up until then," the unflappable de Castella says, "I had just been running my own race, trying to be patient, but from then on I began to attack the hills and run more aggressively. I hadn't panicked and felt that if I could get into a good rhythm and get the Africans in sight, I had a chance."

"Deek" then proceeded to run the next 10km in 30:31, take the lead after fighting off repeated surges by Ikangaa, and win in 2:09:18 despite 90 percent humidity and hills.

PUSHING UPHILL

It's physiologically unsound to make competitive moves up hills unless it's near the end of a race, and there is a psychological advantage to be gained. The few yards someone gains on you by charging up can easily be regained on the downside, especially if you have done your downhill homework. If there is no downhill, apply pressure at the top when the other runner is tired. Runners of your caliber who push up the hills early on are usually sitting ducks if you attack up the final hill(s). Because they expect to run away from you up the grades, it's like a punch in the stomach when you turn the tables on them.

WAITING TO BE OUTKICKED

It happens with alarming regularity in big competition, including the Olympics. Runners with no finishing kick allow the pace to dawdle, thus setting themselves up to get burned at the end. Granted, it's difficult to force the pace all the way, but with a little planning and cooperation, it's not necessary. When up against kickers or after a fast time, recruit one or two other non-kickers and agree to share the pace-making with the agreement that whoever can go at the end does. Even though you may not emerge the winner, it's always better to lose in a fast time than a slow time.

International-class runners, or those vying for team selection, are often too suspicious of each other to enter into such agreements, even when the race is certain to be tactical (slow). One has to admire non sprint-kickers such as Ron Clarke and Portugal's Carlos Lopes, who although rarely setting up pace sharing, were not afraid to force a hot pace during a race's second half. Even though they were sometimes outkicked (for example, Lopes's second place to Viren in the 1976 Olympic 10,000, his 2:08:39 second to de Castella's win in the 1983 Rotterdam Marathon, his second to Beckele Dedele in the 1983 World Cross-Country Championships, and his 27:17:48 10,000-meter second place to countryman Fernando Mamede in 1984 at Stockholm), they still recorded spectacular times and finished higher than they would had they allowed the rest of the field to hang on.

EASING BEFORE THE FINISH
Many important races and places have been lost by relaxing just before the finish line. In *any* race sprint at least two strides beyond the line. Even the world-class have been surprised by a rival with an inspired late kick. If you are hard-pressed at the finish, it will take courage and confidence to resist giving up, especially if you are passed. In the 1983 World Championships, Mary Decker led the 3000 with Tatyana Kazankina (the 1980 Olympic 1500 champion and world-record holder who had beaten Decker in 1980 by nearly seven seconds) on her heels. There seemed to be little chance that Decker could win when, coming off the last turn, Kazankina lit out and in a few strides was beside and then past Decker. "I didn't tense up," Decker recalled, "I took a deep breath, relaxed, and went." So shocked was Kazankina, she sagged and lost second to West Germany's Brigitte Kraus.

NO ALTERNATIVE PLAN
Races don't always unfold as expected, and rivals may quickly detect your strategies and counteract with moves of their own. You may be planning to follow, for example, and find everyone behind you. Therefore, it is smart to have an alternate strategy, and react quickly. The best racers are those who can adjust quickly to almost any situation. Those who panic lose confidence and make mistakes.

TACTICAL TRICKS

There is no limit to the tactical ploys one can invent to fit a particular race situation. Below are a few representative types:

Controlling the pace. Many runners do not realize they can slow the pace by taking the lead. But shrewd tacticians sensing that a slow pace would favor their kick will often surge to the fore and then ease back, hoping the others will be content to follow. It often works because most other runners don't like to overtake and "pull the train."

The pace also can be controlled by running on the leader's shoulder and pressing whenever the pace slips. This pressure and percieved strength is commonly unnerving to a frontrunner hoping to demoralize the competition.

Upsmanship. Roger Bannister tells of a cross-country race where he and another runner had crested a killing, mud-soaked hill and he quipped cheerfully to his adversary, "Well, that wasn't as bad as last year." The other man immediately fell back.

A friend of mine, after fighting neck-and-neck with a rival, finally deliberately gasped out a loud "Araggg!' dropped back 10 yards, collected himself, and then sprinted past looking as lively as possible. The rival, probably about to congratulate himself on having shaken free, caved in at the thought of renewing the duel.

Passing. When passing near the end of a race, do it unexpectedly, quickly, and as deliberately as possible. This is especially true in shorter track races. Because passing on a curve requires that more distance be covered, most track competitors pass on the straights, or accelerate off the turns. For this very reason, most runners don't expect to be jumped entering a turn. If it's a surprise and you get past quickly, you won't have to run wide for long.

In any race, mean business when you pass. Don't just get in front to momentarily bolster your ego, and then ease off and get caught. If you are caught again, at least make your opponent work for it.

COGNITIVE STRATEGIES

Cognition is "knowing," and it's based on both awareness and judgment. It involves choosing what to pay attention to and what to ignore during competition. I've raced indoor one-miles after which I jogged a little before changing back into my training shoes, and *then* noticed I had been spiked in the shin. Upon seeing the holes and blood, it suddenly hurt like hell.

If someone unexpectedly spiked my shin on any occasion other than intense competition, I'd be hopping and howling. But competition is like combat; you often don't realize you are wounded until it's over. I *did* experience extreme fatigue-related discomfort (it's not really pain) during the race, however. This I accepted and monitored precisely.

This little anecdote illustrates two cognitive processes runners knowingly or unknowingly use to cope with nearly unbearble
fatigue. They are *association* and *disassociation*. I disassociated to
ignore the spiking, and associated with my fatigue build-up in
order to parcel out my energies most effectively.

When good, but not great, runners were first studied to determine how they got through "pain zones," it was found that
most of them used wonderfully creative psychological tricks to ignore, divert, or shut out their body's fatigue signals. Methods varied and included "leaving my body" and "escaping into my or
another runner's shadow," mentally building a house, composing
and hearing music, stepping on detested co-workers with each
stride, and pretending to be a powerful piston-driven locomotive.
Each of these disassociative devices was a meditative component
that helped runners tolerate pain and lactate accumulation.

The researchers theorized that elite runners would use even
more sophisticated methods of distraction. Instead, the best runners accepted, monitored, and dealt with their pain in an awesome·
manner. They associated with their fatigue in what is called perceived exertion. Elite runners have an uncanny ability to run right
up to the edge of their limits at every point of a race in a carefully
controlled "pay-as-you-go" strategy of exhausting themselves at
the finish. When lactic acid or fatigue levels become more acute
than they should at any stage, the elite back off ever so slightly. If
they are hurting, but not hurting enough, they increase the effort.

Elite runners are primarly associators and lesser runners are
primarily disassociators, but both methods have their advantages
and their pitfalls. There are times to ignore fatigue and times
when that would be stupid, if not dangerous. If you blast off or jog
at the beginning of a race and don't react to the feedback that
pace is wrong, you'll ruin your race. If, during a marathon you
don't accurately gauge your fatigue, state of dehydration, and so
on, you could either collapse before finishing, or finish with too
much left.

However, there are moments when every runner needs to
momentarily escape or overcome pain. A nearly exhausted Bill
Rodgers held off fast-closing Jeff Wells in the 1978 Boston Marathon after "seeing" the next day's headlines, "WELLS BEATS
RODGERS." If you think back, you rarely were as tired as you
thought during a race. How many times have you crossed the finish and realized you could have run harder, could have passed the

runner in front, could have sprinted at the end? In the thick of competition you believe you can't keep going, but it almost always turns out you could have—by disassociating.

Chanting "tem-po," as described in Chapter 6, is disassociating. It takes your mind off the fatigue and focuses it on maintaing a quick, efficient stride. Laboratory tests with disassociation have shown that it enables you to tolerate greater amounts of discomfort for longer periods, gets you up a tough hill, and inspires you to outrun an opponent you just told yourself you were too tired to stay with.

Roger Bannister reveals a classic example of disassociation in describing his first Oxford-Cambridge mile race. "I was as tired as everyone else," he wrote, "but suddenly for the first time I felt a crazy desire to overtake the whole field. I raced through into the lead and a feeling of great mental and physical excitement swept over me. I forgot my tiredness. I suddenly tapped that hidden source of energy I always suspected I possessed."

Association is the preferred cognitive strategy because you will run a smarter race, but when the opposition is challenging and your body pleads, "I can't take this," you will have to disassociate, throw caution to the wind, damn the torpedos, and charge full steam ahead. F. Scott Fitzgerald could have been describing this moment when he said, "The test of a first-rate intelligence is the ability to hold two opposed ideas in the mind at the same time, and still retain the ability to function. One should, for example, be able to see that things are hopeless and yet be determined to make them otherwise."

RECOVERING AFTER THE RACE

You have kicked through the finish, congratulated yourself on your grand effort, put on your sweats (if it is the least bit cool), and cooled down as soon as you could get going again. Now what? What do you do in the days that follow in order to recover for the next hard training or race? There are two aspects involved here, the physical and the mental, but actually, they are interwoven. Let's look at the physical side first.

PHYSICAL RECOVERY _____
The way to recover fast after a race is to be as fit as possible when the gun goes off. Recovery also depends upon how far and hard

you raced, and the degree of leg damage due to the surface and terrain. After relatively short track races, fit runners can do their long run the next day if the race was on Saturday and you normally run long on Sunday. If you are primarily a track athlete racing regularly, the long run shouldn't be very long or fast anymore. But if you are a marathoner using track races to sharpen, your long run may be quite important and long, and if the next day is the only one available for it, you'll have to carefully monitor your effort to make sure you don't go over the edge. Fortunately, track races are short and anaerobic, and long runs are aerobic, so they don't work the same metabolisms and muscles. But if both runs are hard, you could be stiff and tired for the rest of the week.

After a hard road race Herb Lindsay says, "I . . . allow my body to rest for two days and then come back and start into my training. . . . I don't have to pound my feet into the pavement every day to give myself confidence." A road race takes the place of two hard aerobic workouts, so there's no need to hurry back into training. Road racers don't race as often as middle-distance athletes, so they can afford to take their time, although many runners at the advanced and elite levels can handle a long easy run (18 to 25 miles) after racing up to 10 miles. If you've raced further, there's no immediate need for another long run.

If your legs are sore, biking, swimming, and even walking are excellent ways to get a non-pounding workout. Don't underestimate biking as the main exercise for several days after a long road race. Don't run when your legs are damaged. Give them time to heal. Often when you try to hurry back into training after a hard marathon, you seemingly make progress for a few days, and then get sick or fall apart.

Drink plenty of whatever agrees with you after a race, but avoid alcohol until you are fully hydrated. Beer, a seeming thirst quencher, will dehydrate you further. So will Gatorade. If you intend to party after a race, start with water, fruit juices, pop, etc.

After a marathon eat primarily carbohydrates. Research has shown that it takes several days to replenish your glycogen stores no matter how much you eat. However, don't just pig out on starches and sugars. To get the nutrients you need to recover, eat a fairly wide variety of grains, vegetables, meats or meat substitutes, fruits, and dairy products.

MENTAL RECOVERY _____

Two days after Ron Clarke sets his first six-mile/10,000-meter world record in 1963, he was overcome by depression. After the initial cheering and hoopla died down, he realized that nothing had really changed; the world was the same, he still got aches and pains, he still got tired when he ran.

A letdown doesn't always follow a good performance, but it is not unusual. A week following my two American track records I was shocked that I could average only 5:30 miles during a 5-mile cross-country race. It took nearly two months after my fourth-place Boston Marathon finish to be competitive again. If you have races scheduled for consecutive weekends and they feel like an imposition, don't race the unimportant ones. Pretending your batteries are recharged is a good way to go stale. A few exciting, well-run races are better than allowing weekly racing to become a chore.

Qualifying heats for track events present an inescapable problem. More than a physical ordeal, heats require the ability to focus your attention and emotions on the task at hand. After a heat you must postpone celebration, temporarily turn your emotions off and concentrate on what you'll have to run next. If any man was a master of this, Viren was. Coach Haikkola explained Viren's ability to get through the 5000- and 10,000-meter heats and finals in the Olympics: "After the 10,000-meter final in Montreal, Lasse Viren was not interested in the reaction of the world, or of the people at home, or of the millions of television spectators at the moment of his triumph. He was already thinking about the approaching 5000-meter heat. The ability to concentrate solely on the task at hand was one of Lasse Viren's great advantages. By means of it, he could stand the pressure of the Olympic oval."

The goal in the heats is to come through as easily as possible and still qualify. Unlike sprinters, who can afford the luxury (and often advantage) of running hard and winning, a distance runner who squanders energy before the final is a fool. Attempting to out-psych your opponents with impressive performances before the final is useless if you have no strength left. On the other hand, there's no point in conserving for the final if you don't make it. If your goal is to just make the final, then try to run your best in the heat and do whatever you can in the final. In essence, the heat is your final.

16.

SPECIAL CONSIDERATIONS: ALTITUDE AND HEAT

HIGH ALTITUDE: IT'S BREATHTAKING

There are two basic reasons for training at high altitude: 1) to cope better with races at altitude, and 2) to race better at sea level. A review of the research on altitude training reveals that there is little agreement on the degree to which training at altitude helps a sea-level resident race at sea level, or whether it helps at all. Moreover, it is difficult to draw connections between physiological changes in the body and optimum training altitudes, methods of training, and time at altitude. Much depends upon the individual and his or her event.

But our knowledge need not be limited by what can be proven by science. Runners have ideas and experience of their own. When I first began training at altitude (7640 feet) in 1968, I would run hard, start panting, and exclaim, "Aha, that's the altitude." Everyone who trains at altitude at first fears it to a degree, and overestimates its effects. While puffing through repeat 400s a few days after arriving and blaming the altitude, I reminded myself that at sea level I also panted after 400s. From that moment the altitude never intimidated me. Running at a mile and a half high is no harder or easier than at sea level; only the times are slower. That was a great psychological breakthrough—to realize that I could proceed as usual, albeit slower.

HOW LONG TO ACCLIMATE?

Seated deep in the folklore of altitude training is the notion that if a sea-level resident could not spend more than a week at altitude before a race there, it would be better to arrive just prior to race time. This is not so, but I suspect I know how the idea started. My experience during six summers of high-altitude running camps was that the participants would arrive already foaming at the mouth to show each other how hard they could run. Camp would begin on Sunday, and by Wednesday they were so exhausted, walking uphill to the restrooms was a sizable undertaking.

Acclimation begins the moment you arrive, and if you begin easily, you will improve every day. The effects are greatest the first week, less the second, and diminish thereafter, becoming minimal after six to seven weeks. But you'll never catch up to a high-altitude resident. That's why, at the Mexico Olympics every event from the 1500 meters on up was won by a high-altitude African. From the 800 on down the altitude didn't affect the places, but lessened air resistance certainly accelerated the times. Lee Evan's 43.86 400 remains a world record. Tommie Smith's 19.83 200 and Jim Hine's 9.95 100 remain (in 1984) Olympic records.

According to physiologist Bob Fitts, after six to eight weeks altitude about half of the initial loss in VO_2 max is made up. However, the gain in performance is about two-thirds of the initial loss, probably because anaerobic metabolism is minimally affected, and air resistance is lower. Obviously this benefits those in the shortest races.

ALTERNATING ALTITUDE AND SEA-LEVEL TRAINING

Studies suggest that you ultimately perform better if you are able to alternate periods of altitude and sea-level training. The disadvantage at altitude is that you cannot work at the same intensity (speed) as you can at sea level, and therefore the muscles lose some of their ability to use large amounts of oxygen. Maximum heart rate also is lower at altitude, hence, cardiac output is lower.

There are two ways to approach the problem. One is to drive to lower altitudes once or twice a week to run hard repeats or steady runs, and the other is to periodically spend several (10 to 20) days at sea level. However, this kind of nomadic life-style is generally beyond the means of those other than full-time runners. The only other solution is to move to a high-altitude residence and vacation at *low* altitudes.

OPTIMUM TRAINING ALTITUDE

Most researchers and athletes agree that 5000 feet (1550 meters) is the minimal elevation at which significant acclimation takes place. Ten thousand feet (3250 meters) is about the highest you would want to do regular training. The drop in oxygen saturation in the blood is not linear the higher you go. In other words, the drop in performance in going from 8000 to 9000 feet is much greater than when going from 5000 to 6000 feet. The higher you go, the greater the effect of each additional foot of altitude.

In most altitude settings it is possible to train at various elevations by driving or running to some workouts (When I lived at 8500 feet I could run or drive to a track at 6900 feet to run repeats, or run to 10,000 feet). My gut feeling is that the best regular training should occur between 7000 and 8500 feet. At higher altitudes there's so little oxygen you can't run fast for any appreciable distance. Even when you sprint, the recoveries feel worse and take longer.

THE BODY'S RESPONSE TO ALTITUDE

The physiology of adaption is not well understood, but all you need is a practical grasp of the process. There is no precise relationship between altitude training and change in performance. Few people agree on how and why the body reacts to a lower pressure of oxygen, or why whatever it is that happens doesn't happen to everyone to the same degree.

The factors limiting performance at sea level seem to be ordered differently at altitude. At low elevations the main problems aren't the lungs' ability to extract oxygen from the air and the heart's ability to rush it to the muscles, as much as the muscles ability to use it. At altitude, extracting and transporting oxygen may be relatively more of a limiting factor. At altitude the working muscles could probably use more oxygen if they could get it.

Which means one of the body's reactions to altitude is increased breathing capacity. There also seems to be an increase in hemoglobin concentration as well as total blood volume and several changes in the muscle's oxidative enzymes. But there does not appear to be an increase in sea level VO_2 max in elite runners. Altitude training seems to benefit less fit and average runners most. Some researchers think altitude training is of little or no benefit to elite athletes competing at sea level, although many runners swear to the contrary.

The most obvious bodily reaction to altitude is reduced work capacity. Although E. C. Fredrick says 80 miles a week at 7000 feet is roughly equivalent to 100 miles at sea level, I found that at 7640 feet I was running *more* miles and improving (but I wasn't working my regular job). The effort was the same, but the times were slower. The ability to retain high mileage may be because at slower speeds there is less mechanical stress.

TRAINING AT ALTITUDE

It seemed logical, as I contemplated altitude training for the first time, to arrive already accustomed to anaerobic running. Since running without enough air was going to be a constant problem, I wanted to experience some hard out-of-breath repetitions before I got there. I still think this is a wise prerequisite.

Training at altitude is much the same as at sea level. The first few days, emphasize distance at the expense of speed and effort, otherwise it hits you a few days later. Some of the initial setback is related to dehydration due to dryer air, and can be prevented by drinking more. The rest of the setback is related to various climatic changes and the pressures of travel.

Although physiologist Jack Daniels says that the recovery times between repeats need to be lengthened, I found that for a given effort, recovery took less time. It may be that because of less oxygen, one seems more tired than is the case, or because of the decreased work rate (slower times), one recovers more quickly. Daniels' point, however, is that speed should be the last thing sacrificed. In order to keep the same pace at altitude, either the distance must be shortened, the interval lengthened, or a combination or the two.

Ron Clarke advises against sacrificing long repetitions for a lot of short intervals (200s). Repeat 200s, while making you feel fast, don't develop your ability to run for extended periods. The track training Clarke thinks is best would be something like the repeat 3000-meter intervals he saw Mohamed Gammoudi perform before winning the 1968 Olympic 5000 meters. Gammoudi ran the first kilometer easy, the second kilometer at medium effort, and the last kilometer very hard. Sprints and fast 200s are fine for maintaining leg-speed, but they cannot replace longer intervals or time-trials at or somewhat faster than race pace.

RETURNING TO SEA-LEVEL RACES

It would seem logical to return to sea level and race immediately, before the de-acclimation process begins. Such is not the case. This is dramatically manifest in the experience of the 1972 British Olympic distance runners who went to St. Moritz for pre-Games altitude training. Among the British, Ron Hill was the odds-on favorite to win the gold medal in the marathon. Hill acclimated well enough, but he and just about all the runners stayed on too long, freezing in the mountains and leaving insufficient time to acclimate to Munich's muggy sea-level atmosphere. Without this adjustment period, Hill and most of the other British runners performed poorly.

Ironically, the only British runner to perform way beyond expectation was a woman who became bored at St. Moritz and left early for Munich. In the 1500 meters she set a U.K. record that stood for seven years. Once the others had acclimated to sea level, several of them competing immediately after the Games set lifetime bests. The optimum period of re-acclimation may be from 10 days to two weeks, although much depends upon the athletes, the difference in altitude and the difference in climate (mainly humidity and temperature).

RACING AT ALTITUDE

Racing strategies remain roughly the same, except that whereas in a sea-level race you can back away from an overambitious pace and recover, at altitude you may never recover. Unless your ancestry and normal residence is high-altitude-based, even splits are your best tactic. Use the difference between your sea-level and altitude times to predict the pace to aim for at altitude.

WHEN IT'S HOT YOU'RE NOT

The reason I would rather train in January than July is because the body is far better able to accommodate cold than heat. Cold weather is only a threat to exposed body parts, so you cover up. But after you've stripped to your shorts and shoes, there's little else to remove in the heat.

I learned about heat training the hard way, but it hammered home the lesson. When I went to the National Marathon Championship in 1964 (which was also one of the Olympic selection races), I thought I was fairly well prepared. It would be my second marathon, and although I wasn't concerned with the Games selection, I did expect a personal best. Instead I was to learn the true meaning of preparedness.

The race was held in late May, so I had trained in perfect 50-to-70-degree spring weather. Perfect, that is, for a 50-to-70-degree race. But when the gun went off, the mercury was heading for 96 degrees with high humidity. I headed for disaster. After stumbling into the finish literally near death in 3:25, being hospitalized twice, and collapsing after each release, I realized that no matter how well you trained in cool conditions, you couldn't function in the heat.

A former teammate of mine at the University of Minnesota, Buddy Edelen, had won by 20 minutes in 2:24. Edelen, I later discovered, figured it would be hot, so he trained in five layers of clothing to simulate hot conditions.

Three years later it was my turn. This time it was the National Marathon Champs and Pan-Am Games trials. The race was in Holyoke, Massachusetts, in mid-June. That again meant cool training for hot racing. But not for me. While other runners zipped along almost naked at the beaches, I was sloshing inside a thick sweatsuit, cap, and sometimes mitts. A singular lack of tan earned me the nickname "Nightcrawler" and a lot of stares, but what the hell, if the others wanted to use the "Fly now, pay later" plan, let them.

Sure enough, it was again 96 degrees at Holyoke, and I genuinely appreciated the tans the other runners had. This time I had every detail covered: I drank plenty of water the night before and right before the race to make sure I was completely hydrated. I got rid of my dark singlet and wore a wet white T-shirt which both reflected the sun and refrigerated me as it evaporated dry. I got a white painter's hat with a hanky on the back which, when wet, cooled the blood to my head. And lastly, when the gun sounded, I went out very slowly while the other contenders blasted out like they were running to keep warm.

As the others melted into the pavement, I kept the pace I had started with and emerged the winner by over three minutes. Although I had won, I wasn't the best runner in the field. Another guy came into the race with a time over seven minutes faster than mine, and there were lots of others almost that good. But I was the best prepared.

Even with the Olympic Games up for grabs the next year, the others still hadn't figured it out. Besides having to qualify at 7640 feet we would be on a warm, dry desert in August. Of course, I kept my nylon windsuit on during the 30-mile runs even though the others said I would die, and when the race came I did all that other hot-weather stuff. Again the heat training paid off, and my splits over the five 5.2-mile loops varied by no more that 25 seconds. When I caught and passed Billy Mills, the 1964 Olympic 10,000-meter champion at 15 miles, I knew those extra things I did in my training were about to put me on the Olympic team.

When in 1970 I again donned my painter's hat and T-shirt to run second in the National Marathon Champs on another mid-90s day, a *Playboy* article caricaturized me as having "a weird resemblance to a Foriegn Legionnaire galloping purposefully in his underwear." No wonder runners continue to melt on hot days.

That was many years ago, but most runners still aren't heat training. I see them every spring, already running in shorts and T-shirt when the first robins are still up to their beaks in snow. If there's any chance at all you will have to race in the heat, you must train in it. If the weather is cool during training, you must simulate hot weather.

TRAINING FOR HEAT_____

Heat-train in the spring when it's cool before hot races. As it gets nicer, dress fairly warmly and then 2 to 3 weeks before an anticipated hot race, deliberately try to make yourself uncomfortably warm. If you become acclimatized for heat and race day is cool, you will still perform better. In the summer it's hot enough without heat training. It would be foolish to heat-train for cross-country or fall races when it's cool.

The toughest part about heat training is deciding to do it and resist stripping down on those perfect 50-to-70-degree spring days. Fortunately it takes only between 10 days and three weeks to acclimate to hot weather. If you persist longer, you risk coming apart. It's like hard-easy days; you must back off and recover.

Running at any given speed in heat burns more glycogen than in cool air; therefore, daily heat training not only dehydrates you, it depletes more of your energy stores.

But on those days you heat-train—three or four a week— work fairly hard during the hottest part of the day, if possible. Hot races mean suffering, but heat training spreads out the discomfort so you don't get it slammed to you all at once. Best of all, you will finish way up in the field, and just maybe, you'll save your health or life.

Heat-train roughly every other day, but don't run entirely stripped down on your relief days. Occasionally train hard in cool conditions to maintain confidence that you can still run fast. But

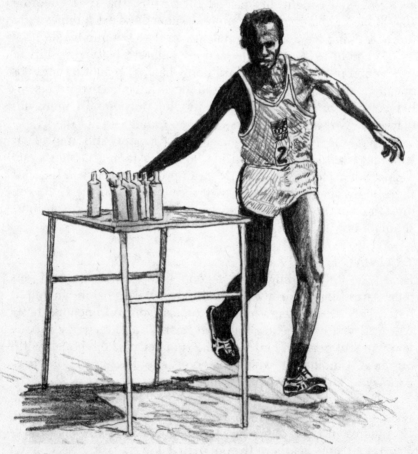

Getting water is critical in any hot race over 10,000 meters.

use most of your heat days for working hard and maximum accli-
matization.

HOW THE BODY ADAPTS

Physiologists have found that after training in the heat the body
kicks in its defenses at a lower core temperature. Sweating begins
earlier, more profusely, and salts are conserved. More blood goes
to the skin to be cooled. Even as the core temperature rises during
the latter stages of a race, the acclimated runner tolerates it better. At 105 to 106 degree core temperature ordinary people are
flattened, but acclimated runners are able to begin their kick.

FLUID REPLACEMENT

A good rule of thumb is drink the (diluted) electrolyte beverages
before the run (race), cold water *during*, and whatever agrees with
you *afterward*. Despite what the manufacturers of commercial
drinks would have you believe, cold water is the least likely to
make you sick, empties the stomach faster and in general does the
job best. Cold drinks also lower your core temperature.

Drink up to a pint 10 to 15 minutes before you begin, long
enough to allow fluids to exit the stomach (but not long enough for
them to make it to the kidneys), and as often as needed during the
workout. If you hydrate properly beforehand, you should never
need to drink during races of 10km or less. Pour the water over
yourself. In long races, begin drinking as soon as possible, *before*
you feel thirsty. Don't pass up drinks because you don't want to
lose ground while drinking. You'll pay back the distance later with
great interest.

During a marathon, try to get enough water in by 20 to 21
miles so that you don't have to drink thereafter. During the final
gory stages of a hot marathon it's difficult to absorb water from the
stomach, so it stays there and makes you sick. In extreme heat and
humidity you can sweat a gallon an hour. During the '68 Olympic
marathon trial when the temperature was only in the high 70s, for
example, although I drank every 2½ miles, I still dropped from
146 to 137 pounds, a 6.2 percent *net* weight loss and double that
needed to cause trouble.

Don't avoid cold sprays from hoses as the U.S. Army advised
Salazar to do before the 1984 Olympic marathon. Common sense
should tell you that a cold spray temporarily restricts your sweat
rate (their objection) because you've been cooled by the conduct-

ing away of heat by the water. Anytime you can get cooled without sweating, you ward off dehydration. Salazar later regretted heeding this advice. Incidentally, in the mid-1960s the U.S. Army said it didn't make any difference whether one wore a black or white shirt in the hot sun. Fortunately, I didn't fall for that one.

RACING

In short races or those with cloud cover, go shirtless. In long races with bright sun, wear the costume described earlier. If you want a constant flow of cold water over your head put ice cubes under your hat.

Keep your head when the gun goes off. Forget time; go for place. If you start sensibly, you'll haul down tons of half-baked kamikaze runners. Be prepared to bail out of a hot race if you begin to shiver, no longer sense heat, or get lightheaded. Without citing the gory details, I want to emphasize that you can ruin your health or even die. If you become nauseated and can't stand after finishing, get medical help. Often, just lying *in the shade* with your feet elevated, drinking and sponging cold water to lower your core temperature will bring you around. Under no circumstances take salt pills. They will dehydrate you further and can kill.

WEIGHT LOSS

As an aside to heat training, NEVER run in rubber suits or sweats on hot days to lose weight. Boxers and wrestlers trying to "make weight" temporarily shed pounds by sweating, but it is just water that has to be replaced.

There are only two ways to lose weight (contrary to what the hucksters claim): reducing calorie intake and burning calories by doing work. If you run to lose weight, go as *far* as you can, because for 150-pound person, running one mile burns about 100 calories, no matter if they are five-minute miles or 10-minute miles. At five-minute miling you just burn them twice as fast. Everyone knows you can run farther on a cool day than a hot one, so run as cool as possible. The weight you lose while suffering and risking your health bundled up in the heat will be almost all water loss, which *must* be replaced.

EPILOGUE

I have likened good training to arranging pieces of a jigsaw puzzle. Now that the pieces are in place, in retrospect the solution looks simple—almost unworthy of the great weight of words used to lay it all out. That is because efficient training is logical and simple. All it requires it that you operate within a physiologically sound framework, avoid unnecessary mistakes, and maintain exuberance in setting and pursuing goals.

Foremost, use your head. Let your emotions excite and activate you rather than incapacitate or frighten you from your mission. Enhance your chances of success by evaluating what you are doing rather than allowing pride and uncontrolled zeal to seduce you into workouts that hinder rather than help.

Efficient training basically means balancing the three kinds of work—aerobic, anaerobic, and speed—over three periods—your running career, a season, and each week. A beginner should devote a greater proportion of the season to aerobic base training because a high VO_2 max is at the root of running fast efficiently. Smart beginners also work on stamina and speed and race track and cross-country rather than become just "marathoners." It is no coincidence that almost every world-class marathoner developed through the ranks of track and/or cross-country.

As you mature, you don't need to emphasize raising your VO_2 max as much, so most of the season is spent on hill (resistance) work, fast repetitions, and speed. How you apportion these various kinds of work depends upon how fit you are when you begin, number of weeks available to train, the race schedule, and your strengths and weaknesses. Although one training goal is emphasized at a time, training is a smooth transition from the easy to the difficult, from one kind of workout to another. Thus, while sharpening your anaerobic skills, you still retain many aerobic workouts and introduce speed.

As some workouts become harder, easy days become necessary. Stress with no let-up always spells trouble. Therefore, rotate the types of hard workouts you do; never stress your aerobic or your anaerobic system two workouts in a row. A hard interval workout could be followed by a relatively hard aerobic workout the next day, but usually you would schedule a recovery before working hard again. It is especially important to get adequate recoveries between hard anaerobic workouts—one to three days of a different kind of work.

Eventually, racing replaces much of the hard training, so a track or cross-country runner competing weekly would greatly reduce the mileage and number of hard intervals. A road runner racing less frequently merely schedules a few easy days after a strenuous race. If you operate within this framework, listen to your body's signals *and* heed them; then it's not difficult to sense when to do what.

There is more to training and racing than workouts, however. Great patience and persistence is needed to get past setbacks, to do first things first, and to train every day. It's tempting to charge ahead for quick, limited results, like marathon hopefuls who never schedule and train for short races.

One must accept, and at times be thankful for, mistakes. They reveal lessons essential to achieving big successes later. Mistakes often instruct best because after you've screwed up, you are more apt to listen.

Innovating to keep your program together means that those who live in Kansas don't abandon hill work, they get on stairways or whatever. It may mean pedaling with your arms and legs (Benoit, for example) during injury, reverting to an indoor hallway to run during impossible weather, or anything to get a workout. This attitude that nothing can stop you is what separates those who succeed from those who alibi and is the key to successfully battling the odds.

Running is more than a world of training, racing and stopwatches. It is the arena where the resourceful underdog can prevail. When you do the little extras such as heat training, skipping, and springing exercises, you discover you *can* change things. When you reach the 20-mile mark of a marathon feeling utterly spent, but finish somehow, you suspect you can conquer other seemingly unbearable events in life. After you discover you can set tough goals and prevail, you realize you can accomplish almost anything you put your mind to. You don't have to look to the marvels of the Benoits, the Coes, the world-class to find your heroes; look inward to your own struggle and discover yourself. What you find may startle you, it may expose you to a whole gamut of emotions, but it will never bore you. And, as Theodore Roosevelt promised, your place shall never be with those cold and timid souls who know neither victory nor defeat.

INDEX